THE POLITICS OF PRIDE EVENTS

Global and Local Challenges

Francesca Romana Ammaturo

First published in Great Britain in 2025 by

Bristol University Press
University of Bristol
1–9 Old Park Hill
Bristol
BS2 8BB
UK
t: +44 (0)117 374 6645
e: bup-info@bristol.ac.uk

Details of international sales and distribution partners are available at bristoluniversitypress.co.uk

© Bristol University Press 2025

DOI: https://doi.org/10.51952/9781529238693

British Library Cataloguing in Publication Data
A catalogue record for this book is available from the British Library

ISBN 978-1-5292-3862-4 hardcover
ISBN 978-1-5292-3867-9 paperback
ISBN 978-1-5292-3868-6 ePub
ISBN 978-1-5292-3869-3 ePdf

The right of Francesca Romana Ammaturo to be identified as author of this work has been asserted by her in accordance with the Copyright, Designs and Patents Act 1988.

All rights reserved: no part of this publication may be reproduced, stored in a retrieval system, or transmitted in any form or by any means, electronic, mechanical, photocopying, recording, or otherwise without the prior permission of Bristol University Press.

Every reasonable effort has been made to obtain permission to reproduce copyrighted material. If, however, anyone knows of an oversight, please contact the publisher.

The statements and opinions contained within this publication are solely those of the author and not of the University of Bristol or Bristol University Press. The University of Bristol and Bristol University Press disclaim responsibility for any injury to persons or property resulting from any material published in this publication.

Bristol University Press works to counter discrimination on grounds of gender, race, disability, age and sexuality.

Cover design: Liam Roberts Design
Front cover image: desiray-green/unsplash

Contents

List of Abbreviations		v
Acknowledgements		vi
Introduction: Out and Proud in the Streets: Pride Events as a Local and Global Phenomenon		1

PART I	**Theorizing Pride Events between the Local and the Global**	
1	Decentring the 1969 Stonewall Riots: Beyond Foundational Myths?	21
2	Towards Progress? Interrogating the 'Kaleidoscope Modernities' of Pride Events	39
3	One Pride or Many? Pride Events between Multiplication and Fragmentation	62

PART II	**Exploring the 'Kaleidoscope Modernities' of Pride Events**	
4	Free to Protest and Celebrate? Exploring Human Rights Issues at Pride Events	83
5	Back to Grassroots? Conflicts and Tensions in Community-building at Pride Events	103
6	A Necessary Evil? Funding, Sponsorship, and the Commodification and Corporatization of Pride Events	125

PART III	**No Pride Without Social Justice: Building the Futures of Pride Events**	
7	Making Space, Creating Place: Disability and the Making of Accessible Pride Events	151
8	Pride on Tow? Environmental Sustainability and Queer Eco-Criticism at Pride Events	172

Conclusion: Pride Events between the Past and the Future: 190
Challenges and Opportunities

References 199
Index 240

List of Abbreviations

AIDS	Acquired Immunodeficiency Syndrome
CoE	Council of Europe
DEI	Diversity, Equality, Inclusion
EU	European Union
HIV	Human Immunodeficiency Viruses
ILGA	International Lesbian and Gay Association
LGBTQIA+	lesbian, gay, bisexual, transgender, queer, intersex, asexual, plus
MENA	Middle East and North Africa
NGO	non-governmental organization
UK	United Kingdom
UN	United Nations
US	United States of America

Acknowledgements

This book would have never existed without the generosity of the Pride organizers from around the world who have responded to my invitation to be interviewed for this project. To them goes my utmost gratitude for their time, engagement with my project, and their enthusiasm. With their work and activism, they strive to make this world safer for LGBTQIA+ (lesbian, gay, bisexual, transgender, queer, intersex, asexual, plus) persons every day.

I am also thankful to those who have believed in this project from the beginning. Right after I finished collecting the empirical data for this research, in the spring of 2022, I went through a process of 'voluntary redundancy' at the institution where I had been working for the last seven years. That experience really shook my confidence as a researcher, and it took me a long time to feel able to engage with my research again. The support of friends and colleagues has been crucial to allow me to overcome these difficult times. For their kindness, generosity, and unwavering support, my thanks go to Maria Federica Moscati, Olimpia Burchiellaro, Leah Bassel, Koen Slootmaeckers, Emma Sheppard, Monica Greco, Carl Stychin, Andrew Moran, Jennifer Melvin, Maayan Geva, Angeliki Sifaki, Silvia Tanzini, Sara Miggiano, Pierluigi Catterino, and Konstantina Georgiou.

Other great colleagues have also helped me to develop and nurture ideas for this book. In particular, I want to thank Momin Rahman, Line Nyhagen, and Phillip Ayoub for reading some of the drafts and giving me feedback at various stages of the production of the manuscript. I also want to thank those who have helped me with developing my ideas further or given me advice on sources and other aspects of my research that I should develop: Rahul Rao, Ayça Çubukçu, Alice Parrinello, Valentina Amenta, Ryan Starzyk and Julian Sanjivan from InterPride, Andy Silveira, Alma Beltran y Puga, Disha Chaudhari, Anne Maureen Syallow, Megha Kayshap, Fabio Corbisiero, Alice Elliott and Antón Freire Varela. I am also grateful to the organizers of *The Sociological Review* Writing Retreat in April 2023, for selecting me as one of the participants, and giving me the opportunity to develop and discuss my ideas with others. Last, I want to thank my editor, Anna Richardson at Bristol University Press, as well as Commissioning Editor Emily Ross, for their help in developing and publishing this manuscript.

In closing, my biggest and heartfelt thanks go to my wonderful partner Sarah. You have always encouraged me, even when I felt I could not meet my deadline, or I thought I had run out of ideas. Your enthusiasm, kindness, and true passion to achieve a more just world have pushed me to pour my heart and soul into this book, with the hope to also contribute to make this world a better place for everyone.

Introduction:
Out and Proud in the Streets:
Pride Events as a Local and Global Phenomenon

I remember us running up a West Side Highway still full of porn and piers, trans and queer sex workers living houseless and making home together. I remember the fierce feeling of free I felt the first time I saw a ragged queer and trans march taking the street. I remember the promise of us, the promise that it could be all different.

Piepzna-Samarasinha, 2019

Why this book?

Pride Events are a special kind of place and space. Ephemeral enough to only last a few hours, sometimes leaving decorations, as well as trails of glitter and sequins behind as the only tangible proofs that they have happened, yet persistent enough to make a difference in the lives of many LGBTQIA+ (lesbian, gay, bisexual, transgender, queer, intersex, asexual, plus) persons who may feel lonely, or isolated, such as mine. I attended my first Pride Event in 2007 in Brussels (during my Erasmus year in the nearby French city of Lille). I was 22 and had not been out as a lesbian woman for long. On that occasion, I decided that I did not just want to participate in the parade, but I signed up, together with a friend, as well as my sister who was visiting me at the time, to volunteer, in exchange for a ticket for the after-party and a t-shirt that I still keep as a cherished memory. On that day we marched in the unpredictable Belgian weather, holding the metres-long rainbow flag, getting soaked to the bone because of the rain; we helped set up one of the stages for the entertainment; and gave directions to the Pride Village to those who needed them. I felt like I had finally found a place where I could belong.

My fondness of Pride Events as a collective moment of queer joy, however, is not sufficient to explain why I decided to write this book, and why I think this book is needed. While I love Pride Events for what they mean to LGBTQIA+ persons and communities, I am also frustrated at how they sometimes become detached from the very people they should represent because of their size or organizational features; how they become politically instrumentalized by political actors who use them as 'proof' of a country's LGBTQIA+-friendliness or 'modernity', and yet these same political actors still discriminate, imprison, or sometimes bomb LGBTQIA+ persons around the world; as well as by the ways in which corporate sponsors take advantage of the need for financial resources by Pride organizers to 'pinkwash' their reputation. While they can be a crucial source of social and political empowerment for LGBTQIA+ persons around the world, Pride Events can become hollow commercial and promotional rainbow husks, leaving behind those who would benefit the most from being heard and represented within the LGBTQIA+ community. This type of sleek and hollowed out Pride Events promotes a homogenizing vision of an LGBTQIA+ community that is deprived of the contradictions, conflicts, and ambiguities that are proper of social movements organizing.

These perplexities do not just reflect my own discomfort with some of the ways in which Pride Events take place, but they speak to broader concerns that are increasingly arising from within LGBTQIA+ communities themselves, as people often feel left out, rather than included, during these events. Pride Events sometimes discriminate and alienate some segments of the LGBTQIA+ community, such as racialized persons, disabled and neurodivergent persons, working-class persons, and trans persons. Some of these people stop going to Pride Events altogether or end up creating their own alternative events where they feel comfortable and included.

Increasingly, critical voices within LGBTQIA+ movements themselves are questioning the identity, role, and objectives of Pride Events. At the same time, however, Pride Events are more popular than ever, having exponentially multiplied across the Global North and the Global South, in both big urban centres and small villages. For some, Pride Events are key moments to celebrate their identities, achievements, and communities. For others, these events do not represent their struggles, their aspirations, or quite simply their experiences. And yet, in a world where attacks to the rights of LGBTQIA+ persons are relentlessly at the top of the agendas of conservative, populist, and right-wing movements across the continents, it is important to reflect about the importance of making Pride Events not only representative of their own communities, but also powerful in addressing issues such as homophobia, transphobia, racism, white supremacy, ableism, and classism.

This book engages with the work of Pride organizers around the world and asks what kind of future Politics of Pride we envision, so we can use these spaces to counter the various forms of discrimination, marginalization, and institutional violence that LGBTQIA+ persons around the world still experience. While this book is ambitious in wanting to cover a vast array of issues relating to Pride Events, as well as adopting a wide geographical approach beyond the confines of Anglophone academia, there are important limitations in relation to the depth of analysis that can be achieved with such a holistic perspective. For this reason, I hope this book will excite and push others who love Pride Events to also interrogate themselves about why we need them, what we want Pride Events to look like, and what world we can build through them.

What is the contribution of this book?

This book is the first of its kind in adopting a global geographical perspective on the study of Pride Events using empirical material. Based on research done through interviewing online 60 Pride organizers from 29[1] different countries and one autonomous territory around the world (see Figure 0.1), in four different languages (English, French, Spanish, and Italian), both in the Global North and in the Global South, this book seeks to put together different strands of studies relating to the phenomenon of Pride Events in a way that has not been done by other scholars.

Because of its interdisciplinary nature and ambition, this book is in conversation with fields such as LGBTQIA+ studies, Social Movements Studies, Critical Human Geography, Decolonial Studies, Human Rights, and International Politics. These characteristics make this book an important contribution to our understanding of the role of Pride Events in a globalized world where LGBTQIA+ rights and lives are simultaneously increasingly celebrated, but also relentlessly at risk from homo- and transphobic conservative forces.

At its core, and to provoke a reflection on the global and local future(s) of Pride Events, this book fundamentally calls into question two main accepted principles of contemporary global and local Pride politics. First, the idea that 'bigger is better', that Pride Events need to inevitably grow in magnitude year on year, regardless of whether they are organized in urban or peripheral, or rural centres. Second, the idea that the existence and/or success of Pride Events automatically signals the entry for a specific country, and its local LGBTQIA+ communities, into the realm of queer modernity, leaving an alleged 'backward' past behind, together with those who refuse to conform.

As for the former idea, this book discusses how endless growth for Pride Events, one that is inevitably sustained by the influx of sponsors, external funders, or other types of interlocutors (governments, intergovernmental organizations, embassies, and so on), inevitably places Pride organizers in the midst of a dilemma: that of serving their communities, while simultaneously

Figure 0.1: Map with country of origin for interviewed Pride Event organizers

becoming increasingly dependent on the whims and the priorities of external funders and sponsors. As of 2025, the growing phenomenon of rollback of DEI (Diversity, Equality, and Inclusion) policies in the US, across several countries in Europe, as well as in countries such as Argentina, in Latin America, show that alliances with both corporate and institutional actors are very risky for LGBTQIA+ communities, as these are often at best performative and are not strongly based on structural changes across these different types of institutions and corporations. While formulated mostly in the form of a provocation, this book asks the question of what it would mean to effectively 'de-grow' (or scale back, or rethink) the very nature of Pride Events, especially the big ones happening in global metropoles around the world, to subtract LGBTQIA+ activism to the whims and priorities of both institutional actors who appropriate LGBTQIA+ rights agendas only if and when compatible with their own electoral prospects, as well as corporate actors who treat DEI, and any other form of inclusivity within the workplace, as a mere extension of their marketing tactics.

As for the second, namely the connection between the creation of Pride Events and the acquisition of a veneer of 'modernity' for the specific country hosting these events, I have suggested that we should go in the direction of refusing the primacy of Western-driven modernity when it comes to LGBTQIA+ rights, all the more in light of the increasing inconsistencies and instances of erasure of decades-long commitments towards these rights across various sites in the Global North. Instead of promoting the idea of a Western linear model of development of LGBTQIA+ rights across the globe, one that uses Pride Events as one of the main measuring tools, we should accept a splintering and fracture of the very concept of 'modernity', one that takes the symbolic form of a kaleidoscope, and refuses to offer a unified, ordered, picture of what the future looks like across the globe for LGBTQIA+ persons. This move does not require an abandonment of our belief or commitment to the respect towards the rights of LGBTQIA+ persons, as this commitment should never wane but only grow stronger in our hearts, work, and activism, but it requires the acquisition of the awareness that linearity and coherence in the obtention of these rights can be put to the service of a civilizing argument that becomes pernicious for activists around the world, because of the impossibility of fully replicating the scale, effects, and consequences of the 'original' Stonewall thousands of times across the globe.

By reclaiming the political nature of Pride Events beyond the controversies existing as to whether these events should be a 'protest' or a 'party' (McFarland Bruce 2016: 21), this book uses the experiences of Pride organizers in different countries and contexts to reflect on why the 'globalization of Pride Events' should not be seen as a mere 'copy and paste' of a Western blueprint, but should be analysed in depth in order to unveil the specificities, interconnections, as well as conflicts and tensions existing in their organization. I argue that Pride Events contribute to the creation of what I call 'Kaleidoscope Modernities', as a form of plural and multi-dimensional sexual and gender modernities that develop across the world beyond the alleged primacy of so-called 'Western modernity' (Rahman 2014b).

The analysis that follows portrays Pride Events as multi-dimensional, layered, and intimately connected to the specific contexts in which they emerge and they are organized, but simultaneously connected to global discourses on LGBTQIA+ rights and politics. The book puts forward a reflection on the process of growth and multiplication of Pride Events, critically analysing the assumption for which 'bigger is better', and appraising the multiplication of Pride Events across different scales. Contextually, the book also analyses another assumption that emerges in relation to Pride Events: that these gatherings should be taken at face value as the tangible 'proof' of a country's entrance into the realm of sexual and gender 'modernity', vis-à-vis countries that persist in refusing to recognize LGBTQIA+ rights around the world. This argument is accompanied by a critical reappraisal of the historical legacy of the 1969 Stonewall Riots whose process of 'mythologization' contributes to create a single-origin story that flattens and overshadows rich and complex histories of local resistance around the world. Last, the book delves into the intricacies of the contemporary challenges faced by Pride organizers in the creation of their events to explore how the 'Kaleidoscope Modernities' of Pride Events unfold in real life and how they splinter our understanding of an alleged uniform and globalized LGBTQIA+ movement across the globe.

This book seeks to ignite conversations in both academic and activist circles on how we nurture the public spaces of Pride Events as democratic, representative, inclusive, free from the dictates of Rainbow Capitalism and Homonationalism, as well as crucial sites where we can collectively imagine and articulate sustainable futures.

Problematizing the growth and multiplication of Pride Events around the world

Pride Events have become a globalized phenomenon across the world, taking place in both big urban centres, as well as small villages, both in the Global North and the Global South (Peterson et al 2018b; Conway 2022, 2023, 2024; Ammaturo 2023; Slootmaeckers and Bosia 2023). As such, they have come to represent the richness and variety of LGBTQIA+ cultures and communities around the globe. At the same time, events that have been established for a long time, sometimes for half a century, have become mass events (New York City, London, Sydney, Mexico City, São Paulo, to name a few), with millions of people attending every year. Across the board, Pride organizers tend to think that 'bigger is better' (Joseph 2010: 2), and that bigger and more sophisticated events show the strength and magnitude of the response of local LGBTQIA+ communities against their local opponents or antagonists. This process of endless growth of Pride Events represents a critical issue that needs to be further scrutinized in light of growing concerns about the increasing reliance of Pride organizers on corporate sponsors that help the creation of bigger than ever yearly events.

At the same time, because of the growing importance of these events in the specific local contexts in which they take place, as well as their steady multiplication across different latitudes, it is necessary to critically interrogate the effects of this proliferation. This is particularly relevant against the backdrop of existing conversations in the literature about the globalization of LGBTQIA+ rights and identities (Altman 1996, 1997; Grewal and Kaplan 2001; Massad 2008; Zhou et al 2021), which scrutinizes the extent to which Western-centric ideas about sexual orientation and/or gender identity are being 'transposed' or 'translated' onto the global stage, and seek to appraise the effects of these processes.

This book argues that the transposition and multiplication of Pride Events is not a neutral process, one that should be taken at face value. On the contrary, through the experiences of Pride activists from around the world, the book discusses how the global multiplication of Pride Events is riddled with tensions between the local and the global dimensions, following processes of 'queer hybridization' (Martin et al 2008). Simultaneously, the book also seeks to overcome the existing 'metronormative' bias of research on LGBTQIA+ issues that subordinates rural or peripheral LGBTQIA+ lives and experiences to those of people living in urban settings (Halberstam 2005), looking at the social and political significance of organizing Pride Events in these marginal locations, often as a direct response to the alienation experienced by LGBTQIA+ persons participating in big urban Pride Events that do not represent them. Contextually, the book also analyses another type of proliferation of Pride Events: that of 'Alternative Events' where specific segments of the LGBTQIA+ community, such as racialized persons or trans persons, can create their own events grounded in more inclusive and intersectional principles than 'mainstream' events.

The mythologization of the Stonewall Riots and the overshadowing of the plural histories of Pride Events

The exponential growth of Pride Events around the world requires an interrogation of their historical roots. This book problematizes the widely received assumption that the global history of Pride Events can be traced back to the events of the 1969 Stonewall Riots in New York City, representing the 'mythical foundation' of the global LGBTQIA+ movement (Armstrong and

Crage 2006: 744). While the historical significance of the 1969 Stonewall Riots is undeniable in firing up the imagination of LGBTQIA+ persons and activists around the world, the book cautions against this process of 'mythologization' that elevates the role of Western LGBTQIA+ movements compared to the subordinated and sidelined local histories of sexual and gender resistance around the world. Research on Pride Events, particularly in the Anglophone world, suffers from this Western-centric approach, one that disregards the coeval histories of sexual and gender diversity (and liberation) across countries.

By creating a dialogue between the histories of Pride movements in the Global North and in the Global South, as well as engaging with Pride organizers' own understanding of this 'myth' and the global history of Pride Events, this book seeks to overcome this Western-centric mythologization of the 1969 Stonewall Riots, acknowledging the limitations of our approach to LGBTQIA+ historiography that can be summarized in the words of American gay historian John D'Emilio (1992: 236): '[B]ecause we have not done a very good job of keeping alive our history of political resistance, we often seem to act as if we were inventing the alphabet of movement building.'

Pride Events have rich and plural histories around the world, histories that transcend the linear temporal narrative of Western social movements that see the 1969 Stonewall Riots as a 'teachable moment' for other activists around the world. In order to critically assess the role of Pride Events in a globalized world, we need to question the Western-centric bias of the historiography of Pride Events, engaging with other accounts from around the world that not only challenge the historical accounts of what prompted the birth of these events for the LGBTQIA+ community, but also crucially, push us to ask ourselves what counts as 'Pride Events'.

'Kaleidoscope Modernities' and the role of Pride Events as harbingers of modernity

A growing number of LGBTQIA+ persons around the world enjoy, year on year, the possibility of taking to the streets and expressing their queer joy at Pride Events. For others, this possibility remains foreclosed because of issues such as criminalization of LGBTQIA+ identities and/or widespread forms of transphobic and homophobic violence, as well as social stigma and social marginalization. In the context of discussions on LGBTQIA+ rights around the world, Pride Events are increasingly seen as representing a sort of 'litmus test' or 'harbinger' of modernity (Ammaturo 2016b; Conway 2016; Slootmaeckers 2017). This book critically assesses and problematizes the process whereby the presence/absence of Pride Events in a specific country contributes to the creation of a dichotomy between 'modern' and 'backward' nations and paves the way to political instrumentalization of these events.

As various authors (Rahman 2014b; Klapeer 2018; Rao 2020) have argued, the use of LGBTQIA+ rights to gauge the degree of modernity and/or democracy relating to a particular country is problematic. First, it creates a hierarchy between countries who have/have not organized Pride Events, with countries who recognize LGBTQIA+ rights (often located in the Global North) being represented as inherently superior (Rahman 2014b), despite their often poor domestic track record on the implementation of these LGBTQIA+ rights. Second, this equation also contributes to the instrumentalization of Pride Events as gatherings that should not be primarily organized to benefit the LGBTQIA+ community, but are needed to impress international donors, embassies, international organizations, and other political actors who may have vested interests in using LGBTQIA+ rights as a form of leverage and bargaining chip (Weber 2016; Lalor 2020; Rao 2020).

This book shows that these processes of conceptualization of Pride Events as key symbols of sexual and gender modernity, allegedly deriving from a Western conception of what counts as 'modern', are part of broader homonationalist narratives (Puar 2007) that posit the Global North as trend-setter when it comes to LGBTQIA+ rights, and the Global South as recipient of these sort of 'civilizational events'. Far from expressing a cynical approach to Pride Events, one that deprives them of the crucial role that these events play for the specific communities in which they are organized, this book shows the complexity of this issue through the experiences of Pride organizers, and warns against the processes of homonationalist instrumentalization that many governments in countries located in the Global North (and sometimes governments in countries in the Global South as well) operate in order to promote Pride Events as the most tangible illustration of how modern or advanced a particular country is, while hiding neocolonial and neoimperialist projects that are often steeped in violence, economic exploitation, and subordination along lines of racial and geopolitical discrimination.

By articulating the concept of 'Kaleidoscope Modernities', as a way to describe the existence of multiple trajectories of sexual and gender modernities existing across the world, this book seeks to counter homonationalist and civilizational discourses that instrumentalize Pride Events.

Beyond the trope of 'protest or party': navigating the challenges of contemporary Pride politics

Oftentimes, Pride Events are presented as joyous, colourful, and loud events that allow LGBTQIA+ persons to freely showcase their identities, meet others, as well as engage in social and political protest. However, historically, events organized for the LGBTQIA+ community, such as Pride Events, are inherently conflictual (Ghaziani 2008), as they have to reconcile different 'souls', instances, and agendas of the various segments of the LGBTQIA+ community (Joseph 2010; McFarland Bruce 2016; Peterson et al 2018b). By centring the various experiences of Pride organizers interviewed for this research, the book explores various areas of conflict and tensions that exist in the context of the organization of Pride Events around the world, trying to carefully portray the interconnection between specific local challenges experienced by organizers (criminalization, violence, social and political oppression), with the bigger issues that all activists face at the global level (capitalism, climate change, global homo/transphobia).

The book identifies a number of tensions and conflicts that are key to understand the contemporary global and local politics of Pride Events pertaining to the areas of human rights, grassroots politics, the commodification and corporatization of Pride Events, the creation of events accessible to disabled and neurodivergent persons, as well as challenges relating to environmental sustainability. Both in the Global North and in the Global South, Pride organizers face significant issues in trying to promote a human rights agenda during the events, while protecting their communities, and having impact at the social and political levels. In the book, I highlight how, sometimes, this hostility to human rights issues, such as in the case of the rights of trans persons, also crucially needs to be combatted from within the community itself (Weiss 2012; Nagoshi et al 2017). Another important challenge explored in the analysis is represented by the growing 'professionalization' of Pride organizers (Butterfield 2016; Paternotte 2016), who increasingly approach Pride Events from the perspective of event management, rather than from a grassroots-based perspective. This process results in alienation from members of the local LGBTQIA+ communities that do not feel represented by the big (corporate) Pride Events (Matebeni 2017; Mbasalaki 2022; Formby 2023). Connected to this tension between the professionalized and grassroots nature of Pride Events is the question of the increasing importance of Pride Events organized in rural and peripheral settings (Ammaturo 2023; Lockett and Lewis 2022; Lewis and Vorobjovas-Pinta 2021). In this book I show how the growth of Pride Events in these peripheral settings is often partly configured as a form of critique to the fact that big Pride Events organized in big cities alienate and marginalize LGBTQIA+ persons living in the countryside or in smaller locales. I see the rise of Pride Events in rural and peripheral settings as an exciting development that can really change our understanding of what Pride should look like, but also what is the very purpose of Pride Events in the first place. Connected to this is the question of the rising importance of 'Alternative Pride Events' (Halperin and Traub 2009; Taylor 2016), such as Black Pride, Trans Pride, Latino Pride, or Dyke Marches, which also challenge the mainstream politics of Pride Events as being exclusionary and too commercialized and commodified.

In this regard, the question of commodification and corporatization of Pride Events (Johnston 2007b; Enguix 2009; Joseph 2010; Ammaturo 2016a; Taylor 2016; Conway 2024), represents one of the most contentious issues that Pride organizers have to contend with. Pride organizers are often limited in the type of event that they can create for their communities because of the financial resources needed. They often resort to having corporate sponsors to raise funds for their events (Peterson et al 2018b). Simultaneously, Pride Events themselves often become 'commodities' that can be branded to attract more people, such as in the case of LGBTQIA+ tourists (Puar 2002; Rushbrook 2002; Bell and Binnie 2004; Dixon 2024). In the book I extensively explore these difficult decisions that Pride organizers take to make their events financially viable, while responding to critique of having 'sold out' to the logics of capitalism. With this analysis I reflect on the need for Pride organizers to consider whether incentives to grow 'bigger and better' (Joseph 2010: 2) are really in the interests of the LGBTQIA+ community, particularly when this growth becomes conditional to the obtention of corporate sponsors. In the book, I argue therefore, that Pride organizers should critically engage with the very concept of wanting to endlessly grow their events, as opposed to nurturing financially viable options that lessen the reliance on corporate actors who predominantly pursue their pinkwashing agenda.

Some challenges experienced by Pride organizers are not as visible as others but are key to the future of these events. In the book, I have addressed two issues that have not been at the forefront of the scholarly analyses of Pride Events: the creation of accessible Pride Events for disabled and neurodivergent LGBTQIA+ persons, and the creation of Pride Events that are environmentally sustainable and do not become complicit with polluting corporations for their practices of pinkwashing. With this analysis, I argue that it is crucial and urgent to bring these two issues to the forefront of the social and political agendas of Pride organizers. Traditionally, Pride Events have not been very inclusive of disabled and neurodivergent persons (Webb 2014; Pieri 2021), with some participants feeling alienated or discriminated against (Stonewall 2018; Kempapidis et al 2023). Increasingly, Pride organizers are adopting 'accessibility policies' to enhance the inclusivity of their events for disabled and neurodivergent persons, but Pride Events are still predominantly organized following able-bodied canons. Making Pride Events accessible represents not only a tokenistic exercise of inclusion, but an invitation to rethink the ways in which LGBTQIA+ persons occupy public space in a way that challenges the interlocking oppressions of compulsory able-bodiedness and compulsory heterosexuality at the same time (McRuer 2008). The question of environmental sustainability also invites us to rethink what Pride Events should look like, and what it means to make Pride Events sustainable. In the book, I argue that Pride organizers need to take seriously the slogan 'No Pride on a Dead Planet' chanted by many participants to Pride Events, as it represents a wakeup call to build cross-movement alliances for a future where climate change can be addressed by a wide range of actors, including LGBTQIA+ persons attending Pride Events.

The complexities of researching Pride Events between the local and the global

Researching Pride Events at the global level is both an ambitious and humbling feat. In approaching this research, my intention has been that of broadening the horizon relating to the study of Pride Events beyond the hegemonic Western narrative of the 1969 Stonewall Riots and their mythical status. However, in doing so, I have been humbled by the vast amount of research that exists around the world about Pride Events in different geographical contexts, and my lack of awareness about them. Building on the recognition of the vastness of the research existing in different contexts, countries, and languages, in this book I suggest that conversations about Pride Events should be articulated in pluralistic and epistemologically open-ended ways, particularly within the hegemonic circle of LGBTQIA+ studies in the Global North, in order to avoid reproducing a singular, progress-driven narrative that flattens the cultural, social, and political complexity of these gatherings for LGBTQIA+ communities around the world.

The language used in this book concerning sexual and gender diversity resorts to the use of the acronym LGBTQIA+ to indicate identities such as Lesbian, Gay, Bisexual, Transgender, Queer, Intersex, Asexual, Plus (to indicate other identities). It is important to note that this language is non-exhaustive when it comes, for instance, to Indigenous genders and sexualities that may not be 'translatable' or confined to this predominantly Western and identity-based model (Picq and Tikuna 2019). For this reason, while the LGBTQIA+ acronym represents the most visible and recognizable terminology to define a wide range of individualities and experiences loosely connected by forms of discrimination relating to sexual and/or gender expression, in the context of this book, this terminology should not be considered epistemologically exhaustive in relation to the plurality of subjectivities that exist at the global level. Furthermore, while the book does not explicitly include 'non-binary' as a part of the acronym utilized, non-binaries' subjectivities are certainly included in the fold of the experiences discussed, including those of several participants to the research for this book. On a different note, the book uses the term 'racialized' to describe broadly a heterogeneous group of people who experience a process of 'racialization',[2] as a process whereby 'racial groups' are created and subsequently assigned specific hierarchical value. When specific identities (Black, Brown, Indigenous, Traveller/Roma) are concerned, I specify this in the context in which it is needed, without generalizing.

Importantly, another aspect to clarify is the use of the expression 'Pride Events' used in this book. A large portion of the literature, until recently, has adopted the terminology of 'Pride Parades' to describe the phenomenon of gatherings by LGBTQIA+ persons related to human rights claims and demands for freedom and equality. In this book, I use the term 'Pride Events' in a broader sense, to include not just 'parades', but also marches, festivals, pop-up events, one-off gatherings, as well as ceremonies and online meetings, to describe a wide array of happenings which have as a common (sometimes loose) red thread the creation of communities for LGBTQIA+ persons at both the global and local levels. In this book, these events are predominantly public, establishing crucial connection with questions of visibility (and who can afford to be visible) discussed by Edenborg (2020). From a methodological perspective, the adoption of the term 'Pride Events' represents a way to obviate problems arising from the inherent polysemic and polyfunctional nature of these gatherings. As their forms, characteristics, part-taking patterns, as well as objectives change, using the expression 'Pride Events' to describe them helps to bring to the forefront the activist dimension of these gatherings, regardless of whether organizers conceptualize them as 'parties' or 'protests'.

At the same time, I am very aware that the use of the term 'event' could be interpreted by some as characterizing these gatherings as in need to be analysed from the perspective of 'event management', as is the case in some of the literature (Lewis and Vorobjovas-Pinta 2021; Lockett and Lewis 2022). This is certainly not my perspective, as I do not intend to emphasize the element of leisure and/or entertainment of these events (although they obviously possess both), but I understand the term 'event' as something that 'happens' and has social and political significance above any other meaning.

For this research, I have carried out interviews online (on Zoom), with 60 Pride organizers from 29 different countries and one autonomous territory around the world. One of the biggest priorities for this research has been the necessity of decentring Western Pride Events as a sort of 'blueprint'. While I have contacted over 400 Pride organizers via e-mail to invite them to participate in my research, as well as publicizing my research call on social media, I have paid particular attention to the inclusion of as many Pride organizers as possible from various countries from the Global South (India, South Africa, Colombia, Bangladesh, Taiwan, to name a few). Often, activists interviewed from these countries were exiguous, and the activists from the Global North are over-represented in the participants. For this reason, the sample of 60 participants for the interviews is to be considered a 'convenience' sample (Etikan et al, 2016), as I have recruited participants that have responded to my call. At the same time, I have also made sure that people interviewed represented a wide range of intersectional characteristics, in terms of gender, gender identity, sexual orientation, 'race' and ethnicity, age, and disability.

I conducted the interviews in four different languages: English, Spanish, Italian, and French. These were the languages that I could access in terms of my personal ability to use them professionally. I am aware that linguistic transactions in these languages contain an element of coloniality, given their historical role of the country of origin of these languages as colonizers of populations, particularly across the Global South. At the same time, given the overwhelming predominance of English as a language to describe the experiences of LGBTQIA+ persons, particularly in academic circles, I intentionally adopted plurilingualism (Andrews et al 2018) to both challenge my own knowledge about Pride Events, as well as offering the opportunity to participants to articulate their experiences in ways that were more authentic to them. This has obviously not been possible for every participant, as I do not speak Mandarin, Norwegian, or Urdu, for instance, but I made an explicit epistemological choice to decentre the hegemony of English as a language through which our knowledge of LGBTQIA+ lives and experiences can be discussed and transmitted. In doing so, I engage with attempts to actively decolonize my methodological approach to research, inspired particularly by the work of Linda Tuhiwai Smith (2021).

Interviews carried out for this research consisted of around ten semi-structured questions that were presented consistently to interviewees. The questions pertained to the following three broad thematic areas, identified both deductively (themes 1 and 2), and inductively (theme 3): (1) the meaning(s) of LGBTQIA+ and Pride activism; (2) the organizational challenges and issues encountered in creating Pride Events; (3) the impact of the COVID-19 pandemic on the organization of Pride Events since 2020. I analysed the transcripts using the software NVivo and coded according to principles pertaining to Thematic (Braun and Clarke 2012) and Discourse Analysis (Gill 2000). Codes were developed in each of the four languages and compared to find similarities. Most codes coincided across languages. Those who were not consistent did not present significant results that needed to be discussed in the analysis. Each participant's transcript was fully anonymized and pseudonymized, to protect their identities.

As a white European researcher working in a Western academic institution, I am aware of my privileges in designing such a research agenda, as well as my complicities with this 'hegemonic' field of study of LGBTQIA+ research that I engage with and seek to critically consider. However, I have tried to the best of my ability to intellectually challenge my epistemological preconceptions on the history and politics of Pride Events, and I hope that I can entice others to do the same by reading this book. In conducting this research, I have felt simultaneously an insider and an outsider (Merton

1972). As an insider, I have felt commonality of intents and empathy with the experiences of Pride organizers who have discussed with me both their personal and professional challenges as LGBTQIA+ persons. As an outsider, however, I had to approach the world of organizing Pride Events as something that is far removed from my personal experience. Furthermore, the geographical distance, as well as the remoteness of the methodological tool used to carry out this research (online interviews on Zoom), has meant that I have had to realize my extraneity to the lived reality of many activists around the world whose experiences, social, legal, and political contexts are very different from my own.

As a queer and disabled cisgender woman, I felt the honour and responsibility to convey and represent the experiences of the people I have talked to in a way that was both authentic, accurate, and respectful. While personal opinions are often hard to disentangle from activists' positionings, I have been careful about labelling the participants' responses to this research as indicative of their posture towards specific themes. On the contrary, I have sought to balance the personal dimension of activism, with the collective and structural elements that shape and constrain individual and organizational choices. In the book, this intention has been achieved by contextualizing as much as possible the claims made by activists in relation to the specific terrains within which they operate, as well as the existing social, cultural, legal, financial, and political landscapes they inhabit. I hope that this research speaks to my intention and contributes to bringing closer the sometimes-distant worlds of LGBTQIA+ activism and academia.

The contents of this book

This book is structured in three parts. Part I, which includes the first three chapters, analyses Pride Events from a theoretical perspective. Chapter 1 discusses how central the 'founding myth of Stonewall' is in understanding the global proliferation and success of Pride Events, arguing for the need to broaden our epistemological horizon in considering the global historiography of Pride Events beyond Anglophone academia. Chapter 2 critically analyses how Pride Events are often considered to be an indication of the 'modernity' of specific countries and how this process is connected to homonationalist and civilizational discourses grounded in the international politics of LGBTQIA+ rights across the Global North and the Global South. For this purpose, the chapter introduces the concept of 'Kaleidoscope Modernities' to pluralize the meaning of sexual and gender modernities around the world from a critical point of view. Chapter 3 problematizes the multiplication and fragmentation of Pride Events from a conflictual perspective, showing that Pride Events are polysemic and polyfunctional for various segments of the LGBTQIA+ communities, and that contestation over their meaning at both the local and global levels contributes to pluralize the idea of one static version of 'Pride Events'.

Part II of this book, consisting of three chapters, centres the experiences of the 60 Pride organizers interviewed for this project to explore five areas where they encounter challenges and tensions in the organization of their events: human rights, grassroots politics, corporatization, disability and accessibility, and environmental sustainability. Chapter 4 considers the importance of human rights as a 'frame' for the organization of Pride Events and shows how Pride organizers articulate rights claims during their events, as well as dealing with hostility from various institutions, such as the government or the police, and from some sectors of civil society, such as organized religions or counter-protestors. Chapter 5 moves to considering the importance of grassroots politics in the creation of Pride Events, as well as the conflicts that arise when LGBTQIA+ persons feel detached from their own community. In particular, the chapter explores conflicts relating to the participation of the police and/or the armed forces at Pride Events, the discrimination of some segments of the LGBTQIA+ community at Pride Events that gives rise to the creation of 'Alternative Pride Events', as well as the proliferation of Pride Events in rural and peripheral settings as an alternative to those organized in urban settings. Chapter 6 delves deeper into some of the conflictual aspects of the global politics of Pride Events by focusing on the growing role of corporate sponsors and commodification at Pride Events. The chapter considers the experiences of Pride organizers in juggling the need for financial resources to organize their events, with the necessity of preserving the principles and values of social justice that are often at odds with the pinkwashing (Puar 2011; Dhoot 2015; Holmes 2022) agendas of corporate sponsors.

The last two chapters of this book, Chapters 7 and 8, constitute Part III of this book and focus on a discussion for a new politics of Pride Events that centres social justice and intersectional solidarity, and imagines radical forms of reconfiguration of practices of mutual care, grassroots politics, and interconnected demands that challenge the extant neoliberal status quo of LGBTQIA+ politics across various global sites. Chapter 7 analyses the challenges relating to the creation of accessible Pride Events for disabled and neurodivergent persons. Currently, Pride Events are not always inclusive of disabled and neurodivergent persons, leading to feelings of isolation and alienation from this event. This chapter explores how Pride organizers tackle the challenge of accessibility. Chapter 8 engages with growing demands by LGBTQIA+ persons around the world to make Pride Events environmentally sustainable. The chapter considers the strategies adopted by Pride organizers as well as raising questions about how corporate sponsors often use Pride Events to 'pinkwash' their reputation as major global polluters.

With this book I hope to offer a comprehensive and exciting overview of the global and local politics of Pride Events from a critical perspective, one that argues that we should protect the significance of these gatherings for LGBTQIA+ persons who take part in them, while simultaneously recognizing that these events can become prey to corporate and political actors who can radically transfigure and hollow out their transformational and radical political potential to imagine new ways of being queer in public spaces in our cities, towns, and in the countryside. At the same time, the book centres the role of conflict in the creation of Pride Events, showing the painstaking process of negotiation between different instances that is needed to create such multifaceted events, and highlighting the ever-growing importance of creating Pride Events that are not just intersectional, inclusive, accessible, sustainable, and plural, but that can be active sites where LGBTQIA+ persons can converge to imagine futures where the achievement of social justice for everyone represents an urgent priority.

Notes

[1] The full list of countries and one autonomous territory contains the following in alphabetical order (number of participants in brackets): Australia (1), Bangladesh (1), Canada (3), China (1), Brazil (2), Colombia (1), Czechia (1), Denmark (1), Faroe Islands (1), France (2), Germany (3), India (1), Ireland (1), Italy (5), Japan (1), Kosovo (1), Lebanon (1), Malta (1), Mexico (4), New Zealand (2), Norway (1), Spain (1), Serbia (1), Slovakia (1), South Africa (2), South Korea (1), Taiwan (2), the Netherlands (1), United Kingdom (9), United States of America (7).

[2] For more information on the concept of 'racialization', its critiques, and its implications, please see Murji and Solomos (2005), Hudley (2016), and Uyan (2021) among others.

PART I

Theorizing Pride Events between the Local and the Global

1

Decentring the 1969 Stonewall Riots: Beyond Foundational Myths?

In both academic and non-academic circles, the 1969 Stonewall Riots (henceforth, Stonewall Riots) in New York City are considered to represent a 'watershed moment', the foundational point of contemporary queer history, and the birth of the global LGBTQIA+ (lesbian, gay, bisexual, transgender, queer, intersex, asexual, plus) movement. During the recent commemoration of the 50th anniversary of the events in 2019, this argument has been articulated numerous times and continues to gain popularity whenever the origins of Pride Events are discussed. On 28 June 2019, at a rally held in front of the Stonewall Inn, the then chairman of Amsterdam Pride, Frits Huffnagel[1] said: 'All the Prides we have in the world, it started here. We are all standing on the shoulders of the people who were here' (Gold 2019). While it is undeniable that the Stonewall Riots have reached a notoriety and significance that transcends the US borders and continue to excite and ignite the imagination of scores of activists across different locales, it is nonetheless reductive to retrace the entire genealogy of social and political resistance at the global scale to one single point in history originating from the Global North. This story of a singular 'origin' also suggests a conceptualization of activism as instant and almost capricious, as if the Stonewall Riots occurred in a historical vacuum and spread like 'wildfire' (Armstrong and Crage 2006: 744), rather than being interconnected with the stratification of different activities and actions, networks, relationships, and conflicts arising between heterogeneous groups constituted by organizations, loosely connected groups, as well as individuals across different spatial and temporal points, in both the Global North and in the Global South.

For this reason, although the Stonewall Riots should be celebrated as a significant moment in the history of social movements that strive to obtain social, political, and legal recognition for LGBTQIA+ people; they should also be fundamentally problematized and contextualized both in relation to global geographies of gender and sexuality, as well as in relation to epistemological questions on how historical knowledge on LGBTQIA+ movements is created, and what narratives are bolstered or favoured to the detriment of invisibilized stories or experiences. The problematization of the Stonewall Riots, therefore, does not intend to detract from the brave actions of activists in New York City who fought discrimination and harassment on those fateful days, but seeks to open up the debate about how we memorialize key moments in the history of LGBTQIA+ movements on a global scale (Altman 1996), who is in charge of this process of memorialization, and what (productive) effects the overwhelming importance given to the Stonewall Riots has had (and continues to have), particularly in relation to the entrenchment of contemporary ideas about sexual and gender 'modernities' that are presented as potentially transposable across the globe, such as through the organization of Pride Events.

This chapter directly addresses this necessity of problematizing Stonewall by engaging with epistemological questions about its historiography and ensuing process of memorialization, as well as considering and analysing critical voices that seek to reshape or resize the significance of this moment in (queer) history, particularly coming from non-hegemonic settings in the context of LGBTQIA+ academic studies and activism, such as Latin America, Asia, and Africa. In light of the global multiplication of Pride Events, as well as their growing diversification in terms of forms, part-taking dynamics, as well as objectives, it is crucial to critically reappraise the role and influence that the legacy of the 1969 Stonewall Riots hold for LGBTQIA+ persons around the world.

Scholars across different fields in the anglophone academy, such as history, sociology, politics, as well as gender and sexuality studies, have engaged in a critical manner with both the events and legacies of Stonewall. In doing so, however, they have mostly kept this exercise confined[2] either to the horizon of the US (Kissack 1995; Armstrong and Crage 2006; Piontek 2006; D'Emilio 2007; River 2015; Duberman 2019) or, in some cases, the Global North (Lippert 2012; Cleminson 2020; Shield 2020). Simultaneously, however, across different locations in the Global South, and particularly in the context of Latin America (but not limited to[3]), hispanophone (Maire 2020; Melamed 2020; Caro Romero 2020) and lusophone[4] (Trindade 2011, 2018; Camargos 2018; da Costa Junior 2022) academic literature has grappled with questions relating to the extent to which Stonewall has been influential in prompting the emergence of autochthonous LGBTQIA+ movements in specific countries (Mexico, Colombia, Brazil, El Salvador, to cite a few) or entire regions, such as Latin America as a whole. In this regard, in order to truly problematize the role, relevance, and legacies of the Stonewall Riots in a way that de-centres Euro-US-centric narratives, and opens up new avenues for both theoretical and empirical analysis of LGBTQIA+ movements at the global level, it is necessary to put these two major strands of literature on the Stonewall Riots, from both the Global North and the Global South, in conversation, in order to challenge hegemonic and homogenizing narratives on the importance of this historical event for the global history of sexual and gender diversity and social movements.

The first section briefly describes the events that occurred on 28 June 1969 in New York from a historiographic perspective, thus trying to offer an overview of various forms in which these events have been described by historians, particularly in the mainstream scholarship emerging from the US. Following this discussion, the section then moves to consider the role of the process of 'memorialization' of these events. On the one hand, emphasis is given to the role of 'memory' in the construction and success of contemporary social movements (Eyerman 2015), including the LGBTQIA+ movement. On the other hand, the section goes beyond the celebratory or descriptive elements of the 'memorialization' process, to investigate the more productive effects that these practices of remembrance and commemoration have on the creation of a unified (Bravmann 1995), abstract, and yet allegedly translatable LGBTQAI+ history across the world.

The second section of this chapter delves deeper into the specific dynamics underlying the creation of the so-called 'Stonewall Myth' which has been a growing concern for several scholars (Bacchetta 2002; D'Emilio 2007; Marcus 2009; Duberman 2019). This section achieves this objective by discussing Barthes' (2009) approach to the question of the 'myth' as a system of communication that is conveyed by specific discourses, as a specific type of speech. This section seeks to demonstrate, by problematizing this process of 'mythologization' of the Stonewall Riots, that the creation of this narrative of univocal origin of global LGBTQAI+ movements across the world forecloses the emergence of alternative genealogies of sexual, gender, and queer resistance, both in the Global South, but also at the periphery of the Global North, thus re-entrenching Western hegemonic discourses on sexual and gender(ed) subjectivities, as well as understandings of sexual 'modernity' (Bravmann 1995: 56) that create, de facto, global hierarchies between subjects and communities.

Last, the third section of this chapter brings to the forefront contributions from within the Global South, particularly from several countries in Latin America (Brazil, Colombia, El Salvador, Mexico), Asia (Pakistan, Philippines, China, and Japan), as well as from Africa (South Africa) in order to reflect on how the creation of this 'myth' has morphed into the rise of Stonewall as a 'metaphor' (Shield 2020: 202) whereby different countries try to trace back the origins of 'their own Stonewall(s)' (Griffiths 2014: 55). While acknowledging the proliferation of these so-called 'Stonewall Metaphors' across different national settings ('Brazil's Stonewall' or 'Colombia's Stonewall', to name a couple), this section also seeks to show the existence of alternative histories and genealogies for sexual, gender, and queer resistance across different locales, which help to scale back the importance attributed to the Stonewall Riots as the original 'beginning'[5] (Piontek 2006: 10) of global LGBTQIA+ activism to show, instead, how sexual and gender movements across the world have often mobilized due to specific local challenges that arose in terms of political structures, policies, and/or specific local events that threatened the local LGBTQIA+ communities.

This chapter helps to both situate and contextualize the importance attributed to the Stonewall Riots as the one founding moment of (global) LGBTQIA+ activism, with the view of proceeding, in the following chapters, to undo this unifying narrative by showing the plurality of histories, challenges, and opportunities that exist across the world in specific settings when it comes to the articulation of a so-called local and global 'Pride Politics'.

Historiography and memorialization of the Stonewall Riots

Protests, riots, uprisings, rebellions, and events of a similar nature are often considered to be key to understand the genesis and/or history of social movements that make demands for specific marginalized or minoritized groups within a society, such as on grounds of gender, sexuality, 'race' and ethnicity, religion, class, disability, migration, and other characteristics or personal circumstances. The literature on social movements is too vast to summarize in this context. However, these key events are considered as breaking or rupture points, which change (often forever) the societies in which they occur (Collier and Collier 1991; Halvorsen 2015; Wagner-Pacifici 2017; Della Porta 2020). These events have also strong cognitive effects on those who take part (Della Porta 2020: 562), for instance through what McAdam (1988) has described as 'cognitive liberation', namely the realization by the participants to an event that their growing number can ultimately tilt the balance, possibly contributing to trigger social change. At the same time, disruptive events such as those mentioned earlier, crucially become objects of 'memorialization' and are subjected to (often) conflicting processes of remembrance (Griffin and McDonagh 2018).

The Stonewall Riots[6] can be considered as an example of a protest event whose process of 'memorialization' has highlighted strong divisions and tensions among activists, in particular LGBTQIA+ activists in the US (but also beyond the US). Much has been written about the events that took place in New York City, starting from 28 June 1969, and lasting for the entire weekend, which involved police raids on the mafia-owned[7] Stonewall Inn bar in the Greenwich Village. While much remains to be ascertained as to 'who threw the first brick?' (Hatfield 2023: 5), as the mythology goes (Waite-Santibanez 2022), it is clear from multiple historical accounts that several people were arrested on that occasion, and that patrons reacted differently to the police raid that night due to the harshness of police intervention,[8] compared to the usual 'bar raids' that it used to conduct against the gay community in New York City (Duberman and Kopkind 1993: 128). The events at the Stonewall Inn, represented a form of 'escalation' of usual bar raids made by the New York City police against LGBTQ people, and one that met fierce pushback and resistance.

Most mainstream scholarship that deals with lesbian and gay history in the US has tried to deconstruct the 'Stonewall narrative' (Kissack 1995: 105), as evidenced by the work of several authors (see D'Emilio 1983, 2007; Carter 2004; Marcus 2009; River 2015; Duberman 2019). However, attempts to diversify the historiographies of LGBTQIA+ social movements in the US, focusing on 'local LGBT histor(ies)' which cover geographical areas such as Mississippi, Pennsylvania, the South, as well as the Pacific Northwest, among other areas (Stein 2005: 613) have also multiplied (see Stein 2000; Howard 2001; Boyd 2003; Beemyn 2013; Kennedy and Davis 2014; Newton 2015). While the events at the Stonewall Inn were undoubtedly spectacular and were used to spark attention on the issue of harassment and discrimination of LGBTQ people in public spaces, it is crucial to point out that police violence and intimidation was a widespread practice across the whole of the US, and one which patrons themselves routinely resisted and pushed back against.

Moreover, discussions on decentring New York City[9] as the main hub in the creation of a US historiography of LGBTQAI+ movement(s), have also been accompanied by scholars' efforts to recentre other marginalized identities that have been often invisibilized after the events at the Stonewall Inn, such as the contributions of women, trans people, and racialized people (and people inhabiting different intersecting identities) to the events of 28 June 1969. While, in fact, the homophile[10] movement[11] managed to use the events at the Stonewall Inn to catalyse attention on the cause of the discrimination and harassment, the focus remained strongly on the issues faced by middle-class, white, gay men. The creation of the Gay Liberation Front (GLF)[12] after the Stonewall Riots, in fact, sidelined the concerns of trans people, Black people,[13] disabled people,[14] and lesbian women, despite their initial involvement in both the events themselves, and their aftermath. Gay male activists, part of the GFL, adopted a masculinist rhetoric that was compounded by suspicions of feminist agendas, which had the effect of marginalizing lesbian women (Kissack 1995: 112).

Trans people also became ostracized within the movement (Kissack 1995: 123) and, in the context of the creation of a historiography of the Stonewall Riots, practices of 'whitewashing' and 'cis-washing' (van Kessel and van Leeuwen, 2019) have also invisibilized the crucial roles of trans people of colour[15] in leading the pushback against the police during that weekend (Gan 2007: 132). The 2025 decision by the National Park Service in New York City to erase from its website any references to trans people who have participated or played a role during the Stonewall Riots and beyond (Nowell 2025), one month after President Trump's arrival to the White House for his second term, represents a worrying reiteration of this trend of 'cis- and whitewashing' of trans people from LGBTQIA+ history, and it is configured as nothing short of an act of 'epistemic violence'.

In centring the importance of trans people during the Stonewall Riots, two key figures[16] (among others) are often mentioned: Sylvia Rivera (a Latinx[17] trans activist of Puerto Rican and Venezuelan descent), and Marsha P. Johnson (a Black trans activist). While some historians, such as Carter (2004, 2019), have cast doubts on Rivera's participation in the events (La Fountain-Stokes 2021), others (Feinberg 1999; Marcus 2009; Duberman 2019; Stein 2019; White 2019) have recognized her central role in the events of June 1969. In the aftermath of the Stonewall Riots, Rivera found herself at odds with the activists of the Gay Activist Alliance (GAA) which she had joined after the Stonewall Riots (La Fountain-Stokes 2021).

In 1970, as an alternative to mainstream 'gay' activism of the time (the one embodied by the GLF and the GAA), Rivera and Johnson created STAR (Street Transvestite Action Revolutionaries) which sought to help trans people, offering shelter and support particularly to those engaged in sex work (Evans 2015). Famous is Sylvia Rivera's speech during the 1973 Christopher Street Day Parade in New York City (precursor to contemporary Pride Events), in which she was prevented from speaking on stage, but managed to get to the microphone anyway, addressing the booing crowds (Rivera 1973):

> You tell me to go and hide my tail between my legs. I will not put up with this shit. I have been beaten. I have had my nose broken. I have been thrown in jail. I have lost my job. I have lost my apartment for Gay Liberation and you all treat me this way? What the fuck's wrong with you all? Think about that! I do not believe in a revolution, but you all do. I believe in the Gay Power. I believe in us getting our rights, or else I would not be out there fighting for our rights. That's all I wanted to say to you people.

Controversies surrounding the role of Sylvia Rivera during the Stonewall Riots represent a relevant illustration of the struggles with the process of 'memorialization' of key events in the history of social movements, such as the LGBTQIA+ movement. Memory is a crucial element for social movements, particularly in relation to how the past is remembered in light of present and future struggles. Social movements remember through forms of iteration and mimetic reference, as well as through commemorative performances (Eyerman 2015: 80), the annual Pride Parades to commemorate the Stonewall Riots being a case in point. Moreover, social movements create collective memories through the recounting of so-called 'memoirs of militancy' (Marche 2015: 273), through which activists themselves offer retrospective access to the history of the social movement itself. The historiography of the LGBTQIA+ movement in the US (but also beyond the US) is full of references to first-hand accounts of activists' experiences (Marche 2015).

At the same time, however, the plurality of voices in the creation of a 'collective memory' of social movements is not a neutral process, but one that carries productive elements: 'while there is always disagreement about how to remember the past, institutionalisation sometimes shapes remembering into its simplest and least controversial form: in these cases a consensus collective memory appears' (Kubal and Becerra 2014: 869).

In this regard, one can argue that the commemoration of the Stonewall Riots, with the creation of the first parade in 1970, de facto represents the emergence of this so-called 'consensus collective memory', one that has helped to crystallize[18] a specific teleological narrative regarding the trajectory of the LGBTQ(AI+) movement and its place in queer historiography, as well as sanitizing specific narratives that might have been unpalatable in terms of reception from mainstream heterosexual public opinion of the time, such as those of trans people and/or sex workers. In an extract of his memoir contained in 'The Stonewall Reader', Mark Segal,[19] journalist and activist, affirmed (in White 2019: 125–126):

> It has been over forty years since the Gay Liberation Front first took trans seriously, but the gay men who wore those shirts with the polo players or alligator emblems didn't want trans people as the representation of their community. Their revisionist history has been accepted into popular culture because they were the ones with connections to publishers, the influence, as well as the money and time to sit back and write about what 'really' happened.

Segal's words clearly highlight the problem with the inclusiveness of trans voices in the historiography of the Stonewall Riots and subsequent activism. Again, the case of Sylvia Rivera's reliability as a participant to the Stonewall Riots is representative of those power structures that (in)validate different forms of queer knowledge. Particularly relevant, in this case, is the role of queer Latinx *testimonios* (Cruz-Malavé 2007: 228; La Fountain-Stokes 2021), which are considered especially important in relation to disenfranchised Latinx as forms of witnessing of abject events that do not just have an individual dimension, but a collective one.

Another question relating to the 'memorialization' of the Stonewall Riots is represented by the use of the term 'riot' itself. While historians and commentators quickly described the events as 'riots' in an exercise of comparison with the historic riots of the 1960s by Black Americans in

Watts, Newark, Detroit, and Harlem (White 2019: xv); later on historians have opted for the word 'uprising' in order to both highlight the relatively small size of the participants to the pushback against the police, as well as arguably elevating their importance to a higher rank than that of a 'riot'.

More in general, these considerations about the process of 'memorialization' of the Stonewall Riots echo concerns raised by Linda Tuhiwai Smith (2021: 32–35) in relation to the importance of decolonizing the epistemological approaches to knowledge-production, particularly through the use and usages of history.[20] Interrogating the process of 'memorialization' of the Stonewall Riots is not just directed at allowing the pluralization of accounts, or inclusivity of narratives (perhaps in a tokenistic way, in some cases), but requires the questioning, at a deeper level, of what role the effort of 'memorializing' the Stonewall Riots produces on queer subjects both within and beyond the horizon of the Global North. This issue becomes particularly pressing in light of a process that runs parallel to the 'memorialization' of the Stonewall Riots: its 'mythologization', which elevates the events of the weekend of 28 June 1969 in New York to the ranks of a 'sort' of ancestral beginning of a universal contemporary history of LGBTQIA+ movements, regardless of how collective (queer) consciousness has arisen across different geographical, social, political, and cultural settings across the world. The next section considers how this 'mythologization' of the Stonewall Riots has occurred, as well as the opportunities and limitations that this process imposes on our capacity to imagine a truly representative global queer activism beyond the confines of the Global North.

The 'mythologization' of the Stonewall Riots: opportunities and limitations for LGBTQIA+ social movements

More than 56 years since their occurrence, the Stonewall Riots have acquired a decidedly mythical character in the historiography and representations of global queer activism around the world. Even writing about them for the purpose of this book comes for me, as an author, with a sort of uncomfortable reverential deference to honour and do justice to a moment in (queer) history towards which I should feel indebted, as a queer person myself. And yet, this exceptional status of the Stonewall Riots in the historiography of the global LGBTQIA+ movement (if we can talk of the existence of such 'globalized' and all-encompassing movement), is one that should be contextualized and, in some measure, problematized. Not because we should undo or disrespect the value of what people who fought back during that weekend in New York did; but because single-origin stories rarely encompass the historical complexity within which social movements arise across different contexts and, as previously discussed, often hide fringes or segments of the population that these movements are purported to represent, such as cisgender lesbian and bisexual women, trans people, racialized people, or disabled people, often at various intersections of their identities.

While these events have undeniably had an enormous symbolic and material importance on the imagination and actions of US-based LGBTQAI+ activists first, and activists around the world at various historical junctures, and continue to reverberate in contemporary conversations about LGBTQIA+ human rights, their elevation to the 'key' or 'founding' moment in queer global history may represent an over-simplification, rooted in Eurocentric narratives about sexual and gender liberation. This emphasis on the crucial importance of the Stonewall Riots elevates events in Western history to the rank of 'universal' events, while obfuscating alternative histories of sexual and gender liberation that emerge from both the peripheries of the Global North itself, as well as from the variety of realities across the Global South.

The so-called 'myth of Stonewall' has been at the centre of scholarly attention. One of the most pressing questions that has been asked is why the Stonewall Riots, but not other similar events, have ascended to the ranks of a 'mythical' moment in both US (and global) LGBTQIA+ history. Armstrong and Crage (2006) have analysed how other comparable events that had happened across various locations in the US did not reach the same level of notoriety and importance, by comparing five[21] different events (including the Stonewall Riots) which involved direct confrontation between LGBTQ people with the police, using the analytical categories of 'commemorability' and 'mnemonic capacity' (Armstrong and Crage 2006: 729).

The Stonewall Riots became 'the' symbol of the gay liberation movement both because of the activists' capacity to frame the event as exceptional or significant (see for instance the role of activist Craig Rodwell in mobilizing New York's press to attend the protest) (Armstrong and Crage 2006: 737–738), as well as because of the choice of a 'commemorative vehicle' (the first parade of 1970 in New York), which *itself* represented part of the very reason why the Stonewall Riots became so central in the historiography of the LGBTQ movement in the US (Armstrong and Crage 2006, 744). Several factors converged in the context of the Stonewall Riots which allowed this episode, among many others, to be 'chosen' or identified as the one that could bring to the forefront the claims of the activists at that particular historical and geographical juncture in the US.

The use of the expression 'the Stonewall Myth' by Armstrong and Crage (2006) to describe the riots, echoes a wide number of scholars (see Bacchetta 2002; D'Emilio 2007; Chauncey 2008; Griffiths 2014; Huang 2019; Caro Romero 2020; Melamed 2020) who have interrogated the emergence of the same phenomenon. The use of the word 'myth', therefore, is not casual, but it sheds light on the social production of an event heralded as exceptional in the history of LGBTQAI+ communities worldwide and, to some extent, still enshrouded by a certain level of mystery (for instance, think about the 'who threw the first brick?' question) as the previous discussion about the challenges of 'memorialization' has highlighted. To this end, it is necessary to reflect further on the process of 'mythologization' of the Stonewall Riots, in order to understand the productive effects that this process has had, and continues to have, on the construction of a seemingly 'global' (Altman 1996) and homogeneous LGBTQIA+ audience worldwide, together with the multiplication of Pride Events across the world that take the Stonewall Riots as a sort of 'ancestral' point of inspiration.

In his book *Mythologies*, French theorist and semiotician Roland Barthes (2009) discussed how every object in the world can become a myth, even the most mundane things, such as astrology, steak and chips, or stripteases. For Barthes (2009: 131–132), a myth is a discourse or form of speech, which requires a certain level of preparation of the 'material' to be communicated. Building on the system of *signifier-signified-sign*, Barthes (2009: 138) argued that myths are constructed in a staggered way: first, through the system of language (*signifier-signified*), and then through 'metalanguage' (the *signifier* is paired with another *signified* and becomes a sign in itself), as illustrated in Figure 1.1 (adapted from Barthes 2009: 138).

Applied to the case in point of the Stonewall Riots, by reworking Figure 1.1, Barthes' theory on the creation of 'myth' can be articulated as shown in Figure 1.2.

Discussions on that (in)famous 'brick' that initiated the Stonewall Riots is the *signifier* that signifies the pushback against the police by people at the Stonewall Inn in June 1969 (the actions themselves being the *signified*). This

Figure 1.1: The creation of a myth

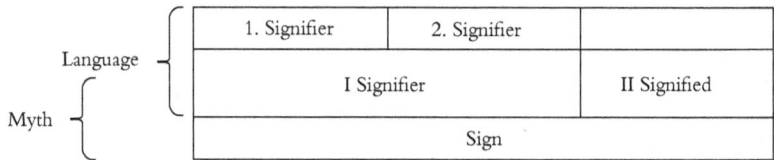

Source: Adapted from Barthes (2009)

Figure 1.2: The creation of the 'Stonewall Myth'

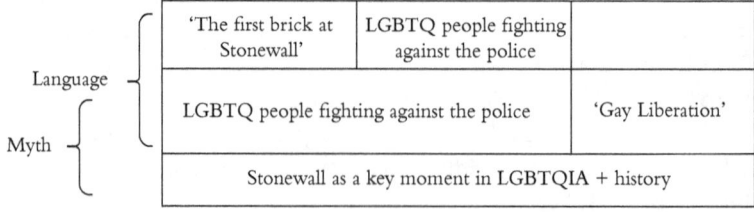

represents a *sign* which can then be used as a *signifier* of the broader concept of 'Gay Liberation' (this being the *signified*). The conjunction of the *signifier* 'LGBTQ people fighting against the police' with the *signified* 'Gay Liberation' then creates a new sign: Stonewall as a key event in LGBTQIA+ history. Barthes (2009: 154) affirms that a myth morphs history into nature, and expands on how the myth is perceived or received:

> [E]verything happens as if the picture *naturally* conjured up the concept, as if the signifier *gave a foundation* to the signified; the myth exists from the precise moment when French Imperiality[22] [Barthes' choice of example] achieves the natural state: myth is speech justified in *excess*. (Barthes 2009: 138)

Myths work by 'taming' the richness of meaning of the *signifier* (Barthes 2009: 140–141), through their form, in a way that Barthes describes as a 'robbery by colonisation' (Barthes 2009: 157). At this point, it is important to reaffirm that while the intrinsic value of the Stonewall Riots is not in question, a reflection is needed on the all-saturating nature of this 'myth' on the capacity to imagine LGBTQIA+ historiography, as well as social movements more broadly. The accounts that lesbian and gay historians present of the past has an impact on the kind of 'lessons' to be drawn from these events, as well as the strategies that can be used in the future (Bravmann 1995: 52). Moreover, for Bravmann (1995: 57) these representations can have a further role, that of constructing what he calls 'the modern homosexual', following Foucault's (1990) formulation. Expanding the horizon beyond the US, and even further afield beyond the Global North, it is possible to observe how the 'mythology' of Stonewall, this discourse on the mythical character of these events, may have an impact on strategies and analyses carried out in contexts in which sexual and/or gender politics bear very little resemblance, if any, to that of the US and/or the Global North, as the facts of Stonewall become both the 'blueprint' for emulation by other activists, as well as implicitly undermining the significance of autochthonous forms of queer, or queer-adjacent, social and political resistance.

The mythologization of the Stonewall Riots has two main effects: first, it invisibilizes prior (queer) history; and, second, it also conceals the existence of (queer) resistance across other locations across the US (Armstrong and Crage 2006: 743; Bravmann 1995), although this argument can be expanded to cover both the Global North, as well as the Global South. The existence of a myth 'naturalizes' a specific reality, as Barthes has suggested (2009: 138). One of the effects of this 'naturalization' of the Stonewall Riots as the turning point of LGBTQIA+ history (both in the US and beyond) has been the creation of a pre- and post-Stonewall era, a distinction 'between oppression and liberation' (Gordon 2005: 317) that has itself acquired almost mythical features. In particular, the creation of this 'mythology' of the Stonewall Riots rests on a retrospective reading of (gay) history, and has limited the political perspectives of activism, such as overreliance on coming out (and visibility) as a political strategy (D'Emilio 2007: 250). Furthermore, defining the Stonewall Riots as the 'key' event of gay liberation renders invisible the 'gay world' that existed prior to these events. To this regard, Chauncey (2008: 2–7) addressed what he believed to be three 'myths' about pre-Stonewall gay life in the US: the myths of *isolation, invisibility,* and *internalization*. These three myths (which can be seen as entertaining a complementary relationship with the 'Stonewall Myth') suggest that a true gay subculture did not exist before the Stonewall Riots because of widespread societal hostility (*myth of isolation*); that even if this gay subculture existed it was extremely difficult for gay men to be aware and access it (*myth of invisibility*); and last, that most gay men uncritically accepted a societal view that labelled them as 'sick' or 'perverted' (*myth of internalization*) (Chauncey 2008: 2–7). These 'myths' hide a much more varied and complex history, particularly in relation to the social and political lives of gay men (other segments of the LGBTQIA+ community are not considered in this context).

Ultimately, this 'metanarrative of Stonewall' (Kennedy 1997) as the periodization of the pre- and post-Stonewall (gay) history, oversimplifies the trajectories of (gay) activism, offers a very homogeneously bleak view on pre-1970s gay politics, as well as overlooking queer resistance beyond the US (Griffiths 2014: 54–55). In turn, the use of a US chronology on gay activism surrounding the Stonewall Riots (a 'before and after' narrative), also impacts how (LGBTQIA+) identities are constituted even beyond the confines of US scholarship (Pérez and Radi 2020: 970). These approaches operate an epistemic reduction of Stonewall almost to an 'empty' myth that becomes transposable across different geographical, social, and political contexts without the need to contextualize it in relation to the specific location, or acting as a quasi-normative device regulating what LGBTQIA+ activism should look like. The next section will address more in depth the question of the polyvocal character of LGBTQIA+ global activism beyond the 'Stonewall Myth', both by analysing the relationship between this myth and national forms of activism across different global locales (predominantly across the Global South), as well as offering perspectives on histories of LGBTQIA+ activism that challenge, either partially or completely, the narrative of the Stonewall Riots as the 'origin point' of all fights.

Decentring Stonewall: towards plural(ized) histories of LGBTQIA+ activisms at the global level

As discussed in the previous section, the mythologization of Stonewall operates a relative flattening of autochthonous historiographies from plural locations beyond the horizon of the US. In doing so, it operates a form of erasure or invisibilization of local histories of resistance, and it could be conceptualized as an articulation of the so-called 'gift of the West to the rest' that Upendra Baxi describes when talking about human rights (2007).

Using the Stonewall Riots as the yardstick or 'origin point' for any other form of LGBTQIA+ activism across the world ultimately reinforces Eurocentric ideas about which (queer) histories count, and whose narratives are listened to, and are elevated to the rank of seemingly 'universal' experiences from which inspiration can be drawn. A solution to this approach can be seen in the attempt to pluralize the histories of queer resistance: 'multiplying the meanings of Stonewall may help us to acknowledge differences among queer people, including differences of race, gender, and class, as well as different approaches to the project of gay and lesbian liberation' (Piontek 2006: 23).

However, on closer inspection, the work of deconstruction that needs to be operated goes beyond the very question of 'multiplying the meanings of Stonewall', as this would still leave us firmly within the confines of Eurocentric narratives without problematizing the alleged universality and significance of this geographically situated historical event. The 'multiplication' effect would still place firmly the Stonewall Riots as the 'original blueprint' to be implicitly or explicitly compared with other events or movements. This is exemplified by the idea of the 'from-Stonewall-diffusion-fantasy', which consists in universalizing the experiences of the US as desirable and to project Western notions of activism and identity at the summit of this process (Bacchetta 2002: 949).

Illustrations of this ambivalence towards the inherent validity of the Stonewall Riots across different activist settings are exemplified by discussions relating to the role of symbolic power exercised from the US (and the Global North) in projecting specific trajectories of queer liberation onto other terrains, particularly across the Global South. Manalansan (1995: 427) described Filipino gay men's ambivalence towards the Stonewall Riots as a validating event in relation to their sexuality, and argued that the 'globalization' of the Stonewall Riots invisibilizes the hierarchical relation between the metropolis and the suburban peripheries, including experiences of migration. On another note, the 'canonization' of the Stonewall Riots risks reproducing homonationalist and homocolonialist projects of 'colonizing' the memories of other LGBTQ movements outside of the US, as discussed by Huang (2019: 70) from the vantage point of China.

Considering these critiques, a more radical approach to decentring Stonewall as the 'origin point' of (global) LGBTQIA+ activism is needed, to offer competing histories that undo the seemingly 'naturalness' or 'universality' of the Stonewall Riots: 'because history refuses to be disciplined into univocality, rather than "a" theory of gay history, we need to develop many complementary and competing theories in order to recognise, help produce, and analyze a surplus of signification of queer pasts' (Bravmann 1995: 61).

Decentring the Stonewall Riots means to make room for that plurality of 'queer pasts' that emerge from different, often 'subaltern', localities in the global geographies of LGBTQIA+ studies. While the first commemoration of the Stonewall Riots in 1970 sparked similar events in countries such as the UK (1972) and Germany (1972) initially, followed by other countries later, this alleged univocal direct genealogy needs to be problematized.

One important strand of contributions to this conversation comes from the context of Latin America, from countries such as Colombia, El Salvador, Mexico, and Brazil to name a few. Several authors, in fact, have reflected on the relationship between LGBTQIA+ movements in these countries, and the so-called 'legacy of Stonewall' or the previously mentioned 'Stonewall Myth'. In analysing the birth of the LGBTQIA+ movement in Colombia, for instance, Caro Romero (2020: 208) has argued that most events organized by local gay, lesbian, or trans activists were not fully connected to the US gay liberation movement. For many local movements, such as the *MLHC* (*Movimiento de Liberación Homosexual de Colombia*) in Colombia, *Entre Amigos* of El Salvador (Maire 2020), the *Frente de Liberación Homosexual* of Argentina (Melamed 2020), *Integración* of Chile (Melamed 2020), *SOMOS* and *Movimento Homossexual Brasileiro* in Brazil (Belmont and Ferreira, 2020), the priorities resided in combating social and political oppression in the context of harsh dictatorships, such as in the case of Colombia, Brazil, or Argentina, or civil war, as in the case of El Salvador. The Stonewall Riots, in these cases, represented often a far-away story that did not really intersect with the local struggles of LGBTQIA+ people in these countries:

> [I]t is fundamental to ask ourselves for which reasons this movement [Stonewall] is recognized as the event that marked and changed our history. ... The fight of white gays who were also, in many cases, middle class, who occupied a bar in Manhattan is capable of representing Latin American homosexuals who, in the same decades, were resisting political persecution during the civil-military dictatorships in the countries of the Southern Cone, for instance? (da Costa Junior 2022: 174; translated from Portuguese[i])

---

[i] See original text: '*é fundamental nos perguntarmos por quais razões este movimento [Stonewall] é reconhecido como o event que mudou e marcou a nossa historia. ... A luta de gays brancos e, em muitos casos, de clase media, que ocuparam un bar em Manhattan é capaz de representar homossexuais latino-americanos que nas mesmas décadas, resistiam às perseguições politicas durante as ditaturas civico-militares nos paises do Cone Sul, por exemplo?*'

Authors writing about Latin America (Trindade 2018; Caro Romero 2020, 2023; Melamed 2020; Maire 2020; Payne 2021) have centred local histories as opposed to the amorphous transposition of a 'Stonewall Myth' in different countries. In several cases, such as Colombia (Caro Romero 2020), Brazil (Trindade 2018: 235), or Mexico (Melamed 2020: 7) the groups or organizations were very close to left-wing parties[23] of either communist or socialist inspiration, rather than autonomous 'gay liberation events'. In the context of the Cold War, moreover, or general suspicion against US politics towards Central and Latin America, solidarity with North American LGBT movements was not seen as particular desirable, as for El Salvador (Maire 2020: 186) or Colombia (Caro Romero 2020: 208) for instance. These narratives counter the 'hegemonic narratives' that foreground discourses on gay liberation and create a dichotomy between the North as the creator of theories and inspiration for activist fights in the Global South (Trindade 2018: 228).

A further reflection to make is that connected to the idea of 'Stonewall as metaphor' (Shield 2020: 202), as the process whereby, while pluralizing the histories of LGBT resistance and liberation, we still use the framework of the Stonewall Riots to define what counts as a 'watershed' moment in the emergence of LGBT(QIA+) activism in specific geographical context. Examples of this process are seen in talking about 'Brazil's Stonewall' (Belmont and Ferreira 2020: 690), or a 'Stonewall español' (Espinosa 2020: 476) or an 'Italian Stonewall' (Cannamela et al 2023), although examples abound in both activist and academic discourses around the world. Arondekar (2020) has offered a poignant critique of the 'Stonewall as a metaphor' phenomenon. Invited to offer a perspective on the legacy of the Stonewall Riots, Arondekar (2020: 3) responded with a refusal to engage in this exercise, asking instead a polemical question: '[D]id the history of the Stonewall Riots create more of a political demand on subaltern collectivities to "produce" their seismic historical event, or did it foreground even more the epistemological division between the West and the Rest?' This question offers a powerful critique of the epistemic constriction to 'identify' a national 'Stonewall moment' that maps onto the model offered by the 'original' events in New York. Refusing to articulate this narrative in relation to the context of South Asia means, for the author, to interrupt this epistemological asymmetry of power relations.

A further insight into this process of decoupling of LGBTQIA+ activism from the 'Stonewall Myth' is represented by the case of South Africa (see also Croucher 2002). The case of the organization GLOW (Gay and Lesbian Organization of Witwatersrand) by Black activist Simon Tseko Nkoli in South Africa shows how embedded in South African politics, and anti-apartheid activism, was the creation of the first Pride march in Johannesburg (Carolin and Frenkel 2019: 512). Nkoli created GLOW as an open challenge to the South African apartheid regime. The first Pride March of 1990 in Johannesburg was a blend between the South African tradition of human rights marches (Women's March in Pretoria in 1956, or the anti-apartheid marches of the 1980s), as well as the 'carnivalesque tradition' of Western Pride marches (Gevisser and Reid 2013: 278). The march displayed both the 'Western aesthetics of Pride', but also hand-painted banners with pictures of Africa, as well as the formerly banned flag of the ANC (African National Congress) Party (Carolin and Frankel 2019: 514–515). On a similar note, albeit in a different context, Payne (2021: 1340) has shown how Pride marches in the city of Chilpancingo, in the Mexican state of Guerrero, have more similarities with local religious and civic traditions, such as the practice of public processions to announce important events, than in the globalized frame of the Western Pride parade.

Challenges of adopting the 'exceptionalization' of the model of US Pride Events also exist in other contexts, such as Japan. The example of Tokyo Rainbow Pride, whose first edition was sponsored by ILGA (International Gay and Lesbian Association) in 1994, shows the problematic normative effects that adopting this Westernized framework can have on local activism (Itakura 2015). The organization of the first parade in Tokyo by ILGA raises questions in relation to the role of international (governmental or non-governmental actors) in the organization of Pride Events around the world, such as in the case of ILGA Europe and the European Union, or specific national governments, such as in the case of Serbia (Slootmaeckers 2017, 2023), or Ukraine (Plakhotnik and Mayerchyk 2023b), to cite a couple of examples.

These critical discussions, coming predominantly, but not exclusively, from different countries from the Global South, show the magnitude of the issue in relation to the overwhelming importance that the Stonewall Riots still play in the narration of a (global) history of LGBTQIA+ movements, but even in the context of the Global North, this epistemic pressure to conform to the 'Stonewall Myth' is evident. Even in the context of the Global North, rich histories of queer resistance, albeit not always linear, have marked the emergence of local LGBTQIA+ movements. These movements have grappled with local histories of oppression, marginalization, and hostility that are often incommensurable with the social, political, and legal circumstances of the US in the 1960s, as analyses have shown (Lippert 2012; Cleminson 2020; Quéré 2022; Shield 2020). For instance, Portuguese and Spanish LGBTQIA+ people living under Catholic and nationalist dictatorships (see the echo with experiences in Central and Latin America), during the 1960s and 1970s, perceived the phenomenon of the Stonewall Riots as being very far removed from their daily experiences (Cleminson 2020: 217–218). In France, one of the founding moves by the FHAR (*Front Homosexuel d'Action*) was the participation in the demonstration on 1 March 1971 for the International Workers' Day in Paris (again, another echo with

Latin American experiences) (Quéré 2022). These examples, together with others, offer a nuanced account of the relationship between local and global imaginaries, as well as specific national and regional circumstances that shape activists' initiatives, and help us to reassess the importance of the 'Stonewall Myth' both across time and space. Exploring these different genealogies of queer resistance across different latitudes represents a key aspect in the process of decentring not only Western narratives on LGBTQIA+ movements but also, more specifically, US-centred narratives, that end up overshadowing the plurality of activist resistance and grassroots organization across different locales around the world (Pérez and Radi 2020: 972). Overcoming the limitations of the so-called 'Stonewall Myth' and the use of the 'Stonewall metaphor' contribute to make our knowledge and narratives on global LGBTQIA+ activisms more diverse, inclusive, and critical of extant global power relations that favour the alleged epistemological superiority of the Global North. What is needed is, therefore, a creative effort to expand the horizon of our imagination and understand that not every form of LGBTQIA+ activism can or should (have) happen(ed) in the shadow of the legacy of the Stonewall Riots.

Notes

[1] In 2020, Frits Huffnagel was asked to resign from the Amsterdam Gay Pride Foundation (AGP) because of comments against refugees he made during a radio interview. See Dutch News (2020).

[2] See notable exceptions such as Manalansan IV (1995).

[3] See for instance Arondekar (2020).

[4] See also scholarship in English on Brazil, such as Silva and Jacobo (2020) or Belmont and Ferreira (2020).

[5] Here I follow Piontek's (2006: 10) analysis of the Stonewall Riots as one of those examples of 'beginnings' discussed by Palestinian-American scholar Edward Said (1968) who argued that these sleek points of origin create a unified and temporally sequenced occurrence of events that suits our perceptual needs.

[6] For a critical appraisal of the use of the word 'riot' in this context, see White (2019).

[7] For more details about the Mafia's relationship with the LGBTQ community in the US, see Crawford (2015).

[8] Duberman and Kopkind (1993: 128) recall, similarly to other historians, how the raid on the Stonewall Inn on 28 June 1969 was different from the others that had been previously conducted. While normally police raids were carried out at least once a month by the Sixth Precinct and owners of the Stonewall Inn were always tipped off by the police before carrying out the raid; this one was carried out by eight detectives from the First Precinct, with no prior warning to the management of the bar, and with potential involvement from Federal Agents, due to some infractions in the selling of bottled alcohol in the venue. In particular, the State Liquor Authority regulation had prohibited until a few years prior, the sale of alcohol to homosexuals, resulting in ongoing practices of harassment at venues where LGBTQ persons used to gather (Duberman 2019: 141).

[9] Carter (2004: 17) also dispels the idea that New York City was relatively liberal when it came to 'tolerance' of homosexuality, compared to the rest of the country; as it seemed to be, in fact, the city where gay men were targeted the most as 'criminals'.

10. The term 'homophile', a synonym for 'homosexual', was used to describe gay and lesbian activism throughout the 1950s and 1960s (D'Emilio 1983: 240).
11. Before the Stonewall Riots, one of the main homophile organizations in the US, with several chapters across the country, was the Mattachine Society, founded in 1950 in Los Angeles, by a small group of men who defined themselves as predominantly left-wing. While, in its inception, the society had a relatively 'radical' approach and outlook on how to combat perceptions of homosexuality as a 'sickness', after only a couple of years from its foundation, more conservative members joined its ranks, pushing for mainstream acceptance for gay people, rather than focusing on a political struggle (Duberman 2019: 93–94).
12. The GLF positioned itself in strong opposition to the perceived conservatorism of the Mattachine Society which supported an agenda of integration for gay and lesbian individuals within mainstream US society.
13. Kissack (1995: 113) discusses the relationship between the Gay Liberation Movement (GLF) and the Black Panthers Party, highlighting how GLF activists such as Jim Fouratt opposed the use of homophobic language by the Black Panthers, while Black Panthers' member Huey Newton tried to persuade the party to support the gay liberation cause. Despite these tensions, the GLF continued to pursue an alliance with the Black Panthers Party.
14. For a consideration of the relationship between gay activism and disability during the late 1960s, see Kunzel (2018).
15. See also the action of two queer activists who painted with brown paint the skin of the white (male-presenting) statues of the Gay Liberation monument in front of the Stonewall Inn in New York, dressed them in feminine attire and placed a placard which read: 'Black Latina trans women led the riots, stop the whitewashing' (Hatfield 2023: 5).
16. For a nuanced critical appraisal of the 'idealization' of Sylvia Rivera and Marsha P. Johnson in tokenistic intersectional terms, see Jill-Peterson (2023).
17. For more information on the experiences of Latinx queer people during the Stonewall Riots, please see Gonzalez (2019).
18. In relation to this, see for example Johnston and Waitt's (2016: 113) discussion on the extent to which Pride parades and marches rely on a 'politics of essentialism', in order to create a sort of 'gay collective'.
19. Mark Segal is an activist and journalist who founded the group Gay Youth in Philadelphia in 1969 and was involved in the Stonewall Riots, as he discussed in his memoir *And Then I Danced* (2015).
20. See for instance Smith's (2021: 33–35) discussion of the critique of Western history in particular, organized around some 'assumptions' about the characteristics or assumptions that are made about what history should be.
21. The five events chosen for the comparison are the Police Raid of a New Year's Ball in San Francisco on 1 January 1965, a riot caused by police intervention at the Compton Cafeteria in San Francisco in August 1966, the Black Cat Raid in Los Angeles on 1 January 1967, the Stonewall Riots of 28 June 1969, and the raid of the Snake Pit Bar on 8 March 1970.
22. Here there is no intention of comparing Stonewall to the concept of 'French Imperiality' of course, but merely a substitution of a relevant example.
23. This is also true elsewhere in the Global North, for instance in France (Quéré 2022).

2

Towards Progress? Interrogating the 'Kaleidoscope Modernities' of Pride Events

Pride Events are becoming a ubiquitous fixture of public life in many countries around the world, although opposition to their organization remains rife in some contexts. According to the organization OutRight International (2023: 8), Pride Events are now organized in at least 101 countries around the world. While encouraging, this process of steady multiplication of Pride Events may overshadow the possibility of looking critically at the role that they play in the broader politics of LGBTQIA+ (lesbian, gay, bisexual, transgender, queer, intersex, asexual, plus) rights at the global level, particularly in the context of ongoing discussions on the nexus between LGBTQIA+ rights, progress, and modernity (see the Introduction to this book). Considering the exponential multiplication of Pride Events around the world (Ammaturo 2023), it is imperative to ask how Pride Events function as 'harbingers of ... modernity' (Conway 2016: np), acting as a sort of 'litmus test' to measure a country's adherence and promotion of democratic principles and institutions and, more symbolically, inscribing the specific country in the fold of 'modernity' or 'backwardness' (Ammaturo 2016b: 59; Slootmaeckers 2017). Pride Events, in fact, act as one of the most 'tangible' illustrations of how LGBTQIA+ rights are implemented and respected in a specific national context, and they can be mobilized to illustrate the existence or absence of this threshold of 'modernity' (Ammaturo 2016b; Slootmaeckers 2023).

This chapter centres the question of the role of Pride Events as markers of 'progress' and 'modernity', trying to disentangle the 'civilizing' aspects of fostering these 'universalizing' ideas about gender and sexual modernity around the world (Hoad 2018: 153). The three sections of the chapter explore different facets of the relationship between Pride Events, progress, modernity, and the globalization of LGBTQIA+ rights and identities. While the chapter obviously critically appraises the role of Pride Events at the global level, the intention is not that of cynically diminishing or devaluing the role that Pride Events play for LGBTQIA+ persons. On the contrary, the chapter seeks to highlight the ways in which Pride Events may become prey to political forms of instrumentalization and/or co-optation, by both governmental and non-governmental actors, that ultimately negatively impact Pride organizers' and participants' ability to create and take part in an event that can be truly empowering and representative of local communities, as opposed to events whose primary objective is that of impressing donors and/or political actors in relation to the country's reputation and/or record on LGBTQIA+ rights.

The globalization of LGBTQIA+ identities (Altman 1996, 1997; Massad 2008), as well as the growing importance of international LGBTQIA+ politics as a tool of both multilateral and bilateral relations between states (Langlois 2016; Richter-Montpetit and Weber 2017; Janoff 2022), have shown the importance of considering the social and political ramifications that these discursive deployments of LGBTQIA+ rights have on individuals around the world. Far from being neutral, discourses on LGBTQIA+ rights are inevitably mobilized as one of the most tangible illustrations of a specific country's journey towards the horizon of Western modernity/modernization (Rahman 2014b; Klapeer 2018; Rao 2020). This process is extremely problematic, as it adopts a sort of 'Darwinian evolutionary narrative' (Hoad 2018: 133), whereby countries that are not considered to be 'developed' (or 'developed enough'), particularly across the Global South (but not exclusively), are expected to 'catch up' with Western 'modernity'.

The first section of this chapter offers a theoretical exploration of the relationship between the concepts of 'progress' and 'modernity' vis-à-vis Western epistemologies. In particular, the section problematizes, through a contextualization with postcolonial and decolonial theories (Dussel 1993; Quijano 1993; Bhambra 2007; Mignolo 2007; Lugones 2016), narratives that separate the Global North and the Global South into two alleged different temporal zones marked, respectively, by either 'modernity' or 'backwardness'. To do so, the section predominantly focuses on the work of Momin Rahman (2014b) on Muslim identities and homosexuality, and Rahul Rao's (2020) analysis on the temporality of LGBTQIA+ rights in Uganda. These two key contributions show the need to disentangle Western ideas about LGBTQIA+ modernities from existing configurations of sexual and gender diversity and plurality around the world, with a particular focus on the processes whereby the application of this Western framework creates a dichotomy between 'modernity' and 'backwardness' that ultimately posits some countries as being in need to 'catch up' or adapt to this existing (globalized) framework of LGBTQIA+ rights.

The second section discusses how Pride Events are held to be the proof of a country's 'advancement' towards modernity and progress (Bennett 2017: 346) in relation to the protection and guarantee of the rights of LGBTQIA+ persons; as well as considering how the advancement in the protection of the rights of LGBTQIA+ persons itself (of which Pride Events represent one of the most visible public representations), becomes, in turn, an alleged marker of 'progress' and 'modernity'. To do so, the section discusses and contextualizes various claims made by activists, governmental, and non-governmental actors in connection to the organization of Pride Events, and maps expectations from these actors in relation to the organization, part-taking, and outcomes of these events (Hoad 2018; Klapeer 2018; Gurok 2022). This section shows the dangers of looking at Pride Events through the lens of 'progress' and/or 'modernity', particularly in relation to the (un)intended consequences that these political discourses may have on the LGBTQIA+ persons in these specific contexts, such as in the case of Serbia, analysed by Slootmaeckers (2023), or in the more recent Israeli practices of 'pinkwashing' during the ongoing genocide in Gaza by waving rainbow flags amid the rubble, and speaking of a fictional Pride Event on one of the region's beaches (see analysis in the second section).

The third and last section starts from the critique of the 'civilizational' model of promotion of LGBTQIA+ rights at the global level to interrogate the multivocality and multidirectionality of different trajectories relating to the concept of 'modernity' for various LGBTQIA+ activist groups around the world. By critically interrogating the work of Eisenstadt (2000) on 'Multiple Modernities' and thinking about the limitations of this model, the section offers an alternative theoretical paradigm that seeks to eschew the Western-based approach to 'modernity' as being inherently a product of the West. The section achieves this objective by putting forward the concept of 'Kaleidoscope Modernities' as a tool that can help us to navigate the complexity of objectives, achievements, and setbacks experienced by LGBTQIA+ communities around the world. By overcoming the Western-centric approach of the concept of 'Multiple Modernities', refuting the assertion of the primacy of this paradigm to understand 'other modernities', the concept of 'Kaleidoscope Modernities' calls for a splintering of our conception of a linear idea of 'progress' or 'modernization', by relying more substantially on that process of syncretic elaboration proper of the theory of 'queer hybridization' discussed in the section below.

What is the problem with 'progress' and 'modernity'? Postcolonial and decolonial approaches to LGBTQIA+ rights and social movements

Discourses on LGBTQIA+ rights around the world are imbued with narratives around 'progress' and 'modernity' (Franke 2012; Chang 2014; Rahman 2014b; Rao 2020). Yet, these narratives can create the false impression that there is a binary opposition between Western countries, in which 'modern' LGBTQIA+ politics is considered to originate, and countries in the Global South that become 'recipient' of these influxes of modernity (Rahman 2014b: 5). To counter this approach, it is instead necessary to embed our analysis in the specific settings where LGBTQIA+ rights are circulated and discussed, thereby problematizing and interrogating these 'trickling-down' or 'contagion' models of LGBTQIA+ social movements and human rights diffusion:

> [W]e need to understand the successes of LGBTIQ politics in their political and sociological context, rather than uncritically reinstating a progress narrative of modernisation that somehow implies the sexual liberation of a pre-social and pre-political identity group of subjects has occurred in the West and now simply needs to be extended to others around the world. (Rahman 2014b: 102)

This approach echoes the model of 'queer hybridization' suggested by Martin et al (2008: 6), whereby Western and non-Western perspectives on gender and sexualities do not exist in cultural silos but are characterized by mutual interconnection and mutual influences. For Martin et al (2008) there are three alternatives to consider global approaches to the study of sexuality (and gender). The first, defined as 'global homogenization' posits the adoption or resistance to forms of sexual Westernization; the second, named as 'local essentialism', relies on the reification of traditional sexualities and genders to the point of denying any external influence; and last, the concept of 'queer hybridization' (the one adopted for this analysis), which emphasizes the mutual influences that exist (and have always existed) between Western and non-Western sexualities (see also Kong 2019: 1907). This third option shows how the delineation of a truly 'Western' trajectory of modernity, particularly when it comes to sexuality, is more of a fiction, than a possible endeavour, as lines of cross-contamination and reciprocal influence are far more significant than compartmentalized understandings of specific Western or non-Western modes of expressing sexuality and/or gender.

Building on this argument relating to 'queer hybridization' (Martin et al 2008), therefore, it is necessary to problematize the notion relating to the existence of an alleged equation between modernity and the West (Dussel 1993; Quijano 1993; Mignolo 2007; Chakrabarty 2011; Morris 2022; Bhambra 2023). By the same token, the notion of 'progress' and its connection to the concept of 'modernity' (Mouzakitis 2017) also needs to be scrutinized. The problematization[1] of the concepts of 'modernity' and 'progress' is central in both contemporary Social Theory, as well as in Postcolonial and Decolonial Theory. However, while postcolonial and decolonial scholars tend to interrogate the role of 'modernity' in the context of the 'colonial/modern world system' (Escobar 2007), social theorists, as well as sociologists[2] have traditionally eschewed this dimension ((Meghji 2021: 1–27; Morris 2022: 1). In so doing, they have offered taxonomies of 'modernity' of different countries/areas, reinforcing the creation of this fictional dichotomy between modernity and backwardness (Meghji 2021). These discourses about modernity have created an almost prescriptive idea about a global order that is linear, universalizing, and leads to the ranking of countries and geographical areas in terms of their teleological trajectory towards a specific embodiment of Western modernity.

Against this backdrop, therefore, the concept of Western 'modernity' cannot be taken for granted. Earlier conceptions of 'modernity', dating back to around the 5th century, tended to portray a relationship between the old and new, by way of comparison (and sometimes imitation) of the 'ancients' (Habermas and Ben-Habib 1981: 3–4; Seed 2002: 3–4). However, it was not until the 15th century that this adjective started to be used to 'criticise the past by portraying the present in a more positive light' (Seed 2002: 6). This tendency to think about time and history through the lenses of modernity, became crystallized throughout the 18th and 19th centuries (Venn and Featherstone 2006: 458), but the idea of 'modernity' as we currently conceive it is the product of the conjunct effect of various factors[3] such as the Industrial Revolution, capitalism, empire building, and white supremacy, among others (Morris 2022: 1).

Decolonial scholars such as Quijano (1993) and Mignolo (2007) have highlighted the direct connection between the emergence of this powerful paradigm of 'modernity' and the establishment of white Western colonial domination across the world, highlighting how 'modernity' is functional to justify colonial domination and exploitation by the West (Bhambra 2007: 68). Bhambra (2007: 68) has gone as far as saying that colonization is not the outcome of modernity, but modernity *itself*: 'modernity has to be understood as formed in and through the colonial relationship – colonization was not simply an outcome of modernity, or shaped by modernity, but rather modernity itself, the modern world developed out of colonial encounters'.

Modernity, therefore, has been built through the exploitation of colonized territories, most notably through the racial and economic domination and exploitation enacted by Western Europe through the transatlantic slave trade, as DuBois and C.L.R. James had already observed in their works (Go 2013: 38; Morris 2022: 7).

A central tenet of the conceptualization of 'modernity', moreover, is the creation of a form of linear time (Venn and Featherstone 2006: 463), guided by the principle of 'entelechia', whereby beings (in this specific context countries, groups, and/or societies) tend to develop towards 'perfection' (Nisbet 1969 in Mouzakitis 2017: 5). This idea of perfection is not neutral, but part of an aspiration towards a form of European 'modernity' believed to be 'singular and superior' in the context of colonization (Quijano 2000, in Conway 2016: 19). This ideal of 'entelechia' can only be realized through the concept of 'progress' (Mouzakitis 2017: 9), as an inevitable, and morally charged, movement towards a necessary development.

The history of the impact of colonialism and imperialism on sexual and gender norms is complex and beyond the immediate scope of this analysis, but a vast body of literature has analysed how colonizers intervened, often violently and punitively, in sanctioning same-sex sexual behaviour and gender diversity across the world (see, among others, McClintock 2013; Lugones 2016; Patil 2017; Schields and Herzog 2021). As Patil (2017: 150) has argued, the effects of the colonial policies on gender and sexuality have had lasting effects not only in the context of the 'colonies' but also, crucially, in the 'post/colonies'. One example of this lasting legacy, for instance, is represented by the persistence of the criminalization of homosexual sexual conduct in many countries around the world that were previously colonized by Great Britain, such as India for instance, through the infamous Section 377 of the Penal Code (Gupta 2006; Han and O'Mahoney 2018; Picq and Tikuna 2019). This process of violent repression by the colonizers of the pre-existing sexual and gender diversity is crucially connected to the concept of 'Western modernity' previously discussed: 'The colonial destruction of native sexualities is more than a mere inability to see otherness. Labelling native sexualities as unnatural justified violent repression, and the heterosexualisation of Indians was as much a process of modernisation as of dispossession' (Picq and Tikuna 2019: 3).

Yet, with the advent of the 20th century, the growing recognition of sexual and gender diversity within the confines of the Global North, a change made possible particularly through the birth of what we would call the 'modern LGBTQIA+ movement', debates started to shift in relation to the primacy of heterosexuality and cisnormativity within Western societies, leading to the emergence of a global discourse of LGBTQIA+ rights. As Rao (2015b: 356) argues, however, the emergence of this global discourse has not been entirely beneficial to locations in the Global South, which have become the object of Western hegemonic discourses on sexual rights, with undertones that are decidedly neo-imperialist. This process has grown over the decades and has been connected tightly to 'modernizing' agendas relating to the safeguarding and protection of LGBTQIA+ rights, but also women's rights.[4]

Focusing on the relationship between Muslim identities and communities, Rahman (2014b) has described the existence of a discourse of Muslim otherness that is often opposed to the idea of a Western (and allegedly superior) modernity relating to homosexuality. These ideas of Western superiority (in this case against Muslims) are triangulated using 'homocolonialism' as a process whereby sexual diversity is weaponized in international relations to prove the existence of a divide between a homonormative space of acceptance in the West, as opposed to a space of 'intolerance' in the East (read also Global South within a broader analytical context) (Rahman 2014b: 121). This process is often carried out through a process of 'pink-testing', as a tool deployed to check whether countries or regions comply with these alleged civilizational standards when it comes to LGBTQIA+ rights (Rahman 2014b: 281). For Rahman (2014b: 124) instead, modernity should be understood as being intersectional, with the intention to overcome the existing essentialism that is deployed to characterize the West/East divide when it comes to issues relating to homosexuality.

The question of modernity and LGBTQIA+ rights, with a particular focus on the politics of time, and its normative use under the guise of 'chrononormativity' (the assimilation of queerness into 'straight time') has also been discussed by Rao (2020: 2) in relation to Uganda. In particular, the designation of communities or countries (in this case Uganda) as being 'out of time' when it comes to the issue of LGBTQIA+ rights is part of a broader colonial and imperialist enterprise that has been grounded on the so-called 'denial of coevalness' (Rao 2020: 1), as the (Western) denial that societies across the world all have the same age and, implicitly, equal value in terms of their historical trajectory towards social change (or modernization?). Similarly to Rahman's (2014b: 121) claim about the use of 'homocolonialism', Rao (2020: 115) has also suggested that the creation of this artificial divide between 'modernity' and 'backwardness' is used towards the deployment of civilizational narratives that make Western intervention needed or 'indispensable'.

Against this background, both authors caution against the invisibilization of the agency of individuals, communities, or countries at the receiving end of these 'civilizational' interventions in various sites across the Global South (Rahman 2014b: 139–141; Rao 2020: 34). The question of agency/subjectivity beyond Western categories (but interconnected with them) is also highlighted by Hoad (2018: 153):

> To assert the universality of a specific historical agent [the 'homosexual'] can, and arguably is, closing down spaces for these participants without replicating the set of historical circumstances which allowed gayness to have historical agency in the West. This is especially so given the unevenness of capitalist development globally. The universalism that promises liberation ends up as oppression.

This promise of liberation, progress, and advancement towards a form of sexual modernity, therefore, contains a seed of disciplining and control (Love 2009: 6), that shuns (Love 2009: 9) or shames (Rao 2020: 38) those who are presumed to be 'backward'.

This rigid and artificial typification between sexual modernity/sexual backwardness can be overcome by analysing the syncretic relationship between Western ideas about LGBTQIA+ rights and local sexual and gender histories beyond essentialism through the concept of 'queer hybridization' (Martin et al 2008). These histories can only be brought to the forefront by widening our gaze and retraining our gaze to perceive the existence of histories of sexual and gender dissidence and resistance between the cracks of an otherwise outwardly alleged heteronormative framework.

Examples that show 'queer hybridization' at work are crucial in retraining our approach to perceive, document, and appraise histories of LGBTQIA+ resistance around the world. Chiang and Wong (2016: 8), for instance, have reflected on the process of sexual 'modernization' in the context of China and have discussed how the disappearance of *eunuchs* in Chinese society during the 20th century was part of a policy of the international repositioning of China as an imperial agent, rather than an object of imperialism itself. In Taiwan, the deployment of LGBTQIA+ rights functions as a marker of modernity vis-à-vis Mainland China, which is framed within Taiwanese politics as being 'backward' (Kong 2019: 1913–1914). This makes the promotion of LGBTQIA+ rights within Taiwan part of the independence and democratization movement. Another relevant example illustrates the interpenetration between the local, regional, and global in the context of Latin America. In the context of Peruvian narratives of development and 'modernization', trying to 'catch up' with other Latin American countries (such as Argentina or Brazil) in relation to LGBTQIA+ rights records, for instance, the dominant narrative is for gay Peruvian men to 'become less *loca*' (become less 'crazy' – as in feminine and loud), in order to be accepted into the fold of modernity in assimilatory terms (Herndon 2016: 12).

Processes of 'queer hybridization' (Martin et al 2008: 6) discussed both through theoretical and empirical analyses, show the necessity of resisting the dichotomizing discourses that simplify the relationship between processes of globalization and localization into a binary. The rise of international LGBTQIA+ politics, the globalization of the LGBTQIA+ movement, and the exponential multiplication of Pride Events around the world cannot be comprehended unless we centre the tensions that activists experience when trying to reconcile local histories of sexual and gender diversity, with unifying global discourses of queerness and identity-based activism originating in the Global North. Pride Events often are key sites where these apparent or alleged tensions and/or contradictions between the local and the global appear and are played out, as they create visible situated moments of articulation of queer identities within the otherwise heteronormative confines of the nation.

The organization of Pride Events as a marker of progress and modernity

With their traditional rainbow symbolism and aesthetics, as well the presence of floats, music, shows, stalls, and (political) speeches, Pride Events seem to have become a global staple of LGBTQIA+ communities, although the global pandemic caused by COVID-19[5] has had a dramatic impact on the cancellation of Pride Events worldwide (Damshenas 2020; Powys Maurice 2021). At the same time, the organization of Pride Events cannot be considered as a given at the global level, as criminalizing legal provisions, as well as other types of impediments or obstacles, may prevent LGBTQIA+ activists from freely organizing events for their communities. For instance, in the 63 countries that still criminalize homosexuality around the world (ILGA World Database 2024), the organization of Pride Events remains impossible (InterPride 2017: 12) because of factors such as the existence of criminal sanctions associated with any expression relating to LGBTQIA+ identities, the inability of LGBTQIA+ activists to register their organization, and/or the social shunning and/or persecution of LGBTQIA+ people in the public domain, such as in the media. At the same time, in countries such as Russia, where homosexuality is not criminalized per se (Russia decriminalized homosexuality in 1993), the organization of Pride Events has also become impossible in recent years (Kondakov 2013; Stella 2013; Ammaturo 2016b), due to existing homophobic laws banning the so-called fictitious 'Gay Propaganda', under Putin's current regime (see Kondakov 2022, 2023). Notwithstanding the formal ban on Pride Events, LGBTQIA+ activists[6] in Russia have continued to organize public protests, often encountering violent state repression (Buyantueva 2022). Even in countries where formal criminalization exists, activists have tried to organize small-scale events, such as in the case of the 2012 'Uganda's Beach Pride' (Nyanzi 2014), or the 2018 Pride Event in the Kakuma Refugee Camp in Kenya (Sopelsa 2018), often facing danger and societal backlash. At the same time, there may also be cases in which no formal criminalization of homosexuality exists in the country, but no Pride Events have been organized to date because of different factors (see OutRight International 2023: 11–12).

While it is beyond the scope of this research to investigate systematically the reasons behind activists' decisions to organize Pride Events in their specific settings, and more empirical research is certainly needed to fill this gap in the current literature, this heterogeneous picture shows that the existence or absence of criminalization of homosexuality in a particular national setting may not be the sole main cause of explanation for the existence or lack of Pride Events, and that it is important to explore activists' agency in making decisions regarding the opportunity to organize these events in light of the existing social, political, and legal circumstances in analysing the phenomenon of (global) proliferation of Pride Events, as well as the existence of political opportunities (Peterson et al 2018b), and/or the possibility to mobilize relevant resources (Ayoub et al 2021). Contextually, we should also consider the inherent value-judgement that accompanies the organization of Pride Events in a specific country or region as an inherently positive development, without considering the possible repercussions that activists can experience in terms of threats to their lives and the safety of their local communities.

Furthermore, it is important to acknowledge that contemporary social movements (among which LGBTQIA+ movements can be included) are a specific historical product of Western modernity (Conway 2016) and, as such, they may adopt (intentionally or unintentionally) a paradigm of Western modernity, imbued with a colonizing logic, and characterized by teleological features of progress, development, and modernization (Conway 2016: 24). As such, social movements play the role of 'modernizers' and they can be considered 'harbingers and measure of democracy, democratisation, and with it, modernity and modernisation' (Conway 2016: 23). It appears inevitable, therefore, that the organization of Pride Events, within the fold of the initiatives by LGBTQIA+ social movements at a global scale, contains in itself a seed of modernization, albeit implicit.

The first question to ask in this regard, therefore, is whether an ideal of sexual and gender modernity needs to be premised on the existence of Pride Events. Can a country ever be considered 'modern' if there are no Pride Events organized by activists?

Pride Events also work as the sites of the articulation of this model of 'queer hybridization', which in some cases can be described as a form of 'hyper-contextualization' (Ammaturo 2023), as I have discussed in my previous work. In articulating the concept of 'hyper-contextualization' of Pride Events, I referred to the process whereby Pride Events are increasingly tailored to represent the specific micro-contexts of locations that may be peripheral and/or rural, thus speaking to the intersection between local and LGBTQIA+ identities (Ammaturo 2023). This process of 'hyper-contextualization' does not just capture the inbetweeness of between the local and the global experienced by activists, but it is more actively configured as a strategic choice to respond to specific challenges existing in local settings that cannot entirely be addressed by mobilizing global(ized) discourses on LGBTQIA+ rights.

An example of how this process of 'hyper-contextualization' may work is represented by the case of Hong Kong, where a shift of tactics from activists from 'parliamentary politics to cultural politics' has emerged, with particular emphasis on the organization of Pride Events, or other public events, because of the impossibility of obtaining legal change in the country (Kong 2019: 1915). In other places, local social and political climates have generated home-grown criticism and scrutiny of the effectiveness of Pride Events. In India, discussions have emerged in relation to the controversial role of Pride Events as a form of panopticon (due to media attention, visibility, and publicity of the event) for participants who may be worried about coming out or being outed (Boyce and Dasgupta 2017: 218). In post-apartheid

South Africa, big Pride Events, such as Johannesburg Pride, function as a performative manifestation of South Africa as a 'Rainbow Nation', calling into question the widespread marginalization of many LGBTQIA+ members of Black South African communities (McLean 2019: 27–28).

These examples exceed the realm of the anecdotal, as they help us to situate across time and space discussions about the importance of considering the organization of Pride Events as being tightly connected to specific social, economic, cultural, and historical contexts that call for an often radical reconfiguration of traditional Pride Events 'repertoires' (Bennett 2017; Ammaturo 2023) to fit the specific needs, priorities, and sensibilities of the specific locale. The existence of these patterns of negotiation between the local and the (Western) global in relation to LGBTQIA+ rights points to the impossibility of neatly dividing countries within camps of 'modernity' or 'backwardness' when it comes to sexual and gender politics, as both the meanings of 'modernity', the tactics deployed to become 'modern', as well as the ideologies attached to these investments into modernization discourses may vary from context to context.

The association of Pride Events with the manifestation of a form of 'progress' within the fold of sexual 'modernity', is both seductive and problematic. Seductive because it responds to an undeniable desire to keep on 'dreaming of a better life for queer people' (Love 2009: 3), even if we may be sceptical regarding the existence of a linear trajectory of history. At the same time, the desire to equate the organization of Pride Events with 'progress' (Bennett 2017: 346) is also inherently problematic, because it buys into 'civilizational narratives' of development that create hierarchies between countries who 'have progressed' and countries that 'lag behind' (Hoad 2018). Furthermore, the reiteration of this dichotomy between 'progressive/backward' countries feeds directly into homonationalist discourses, whereby LGBTQIA+ rights (in this case freedom of expression and/or association) are weaponized at the national level, to create the sexual/racial other, along both internal national lines dividing white LGBTQIA+ friendly populations from racialized (allegedly homophobic minorities), as well as along the geopolitical lines of Global North-Global South (see Puar 2007, 2022; Rahman 2014b). Pride Events can be used to circulate homonationalist narratives (Ammaturo 2016b; Woori 2018), contributing to the consolidation of existing fault lines between those considered to be 'modern' and those who seem to have failed to achieve this status, as well as serving nationalist narratives that ostracize and demonize entire communities for allegedly being 'homophobic'.

The rhetoric of progress/backwardness can be observed in relation to sexual and gender modernity through commentaries from both LGBTQIA+ activists, as well as diplomats, non-governmental organization (NGO) officers, members of international organizations, and members of national governments. While these actors almost never explicitly use the world 'modern' or 'modernity' (Klapeer 2018), they make extensive use of the concept of 'progress', in line with the claim of a direct connection between the concept of 'progress' in relation to LGBTQIA+ rights, and the idea of (Western) sexual and gender modernity (Love 2009: 5; Rahman 2014b: 28; Rao 2020: 38; Puar 2022: 3).

An example of this rhetoric of 'progress' is represented by the 2016 speech by the then German Secretary of State for Europe, Michael Roth, at a Post-IDAHO (International Day Against Homophobia) Roundtable in Berlin on LGBTQIA+ rights in the Western Balkans:

> With these conflicting global trends, a broad development towards LGBTI rights on one side, a backlash on the other side – we may wonder: In which of these two categories does the Western Balkans region fall? ... In the whole region homosexuality is still a social taboo. A lot remains to be improved, but we also see many encouraging signs in the region. ... Several countries like Montenegro have passed strong anti-discrimination legislation, some explicitly out-ruling discrimination based on sexual identity. And after years of bans for Pride Parades, in recent years there were peaceful parades in Belgrade – which I myself joined in 2015 –, Pristina and Podgorica. Sarajevo hosts a queer film festival. (Roth 2016)

Roth's words show the logic of 'progress' at work, particularly in relation to a dichotomized vision of so-called 'global trends' of 'broad development towards LGBTI rights on the one side' and 'a backlash on the other side' in the context of a general discussion on LGBTQIA+ rights in the Western Balkans. The question asked is to which side of this divide do the Western Balkans belong? Do they belong to the camp of (modern) Europe, or to the camp of backwards 'still-not-European' countries? By asking this question, and by using the language of 'development' (Hoad 2018; Klapeer 2018), Roth embraces the narrative of progress/backwardness when talking about the organization of Pride Events, hinting to the fact that Belgrade,[7] Pristina, Podgorica, and Sarajevo are (implicitly) acknowledged as 'developed', because of the organization of Pride Events. This linear understanding of progress is problematic, particularly when 'progress' is haltered and setbacks happen, such as when activists are faced with impediments and political developments that prevent or ban the organization of Pride Events. The case of Serbia, where Pride Events have been organized since 2009, is particularly interesting in this regard, as it shows how these events can, on the one hand, become instrumentalized for the purpose of advancing discourses of Europeanization in the country (Pride Events as a sign of 'Europeanness'); while at the same time become deprived of any political or grassroots element, morphing into what Slootmaeckers (2023) has called 'a ghost pride'.

Similarly to national political actors, national ambassadors (predominantly from the Global North) may play an important role in the reinforcement of this dichotomy between 'progressive' and 'backward' countries when it comes to the organization of Pride Events. Increasingly, diplomatic personnel participate in Pride Events around the world with their own national delegations (see, for instance, the 'Diplomats for Equality' initiative[8]), and/or offer sponsorship and funding of specific events (Butterfield 2016: 46), logistical assistance (that is, offering venues as safe locations), or exercise other forms of 'soft power' (Gurok 2022). This participation, although it is often considered by many ambassadors as politically 'neutral' (Gurok 2022: 45), can be seen as a manifestation of what Hoad (2018: 148) has described as the 'developmental model of homosexuality': 'The rest of the world is understood as equivalent to the past of the now dominant form of male homosexuality in the Western metropolis: we were like them, but we developed, they are like we were and have yet to develop.'

Ambassadors' or diplomatic personnel's participation in Pride Events can be conceptualized as a way to point out this temporal difference between the so-called (Western) 'strong defenders'[9] of LGBTQIA+ rights, and those who yet 'have to develop'. An interesting example in this regard is represented by the participation of diplomats at the annual Seoul Queer Culture Festival (SQCF) (Mee-yoo 2022). During the 2022 edition of the event, the then outgoing Irish ambassador in South Korea, Julian Clare addressed the crowd reminding them that Ireland was the first country in the world that had voted (via referendum) to legalize same-sex marriage, and then added the following: 'In my country, we have travelled the journey from out there to in here, so we know that marriage equality and equality in society is possible. Never ever give up the hope that it can happen.'

Clare's statement is not isolated in its rhetoric, and it would be easy to find similar statements made by other diplomats across different contexts. This statement exemplifies a patronizing tone of 'we once were you, but we show that progress is possible', referring to the struggles of South Korean LGBTQIA+ activists.

Even when diplomatic personnel do not participate directly in Pride Events (for questions of political opportunity), they use these events to 'showcase' their values and portray themselves ('brand' themselves) as visibly queer-friendly:

> Like World Pride, I'm doing a big reception at my residence and I will invite the whole community 'cause in Denmark it's not a controversial thing. ... I will also brand [name of country] as, you know, modern, defending people's rights and of course then you take the opportunity and do something, and you get visibility. (Gurok 2022: 44)

International organizations and NGOs[10] can also play an important role in diffusing these narratives around 'progress' relating to the organization of Pride Events and human rights. So-called 'Rainbow Maps', produced every year by LGBTQIA+ organizations such as ILGA Europe and ILGA World, represent a powerful illustration of how progress in the field is 'visualized' through the use of colour-coded categories used to depict the performance on LGBTQIA+ of each specific country (Rao 2020; Ammaturo and Slootmaeckers 2024). Comparative performances of different countries in relation to LGBTQIA+ rights represent a yardstick for those who seek to achieve a 'better' status. In this regard, another interesting and recent example is the statement made during the 2023 EuroPride in Malta by the president of EPOA (The European Pride Organisers Association), Kristine Garina, who addressed the Maltese LGBTQIA+ activists with the following words:

> Malta, you are indeed a beacon ... of inspiration for progressive government across Europe and beyond. We know, a beacon of hope for activists in countries that have a long way to reach Malta's status. But I want to give a word of caution. You must not lose sight of the fact that LGBTI+ equality is not linear, and we must continue to make progress. (Garina 2023)

The idea that other countries need to 'reach Malta's status' in relation to LGBTQIA+ rights perfectly captures the logics of development towards sexual and gender modernity. This is notwithstanding the fact that, in her address, Garina had criticized Malta's human rights record on reproductive rights and the rights of migrants and asylum seekers, which are strongly in contrast with the 'progressive' approach the country takes in relation to LGBTQIA+ rights.

Moreover, the existence of this alleged 'divide' between countries that support or prevent the organization of Pride Events can also be used by other actors who oppose LGBTQIA+ rights, as is the case for the statement of the Head of the Russian Orthodox Church, Kirill who claimed on 6 March 2022, two weeks after the beginning of the Russian invasion of Ukraine,[11] that the support of Pride Events by Western governments represented a way to understand 'which side of God humanity will be on' in relation to the war in Ukraine. Five years prior to this statement, in 2017, Ukrainian activist Maxim Eristavi, in an online interview (Penman 2017), had claimed that the Pride Parade organized in Kyiv was a sign of Ukraine trying to move away from the colonial orbit of Russia, and back to the 'European family'. Eristavi felt encouraged by the fact that the 2017 Pride Event felt the 'closest it had ever been' to other Pride Events in Europe or the US, thus implicitly operating a comparison between the status quo in pre-war

Ukraine with the attainable (future) goal of reaching the magnitude of big Pride Events in European and US metropolises.

With the ongoing genocide against Palestinians unfolding in Gaza, it is impossible not to consider the implications of 'pinkwashing' (Puar 2011: 139), as a process whereby the promotion of LGBTQIA+ rights[12] is used to mask other forms of human rights violations and Islamophobia, such as in the case of Israel towards Palestinians. A recent and graphic illustration of this process has been a video appearing on various social media outlets, particularly on the platform X (formerly Twitter),[13] during the ground invasion of Gaza by the Israeli forces as a response to the attacks by Hamas on 7 October 2023. In the video, it is possible to see an IDF soldier wearing underwear/swimwear running on a beach in Beit Lahia in Gaza while waving a rainbow flag, followed by another soldier in the same attire holding a plastic chair. The video then cuts to another soldier who makes the following commentary: 'We are here in Gaza. You won't believe this. What's happening here?! My friends. A Pride Parade. I arrived at Nova beach here in Gaza. Look here!'

In this video, pinkwashing works by dividing Israeli and Palestinians alongside lines of 'civility' and 'barbarity', and painting Israel as a progressive state when it comes to LGBTQIA+ rights (Puar 2011: 138), by pointing out the 'surprise' to see a 'Pride parade' happening on the beaches of Gaza. This example is not isolated, as other pictures emerged, in at least two instances of two IDF soldiers holding flags among the rubble caused by the bombardment of Gaza: one rainbow flag with the slogan 'in the name of love', and an Israeli flag with rainbow ribbons on the top and bottom.[14]

The use of the video and the pictures as signs of 'progress' on LGBTQIA+ rights brought about by Israeli soldiers vis-à-vis the Gazan Palestinian population, compels us to question what we mean by 'progress' when LGBTQIA+ rights (and Pride Parades) can be completely decontextualized by existing structural and genocidal violence towards the Palestinian civilian population perpetrated by actors who are persuaded of their alleged 'modernity' in relation to LGBTQIA+ rights, vis-à-vis the rest of the Middle East and North Africa (MENA) region, such as in the case of Israel. Examples like these portray a hollowed-out version of queerness and progress that are only congenial to the spreading of civilizational discourses of inferiority/superiority, and that discount the real lives of LGBTQIA+ Palestinians who may have died while Gaza was turned to rubble in the context of a genocidal project.

This section has discussed the entanglement of Pride Events with both global histories of LGBTQIA+ identities and rights, as well as local experiences of sexual and gender diversity. By looking at the ways in which the local(ized) politics of Pride Events is always crucially situated in the specific context, and yet also cognizant of global political discourses, this section shows the importance of centring Pride Events as crucial sites that should be nurtured for the social and political representation and emancipation of local LGBTQIA+ communities. Simultaneously, and in light of this urgent need to preserve the political and social role of Pride Events across different contexts, the section has critically discussed the perils of adopting this 'modernizing' approach to Pride Events, using them as a proof of the existence of a pattern of 'modernization', 'progress', and/or 'development' in countries that are expected to 'catch up' with Western democracy. By looking at statements of governmental and non-governmental actors, the sections unveil how these civilizational discourses about using LGBTQIA+ rights (and Pride Events more specifically) to become 'modern' create a narrative that implicitly or explicitly ranks the Global North (or some sections of the Global North) as being inherently 'superior' compared to locations in the Global South. The next section will appraise these challenges in relation to a critical reconsideration of the concept of 'modernity' itself, one that needs to be rescued from its current linear and hegemonic configuration as a prerogative of the Global North/West.

Towards 'Kaleidoscope Modernities': pluralizing and problematizing the futures of LGBTQIA+ movements

Having discussed whether ideas of sexual and gender modernity *require* the organization of Pride Events in the previous section, the ensuing question becomes that of whether there are specific features (if any) that these events need to possess. Are big urban Pride Events with hundreds of thousands of participants, celebrity line-ups, floats, and corporate sponsors in the US, inherently more modern than a small-scale event with local *tiendas* selling local products and local artists performing on stage for a *Marcha del Orgullo* in Colombia? The issue becomes not just one relating to entering the realm of 'modernity' through the organization of Pride Events, but the relentless aspiration, or pressure, to become 'bigger and better', to emulate the success of other Pride Events around the world. This pressure to grow inevitably goes hand in hand with the professionalization and institutionalization of NGOs (Butterfield 2016), as well as the global demands of homocapitalism (Rao 2020). These processes can lead to a detachment by activists towards more grassroots segments of local LGBTQIA+ communities, at the advantage of pursuing a 'modernizing' agenda through the cultivation of relationships with national and international institutional actors, sponsors, and corporate stakeholders.

The connection between 'modernity' and Pride Events requires us to reflect on how we measure modernity, how we recognize it, and how we can go against the grain of univocal, Western-centric understandings of modernity. The objective of academic research, therefore, should be to describe the nexus between modernity and Pride Events, as well as problematize it, dissect it, and find new ways in which the thought category of 'modernity' can be applied to the wealth of different queer subjectivities and practices of community-making beyond the Western-centric horizon. To do so, one of the biggest challenges is represented by the (im)possibility of thinking about Pride Events outside the bounds of their original Western-centric matrix, or the 'Stonewall Myth' (see Chapter 1). Can we ever pluralize and de-link the appearance, organization, and meaning of Pride Events?

The ubiquitousness of the rainbow as the global marker of Pride Events (Hagen-Smith 1997; Wolowic et al 2017), driven by the capitalist commodification of these symbols (de Jong 2017), makes it hard for us to have the imaginative capacity to think beyond this aesthetic frame of reference. For instance, we may ask whether initiatives that celebrate gender or sexual diversity, but do not incorporate elements of marching, parading, or rainbow symbols and flags, should even count as 'Pride Events'. Furthermore, starting from the assumption of social movements as harbingers of modernity based on a colonial model (Conway 2016), and having acknowledged the entanglement between Pride Events and Western-centric ideas of sexual and gender modernity, it could be argued that Pride Events can be configured, to a certain extent, as a sort of 'civilizing event', whereby both heterosexual and queer people are simultaneously invited to become 'civilized' through the acquisition of a form of 'Pride Literacy' that can be used as a hermeneutical and experiential tool to navigate public expressions of sexual and gender diversity and/or activism.

Despite its presumed open and inclusive character, and the idea that you can attend 'as you are', Pride Events have always performed forms of exclusion (Schimanski and Treharne 2019; Ammaturo 2023; Formby 2023) towards specific sub-groups within LGBTQIA+ communities (such as cisgender queer women, trans people, racialized people and communities, disabled people, working-class queers, and so on). Contextually, participating in Pride Events requires to be cognizant or to perform certain behaviours, practices, or performances that ensure that one understands the context, and looks like they 'belong'. In this context, it is possible to talk about the concept of 'Pride Literacy', as a form of queer cultural capital,[15] that is expected to be learned/possessed by queer people participating in Pride Events (and, to some extent, by heterosexual onlookers too), premised on a Eurocentric aesthetic, cultural and social conception about queerness. The adoption of rainbow symbolism, the etiquette regarding marching, the centrality of 'pride' as the key emotion to be expressed during the event, the repertoire of music to be played, as well as knowledge of what activities are licit or illicit, welcome or unwelcome during the event, such as the inclusion of 'kink' at Pride Events, interactions with bystanders and other participants, can all be said to be part of this so-called 'Pride Literacy'. The possession of this knowledge enables participants and onlookers to navigate the events and to 'perform correctly', showing the possession of credentials of 'modernity'. Conversely, bystanders or onlookers who threaten or disrupt Pride Events can be said to have failed to acquire that 'Pride Literacy' that enables them to perform as members of a so-called 'modern' society (that respects LGBTQIA+ rights). Without detracting from the right of LGBTQIA+ persons to feel safe in exercising their right to freedom of expression and association during these events, it is necessary to reflect on how Pride Events act as 'civilizing events', creating a rift between those who are willing to become 'modern', and those who resist or resent this invitation, be they participants or onlookers.

One question relates to whether we can ever aspire to disentangle Pride Events from their underlying 'civilizational' undertones. To do so, it is necessary to think creatively about other conceptions of 'modernity' that can be applied to the case of Pride Events, to disrupt that linear chrononormative narrative (Rao 2020) of continuous and endless progression towards a form of queer 'entelechia'. To this purpose, this section will introduce the concept of 'Kaleidoscope Modernities' as an illustrative tool to demonstrate the conflictual, contradictory, and problematic relationship that Pride Events and Pride organizers entertain with the notion of making a country 'modern'. 'Kaleidoscope Modernities' are a specific type of sexual and gender modernity that becomes manifested through the organization of Pride Events across the world and is articulated through the existence of specific characteristics that will be illustrated later.

One of the most popular and discussed alternatives to a Western-centric concept of 'modernity' is offered by the concept of 'Multiple Modernities' proposed by Eisenstadt (2000).[16] According to this formulation, 'modernity' should be seen as a continuous constitution and reconstitution of cultural programmes at the global level (sometimes radically different from each other) that transcends the simple transposition of Western modernity across the world and is premised upon the creation of a distinct 'social *imaginaire*' (Eisenstadt 2002: 27–28). In identifying the existence of multiple 'cultural programmes' that develop distinctly but interrelatedly this approach has the merit of problematizing the equation between modernity and Western ideas of social change rooted in 'progress' (Mouzakitis 2017: 8), While the univocal relationship between the West and modernity is weakened through the theory of 'Multiple Modernities', the West is still considered as the source of modernity and represents a 'basic reference point for others' (Eisenstadt 2002: 27). Hence, while Eisenstadt 'pluralizes' the configurations of 'modernity' *in situ*, he still accords the primacy of thought to the West, thus reinforcing a hierarchy between Western and non-Western embodiments of 'modernity' following a derivative logic. Scholars[17] (see, for instance, Wagner 2010; Delanty 2016; Bhambra 2023) have criticized this approach for reproducing this Western-centric lineage for the idea of 'modernity'. For Bhambra (2007), the concept of 'Multiple Modernities' presumes the development of the concept of 'modernity' in the West in isolation from locations beyond the horizon of the Global North, as if there were '*separate civilisations*' (Bhambra 2007: 68), rather than considering that the very Western idea of 'modernity' was forged through colonial domination (Prakash cited in Bhambra 2007: 68). For this reason, the concept of 'Multiple Modernities' still purports an insular genesis of this concept detached from global non-Western influences which, ultimately, reinforces the alleged primacy of the West vis-à-vis, particularly, the Global South.

This critique of the concept of 'Multiple Modernities' appears useful in the context of an elaboration of a paradigm of sexual and gender modernity that seeks to eschew this framework of alleged Western 'superiority'. This process can be articulated as follows. Following a linear 'modernizing' approach to LGBTQIA+ rights at the global level, we could posit the Stonewall Riots as the 'founding' moment of modern LGBTQIA+ activism (see Chapter 1), whose philosophy, practices and ideals subsequently spread around the world, giving rise to LGBTQIA+ social movements, as well as the creation of Pride Events in different countries, almost as a 'blueprint' of the original. However, following a 'Multiple Modernities' approach, we could complicate this picture to say that, while the 1969 Stonewall Riots remain the 'point of reference' for LGBTQIA+ movements across the world, distinct patterns have been created and elaborated in different locales. This approach would still not challenge the 'primacy' of the Stonewall Riots. Alternatively, and more in line with the approach chosen for this book, explored particularly in Chapter 1, we could argue that the Stonewall Riots do not represent a privileged historical point in the 'modern' history of LGBTQIA+ movements, but one that has become such through the inscription of a preference for a historically and geographically specific form of LGBTQIA+ activism, and one that presents many shortcomings (see exclusions of different segments of LGBTQIA+ communities). This last approach does not seek to downplay the importance of the Stonewall Riots, but problematizes the creation of the 'origin story' as a form of inscription of Western 'primacy' in the history of sexual and gender diversity.

This argument contributes to the articulation of a concept of 'Kaleidoscope Modernities' as a continuous process which builds on the notion of 'queer hybridization' (Martin et al 2008), and 'hyper-contextualization' (Ammaturo 2023), recognizing both the autochthonous and global elements participating in the creation of contemporary forms of LGBTQIA+ activism that are, simultaneously local and global, in a situation of coevalness, rather than chrononormative superiority/inferiority of different locales (Rao 2020). The concept of the kaleidoscope here is used as a symbolic device to express the tension between the linear and homogenizing aspect of global(ized) queer cultures, as opposed to the different chromatic configurations that exist across LGBTQIA+ communities around the world. Kaleidoscopes use diffraction to complicate our understanding of light and colour. Similarly, the 'Kaleidoscope Modernities' of Pride Events show us the fragmentation of allegedly 'rainbow' realities, into myriad specks of colours, lights, and shapes. The concept of 'Kaleidoscope Modernities' contains in itself the critique to the idea of the 'primacy' of the Stonewall Riots as the founding moment for contemporary LGBTQIA+ activism, questioning not only what are the colonial conditions of violence that have suppressed sexual and gender diversity across the world (Matebeni 2014; Rodriguez 2017; Delatolla 2020), but also, crucially, how colonial violence has simultaneously stifled, repressed, and criminalized freedom of expression and freedom of association in the Global South in general (Thomas 2012; Lawrence 2013; Von Holdt 2013) as a key element to maintain power and oppression.

The proliferation of Pride Events around the world needs to be conceptualized starting from the joint analysis of how domestic forms of patriarchal, heteronormative, and cisnormative cultures converge with the colonial homo- and transphobic legacies, as well as being compounded relationships with the concomitant suppression of freedom of expression and association in former colonized territories, as well as domestic instrumentalization of sexual and gender expression for (homo)nationalistic purposes. Without romanticizing the existence of pre-colonial forms of sexual and gender diversity, which were still often understood within patriarchal, heteronormative, and cisnormative cosmologies and paradigms, the suppression of gender and sexual diversity and the suppression of freedom of expression and association (although these are technically categories instituted through contemporary human rights regimes) in the Global South during colonialism form part of the same process of suppression of different forms of personal and political agency, through the exertion of a form of physical, psychological, and epistemic violence which invalidates autochthonous forms of knowledges as being 'traditional' or 'premodern'; ultimately impacting the ability of individuals to imagine their own futures and, in turn, of conceptualizing what social change (or progress, or modernity) means for them and their respective communities.

The concept of 'Kaleidoscope Modernities' can help to analyse the tensions that Pride Events organizers around the world navigate in relation to the dyad traditional/modern. Although we may think about Pride Events as a relatively recent phenomenon – the first Pride Event, in New York, is only 55 years old! – we can now consider the existence of a sort of 'canon' for the organization of Pride Events. This 'canon' is characterized by a temporal (and spatial) distinction between 'old' and 'new' Pride Events, marked by a set of challenges or tensions that contribute to implicitly define how 'advanced' the specific event seems to be, compared to the 'big' events (see again, for instance, NYC Pride). Looking at Pride Events through a kaleidoscope, rather than a 'clear' lens, shows the complexity and changing architecture of these phenomena across locations, with their specific configurations each time we twist the kaleidoscope itself.

Through the empirical analysis of 60 interviews carried out with Pride Events organizers around the world contained in Part II, this book identifies five major tensions that contribute to the articulation of the concept of 'Kaleidoscope Modernities' in relation to Pride Events. The first tension relates to the enjoyment of human rights in the context of Pride Events (Chapter 4), particularly freedom of expression and assembly, with some events unfolding peacefully and without disruptions, while others become the object of harassment from opponents and hate groups, as well as encountering administrative obstacles and/or outright bans by national authorities. Achievements relating to the rights of LGBTQIA+ persons are often fragmented, contradictory, and accompanied by equally strong campaigns to oppose or curtail them. Pride Events constantly address this dyad of progress-backlash and are sometimes themselves transformed in sites of dispute and confrontation.

The second tension relates to the number and size of the events, with bigger events traditionally considered to be the marker of success and/or progress, and smaller, less institutionalized events often aspiring 'to go big' to catch up with the most well-established events (Chapter 5). The dimension of the Pride Events, and the relentless aspiration to make these gatherings bigger, year on year, represents a crucial problem that invests Pride organizers, as it requires them to actively engage with the nexus of growth-progress. Connected to the second is the third tension, which concerns the participation of commercial actors and corporate sponsors to the organization or the unfolding of Pride Events (Chapter 6) which is often considered as a sign of 'progress' in the context of global homocapitalism (Rao 2015), but which often creates alienation and dissatisfaction among participants. The ubiquitousness and inescapability of capitalistic structures within which social movements, including LGBTQIA+ movements operate, create true dilemmas for organizers that seek to reconcile their desire to create events for their communities, with internal pushbacks relating to the ethical frameworks within which these choices are often made.

Last, the book identifies two major areas where the concept of 'Kaleidoscope Modernities' can help us understand the multifariousness of Pride Events as global social phenomena. The articulation of Pride Events activism, namely the inclusivity of Pride Events for disabled LGBTQIA+ persons (Chapter 7), and the question of environmental sustainability (Chapter 8) speak to the future challenges that LGBTQIA+ movements face when thinking about how to ground their activism in social justice from an intersectional perspective and across single-issue mobilization.

These conversations about disability and environmental sustainability show the potential, as well as the possible contradictions and trade-offs, existing between advocating for LGBTQIA+ rights and pursuing a social justice agenda that is bold in imagining radically just futures.

These five issues directly offer insights into how different 'Kaleidoscope Modernities' may emerge at the crossroads of specific sites, histories, and organizational cultures and experiences in relation to Pride Events, and what are the internal tensions, contradictions, and struggles that Pride activists (and participants to these events) have to grapple with, in order to make sense of the trajectory of their own LGBTQIA+ advocacy or liberation movements.

Starting from the assumption that the organization of Pride Events can in itself be used to signal the entrance into a presumed era of sexual and gender modernity (Ammaturo 2016b; Slootmaeckers 2023), we also have to consider how, for instance, big Pride Events (again, think about NYC Pride) seem to possess the following features: they are big events organized on a massive scale where no apparent disruption or impediment takes place; they are backed by a substantial (and potentially ever-growing) number of corporate sponsors; they showcase inclusivity through a range of actions, such as the inclusion of the police or armed forces, the inclusion of disabled people, the inclusion of previously marginalized segments of the LGBTQIA+ community; as well as nodding to a sustainable future where the environmental footprint of the event can be significantly reduced. The 'blueprint' of big successful Pride Events inevitably becomes a model for small-scale, peripheral, newly established Pride Events which aspire to become as successful as the 'big ones', in order to both appeal to members of local LGBTQIA+ communities, as well as projecting an image of being 'modern' and attuned with global LGBTQIA+ politics and social movements.

Notes

[1] It is beyond the scope of this chapter to thoroughly map the literature on modernity and progress in both sociology and decolonial and postcolonial studies, so this overview will inevitably present some important limitations in the range of works approached and discussed.

[2] For a decolonial approach to social theory, please see Meghji (2021) and Bhambra (2023).

[3] Habermas and Ben-Habib (1981: 4) also highlight the role of the Enlightenment philosophy on the development of the concept of 'modernity'.

[4] In this regard see, for example, the concept of 'femonationalism' (Farris 2017) as the weaponization of women's rights to push for civilizational (and nationalist) narratives grounded in alleged Western and white feminist 'superiority'.

[5] See Part II of this book for more information on the impact of the COVID-19 pandemic on the organization of Pride Events worldwide.

[6] Russian LGBTQIA+ communities currently face renewed challenges, due to the designation, in the early months of 2024, of the LGBTQIA+ movement as a 'terrorist organization', by the Rosfinmonitoring (The Federal Service for Monitoring, the financial Russian watchdog). This decision is in line with a judgment by Russia's

Supreme Court issued in November 2023, which called for the ban of the so-called 'International LGBT social movement', under request of the Russian Justice Ministry. This designation by the Rosfinmonitoring could see the freezing of assets of Russian LGBTQIA+ organizations, as is already the case for organizations designated as 'terrorist' in the country (Woodmass 2024).

7   For a thorough analysis of Pride Events in Serbia please look at Slootmaeckers (2023) and Bilić (2016), particularly in relation to the cancellation of Pride Events in the country. For the incidents that occurred during the 2022 EuroPride in Belgrade, please see Gavranovič (2023).
8   For more information see *Financial Mirror* (2022).
9   See the website of the External European Action Services on LGBTQIA+ rights, where it is claimed that:

> The EU stands up for human rights of LGBTIQ+ persons. We are currently seeing a clear backlash against the human rights of LGBTIQ+ persons, with sharp increases in hate speech and discrimination. The EU is a strong defender of human rights of LGBTIQ+ persons globally. Equality and non-discrimination are part of our core values, as emphasized in the Universal Declaration of Human Rights, the European Treaties, and the EU Charter of Fundamental Rights. (www.eeas.europa.eu/eeas/pride-heroes-celebrating-pride-month-2023_en, last accessed 3 April 2024)

10 See for instance Klapeer's (2018) analysis of the role of the Dutch NGO 'Hivos' (HIV NGO) that has been one of the first in the world to include LGBTQIA+ rights advocacy within the context of development policies.
11 For an analysis of the impact of the Russian war in Ukraine on LGBTQIA+ rights, see Shevtsova (2022).
12 For an analysis of Tel Aviv Pride as a manifestation of 'pinkwashing', see Stallone (2019).
13 Malekafzali, S. (@Seamus_Malek). 2024. IDF soldiers wave the Pride flag as they run on the beach near Beit Lahia, a city in northern Gaza that has been virtually destroyed by Israeli military bombardment. [X/Twitter] 9 January. Available at: https://x.com/Seamus_Malek/status/1744850408630075683?s=20, last accessed 4 April 2024.
14 Leekern (@leekern13). 2023. Under Hamas, being gay means death. Israeli Yoav Atzmoni wanted to send a message of hope. See his story below. To Gaza's hidden LGBTQ+ community: STAY HOPEFUL of a future where you can live and love free of Hamas! [X/Twitter] 12 November. Available at: https://x.com/leekern13/status/1723807905835585996?s=20, last accessed 4 April 2024.
15 See Ward (2003) for a use of Bourdieu's concept of 'cultural capital' in the context of Pride Events in Los Angeles.
16 Eisenstadt's formulation of 'Multiple Modernities' was a direct response to both Fukuyama's argument on 'the End of History', as well as Huntington's thesis of the 'Clash of Civilisations' (Mouzakitis 2017: 8).
17 The literature on the concept of 'Multiple Modernities' and ensuing critiques is much more developed but cannot be properly addressed in depth in the context of this chapter.

3

One Pride or Many? Pride Events between Multiplication and Fragmentation

With millions of people around the world taking to the streets every year, whether it is to protest, celebrate, or party, Pride Events have become a true global success story. The 'globalization' of Pride Events (Markwell and Waitt 2009; Ammaturo 2023; Slootmaeckers and Bosia 2023) is tightly connected to the broader phenomenon of the so-called 'globalization of LGBTQIA+ [lesbian, gay, bisexual, transgender, queer, intersex, asexual, plus] identities/ rights' (Altman 1996; Boellstorff 2016; Paternotte and Seckinelgin 2016; Szulc 2018; Muparamoto and Moen 2022), which interrogates how Western categories relating to gender identity and sexual orientation have been adapted, transposed, or adopted across the world, not without tensions, limitations, or criticalities.

This chapter discusses the growing multiplication and differentiation of Pride Events across the world as an illustration that Pride Events need to be understood in the plural, rather than using one homogenizing Western/ Eurocentric mould. Ultimately, it shows that conflict is a vital part of Pride Events that is too often underestimated and minimized. Acknowledging the conflictual nature of Pride Events, instead, enriches both our theoretical, as well as empirical, understanding of this phenomenon, working towards an ever-sharper configuration of a framework of 'Kaleidoscope Modernities' engendered by the never-ending negotiations enacted by social actors participating in the creation of Pride Events.

The multiplication of Pride Events worldwide cannot be taken as a given. On the contrary, it is necessary to investigate critically their growing importance and success considering different aspects: first, the significance of this growth in relation to the 'globalization' of LGBTQIA+ rights; second, the proliferation of Pride Events beyond the traditional horizon of the city; and last, the increasing 'splintering' of Pride Events into differentiated initiatives that are either antagonistic to 'mainstream Pride Events' (see 'Alternative Pride') or seek to specifically cater for segments of the LGBTQIA+ community, such as trans people, queer women, and/or people of colour. Furthermore, despite a perception that research on Pride Events remains limited in the context of the Global South (Conway 2024: 5), there is an undisputable wealth of research in Spanish and Portuguese languages that covers a wide array of countries in Central and Latin America. This corpus of research on Pride Events offers a good opportunity not just to 'diversify' current entrenched academic knowledge about Pride Events at the global level, but also to challenge our own Anglo-hegemonic epistemologies[1] in the context of knowledge production and diffusion.

While scholars have recognized that Pride Events are multiform, different, and are organized in accordance to the local needs of the communities, as well as the local cultural, social, political, legal, and economic settings in which they take place (Markwell and Waitt 2009; McFarland Bruce 2016; Wahlström 2018), this element of diversification and heterogeneity has not been systematically interrogated in light of processes of 'globalization of LGBTQIA+ identities/rights', but has almost been taken for granted, except for a few interventions in more recent literature (Ammaturo 2016b, 2023; Ghaziani 2021; Slootmaeckers and Bosia 2023; Conway 2024). The existence of a predominant descriptive, rather than analytical, academic approach to Pride Events, contributes to fostering the idea that we are simply dealing with 'adapted versions' of a Western/Eurocentric blueprint within and beyond the Global North, rather than pushing us to critically interrogate the relations between the global and the local that underpin the creation of these events around the world.

To a similar extent, we can also observe a relative lack of problematization, or critical inquiry, into the multiplication of Pride Events around the world beyond the 'metronormative' (Halberstam 2005) horizon that privileges urban settings as the privileged site for the organization of these events for LGBTQIA+ communities and posits peripheral and/or rural locations as inhospitable for welcoming queer life (Halberstam 2005; Stone 2018; Ammaturo 2019). Increasingly, both in the Global North and in the Global South, Pride Events are organized beyond the big urban metropoles, in small(er) cities, towns, and villages (Shah 2015; Ammaturo 2019, 2023; Barreto 2020; Bernieri Ponce and Larreche 2021; Lewis and Vorobjovas-Pinta 2021; Conner and Okamura 2022; Lockett and Lewis 2022; López Sánchez and Rodríguez Domínguez 2023). The multiplication of Pride Events in peripheral and rural locations can shed light on the negotiations enacted between the levels of the local and the global, interweaving processes of 'hyper-localization' and 'hyper-contextualization' (discussed in Chapter 2) of Pride Events (Ammaturo 2023), which interrogate both issues of politicizing peripheral and rural queer life, as well as considering how notions of belonging and inclusion for LGBTQIA+ people are strategically negotiated beyond the horizon of the city.

Additionally, the issue relating to the organization of Pride Events brings to the forefront the centrality of conflict and disagreements, as well as fragmentation and separatism in the organization of and taking part in these events, which all remain relatively under-researched aspects. While scholars have addressed the existence of conflicts and internal rifts between different segments of LGBTQIA+ communities that have happened in the aftermath of Stonewall and soon after (Kissack 1995; Armstrong and Crage 2006; Cruz-Malavé 2007; Ghaziani 2008; Kunzel 2018; Duberman 2019), there is not a systematic approach to charting current divisions, conflicts, and 'infighting' (Ghaziani 2008) that characterize the contemporary politics of Pride Events, and have increasingly led to the organization of so-called 'Alternative Pride Events', such as Black Pride, Trans Pride, or Dyke Marches, to name a few.

As Pride Events multiply and fragment at the global level, it is crucial to adopt a systematic[2] approach to the tensions that crosscut their organization, forms of participation, as well as audiences. These divisions and disagreements are, in fact, at the heart of the various challenges encountered by Pride organizers, ranging from issues of depoliticization of Pride Events and disappearance of the grassroots connections with local communities, to the growing corporatization and commodification of these events, to issues of inclusivity and representation of various segments of LGBTQIA+ communities, as well as economic and environmental sustainability. Bringing the question of conflict, divisions, and tensions to the forefront of the analysis, allows us to consider the contemporary politics of global(ized) Pride Events beyond the narrow frame of 'modernity' (see Chapter 2), and enables us to be critical about successes and setbacks for Pride organizers around the world, without losing sight of the specificities of each context.

This chapter has three parts. First, it addresses the multiplication of Pride Events at the global level, reflecting on the significance of this multiplication beyond Eurocentric ideas of LGBTQIA+ mobilization. Second, drawing from the concepts of 'hyper-localization' and 'hyper-contextualization' of Pride that I have developed in my previous work (Ammaturo 2023), the chapter moves to show that Pride Events are not homogeneous in their organization, symbolism, and function but that they often present a blend between global discourses on gender and sexuality, and local heritage, culture, and social and political contexts, even at the micro level of rural locales, where these events are increasingly take place. Last, the chapter analyses the growing controversies arising within the organization of Pride Events, particularly in relation to the lack of inclusion for specific segments of the LGBTQIA+ community (trans people and racialized people), as well as challenges from left-wing sectors of the LGBTQIA+ movements, which often culminate with the creation of 'Alternative Pride Events'.

The more, the merrier? Contextualizing the multiplication of Pride Events around the world

When it comes to the exponential proliferation of Pride Events around the world, we may be tempted to ask whether we are moving towards a 'movement society' (Meyer and Tarrow 1998) or a 'movement world' (Goldstone 2004: 335), as some scholars have argued, commenting on the success of different social movements, including those fighting for the recognition of LGBTQIA+ rights. The multiplication on a global scale of these events for LGBTQIA+ people, as well as their diversification and penetration in both urban and rural areas, requires us to interrogate this 'success story' and critically appraise its potentialities and limitations. For this reason, it is crucial to start from a contextualization and critical appraisal of this multiplication across time and space.

As already mentioned in Chapter 1, the NGO Outright International (2023: 8) lists a total of 101 countries in the world that organize at least one Pride Event on their territory, with 61 countries now also organizing events outside of their capital cities. The 2016–2017 Report by the International Association of Pride Organizers, *InterPride* (2017: 12), mentions the existence of a total of 971 Pride Events organized by the date of publication (more events have certainly been created since the report was published). In the same report, the then vice-president of the organization, Frank van Dalen (InterPride 2017: 10), reflected on the growth of the movement:

> With the exponential growth of the Pride movement in recent years, new opportunities have arisen. If every Pride leaves a positive footprint in the local community, collaboration can actually be reached on a global level. With millions and millions of people visiting Pride Events, we are a movement that can make a difference. What is visible cannot be ignored and has to be dealt with. No other movement like the Pride movement has the power to make our community and its desires visible – showing solidarity in numbers, disclosing wrongdoings, and celebrating victories empowers others to continue their battles.

Van Dalen's words summarize well the intentions behind the desire of professionalized Pride organizers to 'scale up' events and help with the spread of Pride Events around the world: visibility, solidarity in numbers, 'in your face' political protests, exorcising discrimination through the playful celebration of sexual and gender difference, they all seem to be successful ingredients to advance the claims and rights of LGBTQIA+ people worldwide. The reasons behind the multiplication of Pride Events on a global scale are complex and cannot obviously be reduced to a single buzzword such as 'globalization', as we may be tempted to do. At the same time, it is undeniable that the globalization of the LGBTQIA+ movement (Altman 1996), through the professionalization (Joseph 2010; Butterfield 2016; Paternotte 2016) or 'gentrification' (Schulman 2013; Burchiellaro 2023; Conway 2024) of its activism, and the institutionalization[3] of LGBTQIA+ rights in the international arena (Langlois 2020; Velasco 2018), have definitely helped to project Pride Events as a sort of 'crown jewel' of LGBTQIA+ movements, both in the international and domestic arenas. The organization of Pride Events becomes a sort of pinnacle of organizational capacity and is built on the premise that, in order to show the growing number of self-accepting LGBTQIA+ people, as well as the support of their allies, these events have to become 'bigger and better' than the previous year's (Joseph 2010: 2), often counting on big budgets that include expenses such as security, celebrity line-ups, and impressive logistical infrastructures.

The desire of growing in size in specific locations (see also Peterson et al 2018b: 124), also corresponds with a wish to grow in terms of geographical spread, as we saw from the quote from van Dalen (InterPride 2017): there is strength in numbers. This wish for Pride Events to be 'transposed' across geographical contexts, however, cannot be taken at face value, and requires an interrogation in terms of the role of Pride Events in participating to the construction of idea(l)s of modernity/modernization in specific national or regional settings (see Chapter 2). While critical research on the issue of the 'transposition' of Pride Events remains relatively limited, there are growing contributions to this discussion on the diffusion of Pride Events as a specific format within a specific 'frame' (Bennett 2017). One example is the concept of the global transposition of Pride Events as an act of 'geo-temporal dislocation', which leads to the use of specific temporal strategies to be appropriated and/or instrumentalized by both national and international political actors (Slootmaeckers and Bosia 2023: 8). While we should always acknowledge the central role of activists, and their agency in organizing such complex events, the act of romanticizing the growth of Pride Events as a neutral mark of the increasing 'acceptance' of LGBTQIA+ persons at the global level may lead us to avoid difficult questions. These questions relate to Pride Events as being imbricated in issues of representation, respectability, 'civility'/'civilizing' of allegedly backwards populations (see Chapter 2), as well as questions relating to the commodification of LGBTQIA+ identities, and the aligning of LGBTQIA+ activism with (homo)national(ist) political agendas.

One of the visible effects of the globalization of Pride Events has been that of creating 'stable, normative, understanding of what Pride Events are' (Bennett 2017: 349). This means that the multiplication of these gatherings is accompanied by an expectation of what Pride Events should look like, what messaging they should contain, as well as which tactics they should deploy (see the discussion in Chapter 1 relating to the acquisition of 'Pride

Literacy'). Although it remains undeniable that the format, symbolism, and tactics deployed around the world are often (if not most of the time) inspired by the format of Pride Events popularized after the Stonewall Riots of 1969 in the US, to create this equivalence between US-based Pride Events and a seamless transposition elsewhere would lead to an invisibilization of the histories, the agency, and the specificity of social, political, and legal struggles of LGBTQIA+ activists around the world.

At the same time, the creation of global and regional events such as World Pride and Europride (Peterson et al 2018b: 24) has certainly helped to crystallize and consolidate those 'normative expectations' discussed by Bennett (2017: 349). Hence, while we can acknowledge the globalizing role that events such as Europride or World Pride have had in sparking the imagination of scores of activists everywhere, we need to be cautious in over-determining the importance and pre-eminence of these 'Rainbow Imaginaries' in the global activation and mobilization of activisms based on issues relating to sexual orientation and/or gender identity. 'Rainbow Imaginaries' are powerful and hegemonic frames through which Pride Events have come to be imagined across boundaries and include semiotic, aesthetic, aural, and symbolic representations of Pride Events as predominantly characterized by the use of the colours of the rainbow, the reproduction of specific music or sounds, and embodied expectations for individuals to occupy and move through space following the script of a procession or a march. As every hegemonic discourse, however, 'Rainbow Imaginaries' can be used to create auras of conformity, rather than contribute to challenging the hetero-patriarchal status quo.

One illustration of the problem inherent in the creation of a global 'Rainbow Imaginary' of Pride Events is shown in the documentary *Pride Denied*, directed by Kami Chisholm (2016). A substantial part of the documentary was filmed during the 2014 edition of World Pride that was held in Toronto, Canada, showing the discrepancies between sleek, tourist-oriented events, such as World Pride, and the realities lived by other segments of the local LGBTQIA+ community, such as trans people, homeless, and/ or sex workers and drug users who became targets of the so-called 'TAVIS' (Toronto Anti Violence Intervention Strategy), aimed at 'cleaning up' the streets of Toronto on the eve of the event. The 2014 Toronto World Pride felt like an exclusive white, middle-class, respectable, and commodified event from which many queer Torontonians were themselves excluded.

Fantasies of unbound mobilities that are articulated through the rhetoric of World Pride[4] also come into question when the rights of LGBTQIA+ migrants are interrogated. In 2021, Black Ugandan LGBTQIA+ activists who had been invited to participate in the 2021 Copenhagen/Malmö World Pride were stopped at the Swedish border, ironically while they were on their way to the *Refugee, Borders and Immigration Summit* organized as part of the World Pride celebrations (Saleh 2023). Casting Pride Events as a global event, while underestimating the entanglements with homonationalism (Puar 2007), homocapitalism (Rao 2015a), as well as the violence of border regimes (Holzberg et al 2022; Sajjad 2022) in Europe and across the Global North represents a problem if we truly want to detangle LGBTQIA+ activism from Western-centric practices and explanatory and activist frames.

Criticalities also exist in relation to the organization of Europride, particularly in the context of processes of Europeanization through the adoption of LGBTQIA+ rights (Ayoub 2013; Ammaturo 2015; Binnie 2016; Slootmaeckers 2023) across the continent. The most paradigmatic case, albeit not the only one, is represented by the 2022 edition of Europride held in Belgrade, Serbia. On 10 August 2022, the Serbian President Vučić announced the cancellation of the event, citing safety concerns about the ability of protecting participants from right-wing counter-protesters. Organizers responded confirming that they would go ahead nonetheless, as a ban would be unconstitutional (Civicus Monitor 2022). The government finally banned the event, despite a legal challenge from the organizers, receiving intense backlash from EU Equality Commissioner Helen Dalli and the Commissioner for Human Rights of the Council of Europe (CoE), Dunja Mijatović. While the 'walk', which had been authorized by the police, went ahead with a shortened route, violence against participants broke out from right-wing counter-protesters, leading to at least ten people (if not more) being attacked and injured (Civicus Monitor 2022). This case shows the instrumentalization, by both nationalist forces, as well as actors involved in the process of 'Europeanization' (such as the CoE or the EU), of an event that should have been empowering and representative for the local LGBTQIA+ communities. Similar to what had happened to the 2014 edition of Pride in Serbia, which became hostage to similar altercations across the political divide thus being labelled as a form of 'ghost Pride' (Slootmaeckers 2023), the 2022 Europride in Serbia shows the danger of wanting to 'expand' the reach of Pride Events to the maximum field of capacity, without considering strategies and tactics that are truly empowering (and safe) for the communities on the ground.

At this critical juncture between the global and the national, the multiplication of Pride Events across different locales around the world also raises the question of a global strategy based on 'becoming visible'. This form of political visibility is exercised in direct response to the historically widespread processes of erasure of LGBTQIA+ people and their experiences in the context of public life, and normally seeks to challenge received stereotypes. And yet, as Edenborg (2020: 353) has warned, the politics of 'visibility' can also be a double-edged sword for some LGBTQIA+ people, particularly those who find themselves at crucial intersections between sexual orientation, gender identity, 'race', disability, and/or migration and nationality status, and may become the subject of intense scrutiny and, in some cases, the targets of compounded forms of discrimination. The process of becoming globally visible, framing or reframing one's sexual orientation and/or gender identity within the perimeter of the global politics of queer visibility of Pride Events, may lead to the distribution of differentiated forms of risks/benefits in terms of violence and harassment, with those inhabiting a relative position of privilege being relatively more sheltered from violence than those who inhabit intersections that may put them in a situation of multiple disadvantage. The aforementioned cases of the 2022 Europride in Serbia, or the episode regarding the two Black Ugandan activists at the 2021 World Pride in Copenhagen/Malmö offered by Saleh (2023), exemplify the limits of a global politics of queer visibility, showing that visibility is often, unfortunately, accompanied by vulnerability to widespread atmospheres[5] of homo- and transphobic violence.

Despite the existing hegemony of aforementioned 'Rainbow Imaginaries', therefore, it is key to reiterate that heterogeneity is a key characteristic of Pride Events. As has been discussed earlier in this chapter, several authors have recognized this peculiarity but have not engaged with a thorough consideration of what is the process behind it, and why it matters for an event such as Pride to become 'adaptable' or 'translatable' across contexts, even beyond its Western/Eurocentric initial framework. In this context, Bennett (2017: 348) has used the work of Snow and Benford (1999) on 'frame diffusion' to explain how Pride Events 'spread' across contexts. The three possible types of frame diffusion identified by Snow and Benford (1999: 26) are *reciprocation, accommodation*, and *adaptation*. *Reciprocation* corresponds to a mutual process in which both the transmitter (think about the 'original' frame of Pride in North American and/or European contexts) and the 'adopter' (new locations/actors engaging with the idea of 'Pride Events') engage in a process of diffusion. *Accommodation* represents more of a 'top-down' process, proceeding from the actions of the 'transmitter' to accommodate the original frame in a specific location or context (Bennett 2017: 348). *Adaptation*, on the contrary, flips this process, placing the agency firmly in the hands of the so-called 'adopter' who enacts the diffusion of the frame strategically and purposefully (Bennett 2017: 348).

In order to describe this process of diffusion of the 'frame' of Pride Events, Bennett chooses the last type of *adaptation* as a 'process of discursive and semiotic recontextualization of social practices'. Pride Events, in fact, are inherently polysemic (Joseph 2010: 303), as they can acquire different (and sometimes even competing, as will be shown in the next section of this chapter) meanings for both participants and/or organizers. The very polysemic character of Pride Events, however, can also be at the origin of conflicts regarding whether Pride Events should push for assimilation and inclusion within society, or whether they should articulate a desire to alter social structures altogether (see next section of this chapter). The hypothesis advanced by Bennett (2017) usefully highlights the role of agency of activists, in the diffusion of any social movement frame, rather than just positing a 'top-down' approach. In this regard, we could think about the diffusion of frames such as that of the *#MeToo Movement* (Lee and Murdie 2021), or the *Fridays for Future* movement (Beckh and Limmer 2022) in relation to how activists and organizers strategize to frame their claims, maintaining a balance between the specific cultural, social, political, legal, and economic features of the local setting, and global demands that these movements seek to advance or vindicate.

This problematic assumption about a 'core' of Pride Events discussed by Bennett (2017) also manifests itself in Ghaziani and Baldassarri (2011: 197), who have described the common 'corpus' of ideas or concepts that organize the very phenomenon of Pride Events as 'cultural anchors'. These are 'recurring' ideas that are mobilized by actors across different contexts, thus creating a sort of 'thin coherence' across different types of Pride Events. Elements such as 'coming out scripts', the 'parade format', as well as the 'rainbow iconography' (what I have previously termed 'Rainbow Imaginaries') can all be described as examples of 'cultural anchors' that bond, ideally, Pride Events organizers across different contexts (Peterson et al 2018b: 72).

The idea of the cultural anchors of Pride Events should be scrutinized in relation to the assumption that convergence is always to be expected or desired around three main elements: a politics of 'visibility' or 'visibilization', an assumption about the spatial and embodied performance of Pride Events through the form of the 'parade', and a specific aesthetic to be employed/ deployed during Pride Events (through the deployment of a 'Pride Literacy' and 'Rainbow Imaginaries'). These elements, or cultural anchors, in this regard, could be seen as having the potential of becoming more prescriptive than descriptive. Rather than being used to describe a sort of already 'existing common denominator' between these events, these cultural anchors can be used to prescribe what a real/successful/intelligible Pride Event should look like. This critical approach does not deny their ubiquitousness or relevance in many contexts but pushes us not to take the presence of these elements or 'features' for granted or to expect them at any iteration or example of a Pride Event.

Mapping Pride: a critical social geography of Pride Events between the local and the global

In the urban anonymity of big centres, where huge groups of people take to the streets, Pride Events create a rupture in both the straight geography and time of the life of the city. However, the existence of a relatively recent trend that sees Pride Events increasingly organized outside of the traditional sites of big cities and metropoles is starting to challenge the pre-eminence of urban settings as the privileged sites to organize these gatherings. Pride Events that happen in rural or peripheral locations[6] defy the traditional 'metronormative' (Halberstam 2005) character of research on LGBTQIA+ identities and experiences, which posits that the privileged site for the flourishing of queer life is the city. In fact, rural or peripheral locales are routinely thought to be 'inhospitable' to LGBTQIA+ and, possibly, even more so when thinking about hosting a 'visible' event that showcases LGBTQIA+ subjectivities and experiences, as I have discussed in my previous work (Ammaturo 2023: 3). Place, or 'emplacement' of Pride Events, is a key element of the articulation of collective and individual identities, as well as the identification of protest strategies (Ghaziani 2021: 4).

A tradition, predominantly in the context of North America (US and Canada) and Australia, of studying rural LGBTQIA+ life has been established[7] since at least the 2000s (Waitt and Gorman-Murray 2008; Gray 2009; Herring 2010; Kazyak 2011; Gorman-Murray et al 2013; Gray et al 2016). In Latin America, this field is also growing in importance, with several authors increasingly looking at rural life in different countries across the continent (Gaona and Ficoseco 2015; Duarte and da Silva 2023; Erazo-Gómez et al 2023; Galyon 2023). In Europe, attention is also growing (Bell and Valentine 1995; Kuhar and Švab 2014; Ammaturo 2019, 2023; Barreto 2020; Araque Barboza et al 2023; Jukes 2024), with huge potential for exploring the multifarious configurations of queer European ruralities. Research on rural LGBTQIA+ life often builds on Halberstam's (2005) critique of 'metronormativity', to counter stereotypes about queer life in rural settings as being suboptimal, incomplete, or unfulfilling, showing, instead, its intricacies, complex negotiations between competing ideas of 'tradition', as well as the construction of a network of allies.

Specifically in relation to Pride Events, research focusing on the organization of these events in rural locales is still comparatively limited if compared to research that adopts a metronormative approach, but a growing number of scholars are starting to take notice of this phenomenon, both in the Global North (Ammaturo 2019, 2023; Barreto 2020; Lewis and Vorobjovas-Pinta 2021; Conner and Okamura 2022; Lockett and Lewis 2022) and in the Global South[8] (Shah 2015; Bernieri Ponce and Larreche 2021; López Sánchez and Rodríguez Domínguez 2023). While we may be tempted to neatly divide urban and rural spaces where Pride Events are organized into either friendly/or unfriendly spaces (Peterson et al 2018b: 164) and create an equivalence between urban settings as being more hospitable and rural locales as being less hospitable to LGBTQIA+ activisms, empirical evidence suggests that the situation is more complex.

In my previous work (Ammaturo 2023), I have looked at the issue of the multiplication and rising significance of Pride Events in rural/peripheral locales through the concept of 'glocalization' that hinges on the dilemma between 'heterogenization/homogenization' (Giulianotti and Robertson 2006: 173). If we reject the idea that globalization always happens as a blanket transposition of ideas originating elsewhere (often in the Global North, like in the case of Pride Events), and we posit, instead, that actors engage in a meaningful process of negotiation between the local and the global – 'glocalization', we will then have to consider what are the options in this context. We can see, therefore, how the tendency to 'homogenize' Pride Events across locales can be described as a form of 'hyper-localization' (Ammaturo 2023: 4) whereby Pride Events effectively have the potential (and in some cases the effective capacity) of spreading 'everywhere', even to the most remote of villages. At the same time, the 'heterogenizing' element of this negotiation, which somehow seeks to counterbalance the process of 'homogenization', is represented by the phenomenon of 'hyper-contextualization' (Ammaturo 2023: 7), whereby Pride Events are made to be relevant in light of local history, traditions, and heritage, often to legitimize respectability and belonging in the local community, as well as in the polity[9] at large (Ammaturo 2016a). As I have discussed, this process of hyper-contextualization often requires or engages with a sort of 'reinvention' of the straight past of traditions, such as in the cases analysed in relation to the contexts of Italy or the United Kingdom (Ammaturo 2023), where local symbols (of gastronomy[10] and/or local history[11]) are reimagined to be 'inclusive' of LGBTQIA+ identities. This process is observed well beyond the context of the aforementioned study.

Several other case studies (in Spanish and French), particularly in the context of Latin America (Mexico,[12] Ecuador, Argentina[13]), show how Pride Events in peripheral locations often transfigure, partly or fully, the very meaning of those events, to strategically pursue specific objectives and/or claims that make them relevant in the specific context. One of the most interesting case studies, that has already been cited in the first chapter of this book, is the case of the Pride Events organized in the city of Chilpancingo, in Mexico (Payne 2021), where activists have drawn from Christian iconology (crucifixions, Catholic iconology), as well as anti-colonial traditions (the participation of *chinelo dance* – a type of dance developed in the 19th century to mock efforts to Europeanize Mexico), in order to strongly root events that could be(come) controversial in a small(er) community, through the subversive use of 'traditional' elements of local cultures. In Ecuador, a group of trans(feminine) people, who have name themselves 'Ñuca Trans', have 'appropriated', starting from the 2008 edition of the *Marcha del Orgullo LGBTI* in Pomasqui (north of the Ecuadorian capital of Quito), the traditional dance associated with the Inca-inherited ceremony of the *Inti*

Raymi (Festival of the Sun) (Venegas Ferrin 2017). With this process, the members of 'Ñuca Trans' have claimed back their indigenousness through their trans identity, in a context in which knowledge about gender diverse individuals (*Warmishina*) in Inca societies has been marginalized and/or forgotten (Venegas Ferrin 2017: 79).

Another interesting aspect of the transfiguration of Pride Events relates to the fact that rural or peripheral locations also often engage with Pride Events with a particular relation to the territory, often showing a marked form of 'eco-sensibility'[14] that may be different in terms of priorities or themes compared to urban settings. Some case studies have shown the emergence and existence of a marked interest in themes relating to the preservation and/or restoration of a decayed, compromised, or at-risk local natural environment on the part of local Pride Events organizers and/or participants (Ammaturo 2019; Barreto 2020; López Sánchez and Rodríguez Domínguez 2023). For example, the Festival '*Agrocuir*' in Monteroso, Galicia, organized in this part of Spain since 2014, with traditional music, workshops, plays, and other events, is inescapably related to Queer Eco-Criticism (Barreto 2020; Mortimer-Sandilands 2010): 'An *Agrocuir* politics insists on the impossibility of a sexual liberation that does not include the protection of nature, especially for those non heterosexual people who live in rural [spaces] and who fight against various systems of socio-economic, cultural, and sexual oppression at the same time'[i] (translated from Galician, from Barreto (2020: 17)).

This example highlights, as has already been pointed out in another case study I undertook in 2019 relating to the subregion of Salento, in south-eastern Italy (Ammaturo 2019), that there is a growing sensibility towards a joint articulation of environmental issues, as well as social, economic, issues that affect queer people living in peripheral and/or rural locales. While, therefore, rural locales are often posited as 'immobile' or 'stuck in time' (Herring 2010; Parrinello 2021), when it comes to LGBTQIA+ activism, the truth is far more dynamic, as these locales articulate in intersectional terms issues relating to the environment, lack of economic opportunities, and/or other forms of intersectional oppression, including homophobia, transphobia, and racism.

Research on experiences of organizing Pride Events in rural and/or peripheral settings has shown the necessity of balancing many different (and competing) interests (Venegas Ferrin 2017; Ammaturo 2019; Forstie 2020; Lockett and Lewis 2022; López Sánchez and Rodríguez Domínguez 2023),

---

[i] See the original in Galician: '*Unha política agrocuir insiste na imposibilidade dunha liberación exual que no inclúa unha defensa de natureza, sobre todo para aqueLos persoas non heterosexuais que viven no rural e que loitan contra vario sistemas de opresión socioeconómica, cultural e sexual ao mesmo tempo*' (Barreto 2020: 17).

that is often manifested in the choice of less 'in your face' tactics, and more articulated forms of micro-politics that seek to create alliances with local actors, to enhance the acquisition of what Joseph (2010: 28–31) calls 'social capital' (borrowing from Bourdieu) when it comes to the organization of Pride Events. More needs to be done to put rural Pride Events on the map of researchers and scholars, particularly given the anti-rural bias (Herring 2010) that remains widespread in LGBTQIA+ scholarship. However, Pride Events organized in rural and/or peripheral settings have the true potential of complicating (and sometimes subverting) what we know about the seemingly hegemonic narrative of Pride Events, as a blanket transposition of the triad of 'coming out story', 'the parade format', and the 'rainbow iconology', as the key cultural anchors (Ghaziani and Baldassarri 2011) of Pride Events that we have previously discussed. More discussions on Pride Events organized in these often forgotten (or misunderstood) settings can only help us to enrich, complicate, and nuance our current understanding of this type of activism beyond the horizon of the city. This also contributes to doing justice to significant segments of various LGBTQIA+ communities and individuals living in geographically 'marginal' settings who do not often see their stories showcased.

United in Pride? Conflict and differences in the organization of Pride Events

'Emotional contagion' (Britt and Heise 2000), the idea that emotions[15] travel through a crowd[16] (people feeling proud of being LGBTQIA+ may lead others to feel the same), is central to the way in which Pride Events work, mobilizing feelings of pride to counter feelings of 'shame' (Munt 2019). Although Pride Events may give the impression of fostering community cohesion, solidarity, and mutual recognition between different segments of LGBTQIA+ communities, as well as (hetero/cis) allies, their histories and realities contain a key element of conflict and infighting (Ghaziani 2008). While the history of conflict and disagreement in the organization of and participation in Pride Events has not been erased, it has certainly not widely been showcased by scholars and activists. In the face of intense ongoing hostility towards LGBTQIA+ communities coming from right-wing, populist politics, as well as so-called 'anti-gender movements' (Liinason and Sasunkevich 2023; Ayoub and Stoeckl 2024; Sipos and Bagyura 2024), the intention of offering a united front in the face of homo/transphobia might be perceived by organizers as being more of a priority than highlighting internal disagreements.

As Ghaziani (2008: 3) has pointed out, however, 'horizontal hostility' – the incessant infighting within minority groups – is a ubiquitous feature of social movements, and political life in general. LGBTQIA+ social movements are not exempt from these forms of infighting. Ghaziani (2008: 5) identifies two main issues that are at the core of disagreements for LGBTQIA+ activists:[17] the issue of *strategy* and the issue of *identity*. When we think about disagreements relating to *strategy*, we are effectively dealing with organizers' ideas about what Pride should be for or what its demands should be. In relation to the question of *identity*, which is not at all necessarily divorced from questions of *strategy*, we can think about how representative Pride Events are, and whether alternative events can better convey or showcase the priorities or needs of marginalized segments of the communities (McFarland Bruce 2016: 7), such as LBTQ+ women,[18] racialized minorities, disabled people, working-class people, trans, non-binary people, and/or asexual people.

Questions relating to *strateg(ies)* to be embedded in Pride Events have been ubiquitous, including for the first Pride Event organized in the aftermath of the 1969 Stonewall Riots (Ghaziani 2008: 27). Talking about Pride Events in the context of their emergence in the US in the early 1970s, Armstrong (2002: 85) has identified three main strands holding opposing (sometimes mutually excluding) views on what Pride Events should be like: 'Gay Pride' (focusing on visibility, and the articulation of a 'positive gay identity'), 'Gay Power' (whose agenda is revolutionary and anti-capitalist), and 'Gay Rights' (which adopts a homophile,[19] strongly assimilationist logic in relation to inclusion into heteronormative societal structures). While this Euro/Western-centric theorization may be of limited applicability in relation to the global development of Pride Events, judging from emerging patterns across different global locations, it can be argued that assimilationist (Gay Pride + Gay Rights) segments of the communities have successfully managed to shape Pride Events, compared to the more 'radical counterparts'. This has potentially led to both a taming of radical messaging of these events (Joseph 2010: 307), as well as to a sharp rise[20] in the number of participants (Peterson et al 2018b: 10–11).

In relation to the choice of *strateg(ies)* to be deployed during Pride Events, the main issues of contention can be articulated as follows:

1. The organization of an event focusing on celebration, fun, and playful articulation of LGBTQIA+ identities VERSUS the adoption of a protest framing that conveys and advances complex political requests (McFarland Bruce 2016: 21).
2. A desire to push for assimilation of LGBTQIA+ people within mainstream society VERSUS a desire to radically challenge and change institutions and structures (capitalism, the police and the armed forces, the family) that are perceived to limit the expression of LGBTQIA+ identities, experiences, and subjectivities (McFarland Bruce 2016).
3. The adoption of 'single-issue parades' (just focusing on LGBTQIA+ equality) VERSUS the creation of 'multi-issues events' (forging alliances

across axes of discrimination – such as in relation to questions of race and class) (Peterson et al 2018b: 11).

These debates and issues are far from having been 'resolved' once and for all and remain, instead, at the heart of the contentious politics that characterize the very essence of Pride Events as a phenomenon that allows the expression of myriad subject positions, sometimes even in partial contrast to each other (McFarland Bruce 2016: 65–66).

Despite this growing institutionalization of reformist and assimilationist framing of Pride Events, events that explicitly position themselves in opposition to so-called 'mainstream' Pride Events are growing at the global level. While this phenomenon is more visible in the Global North (and particularly in the US and Canada), it also exists[21] in the Global South, in Latin America (Hernández Mosquera 2015; Capasso 2019; Guerrero 2019), as well as in Hong Kong, India, and South Africa, as recently discussed by Conway (2024). In the context of the Global North, 'Alternative Pride Events' began to be systematically organized since the 1990s (Peterson 2018b: 23). The main types of events that are organized as an alternative to 'mainstream' events can still be categorized within the dyad of *strategy/ identity*: while some adopt a holistic approach in challenging the very idea of what Pride Events should be, others focus on increasing representation and celebrating often marginalized segments of LGBTQIA+ communities, with overlaps between the two.

The ever-growing commercialization and commodification of Pride Events across the world, whereby Pride Events become increasingly entangled, and in some cases dependent on, corporate sponsorships for their organization (Johnston 2007a; Enguix 2009; Joseph 2010; Ammaturo 2016a; Taylor 2016; Conway 2024), offers a key point of opposition from some segments of LGBTQIA+ communities (see Chapter 6). Many 'Alternative Pride Events' adopt a strong anticapitalistic, anticommercial ethos, framed as a reaction or form of opposition to these widespread processes of commercialization/commodification, as the international success inspired by the 2002 Alternative Pride Event 'Gay Shame' organized in the US from 1998 to 2013 shows (Taylor 2016: 36–37). In South Africa, events such as Soweto Pride and Khumbulani Pride, as well as networks such as the 'Alternative Inclusive Pride Network', have offered resistance and opposition to the affluent, middle-class, white, capitalistic events organized in major cities such as Johannesburg and Cape Town for Black LGBTQIA+ South Africans (Mbasalaki 2022: 53; Conway 2024: 5).

Another important point, still relating to *strategic* framing of Pride Events, is the question of the participation or representation of the police and/ or the armed forces at these gatherings, often perceived to be vehicles of homonationalist messages about citizenship (Ammaturo 2016a; Russell 2018;

Wahab 2020; Berg 2024). In this regard, the participation of the police at Pride Events is materialized either through the presence of a parading contingent of police officers to be included in the body of the march/parade, alluding to the inclusivity of the police and/or the armed forces as an LGBTQIA+ employer (Berg 2024); or in their professional capacity in offering policing and security during the events (Piña 2022: 4). In both cases, the participation of the police has sparked the reaction and opposition of various segments of LGBTQIA+ communities, and in particular those who highlight the history of brutalization and violence that the police has historically played not just towards LGBTQIA+ communities in general but also, more specifically, to racialized populations, trans people, and/or other marginalized individuals, such as HIV-positive people, sex workers, and homeless people. In this regard, in 2016, a *Black Lives Matter* Chapter in Toronto (BLM-TO) successfully managed to ban altogether the presence of police officers attending Pride in a professional (not individual) capacity (Russell 2018; Holmes 2019).

The second type of Alternative Pride Event, which centres around the notion of *identity*, is represented by the constellation of events that focus on specific subjectivities, such as Black Pride, Trans Pride, and/or Dyke Marches, to name a few examples.[22] Pride Events that holistically challenge the white-centred or, sometimes white supremacist,[23] framing of Pride Events (Piña 2022) are growing in importance across different locations, in both the Global North (see Baez 2019; McNeill and Smith 2021; Yarborough 2022) and the Global South.[24] The creation of events such as 'Black Pride' (Smith 2020) or 'Latino Pride' (Kenttamaa Squires 2019) shows the need of decentring whiteness from Pride Events, and offering alternatives to individuals that may be more meaningful to them, often situated in more familiar environments, compared to mainstream Pride Events (McFarland Bruce 2016: 200).

Historically, one of the main challenges to the male-centred nature of Pride Events (Ghaziani 2008: 28) has been the creation of alternative events focusing on LBTQ+ women's subjectivities and priorities. The main type of events of this kind has been that of Dyke Marches that had sporadically been organized in the US since the 1970s but had not become institutionalized until the 1990s. Since then, Dyke Marches have become a recurring event in many cities across North America (and occasionally beyond it, for example, in Berlin and London). Some of the main features of these events are the intention to react to the growing depoliticization of mainstream Pride Events (Currans 2012: 74), the creation of alternatives to male-oriented events that monopolize and invisibilize women's experiences (Ghaziani 2008: 28), as well as the possibility of welcoming individuals (including trans people) who do not feel welcome at mainstream events (Podmore 2016: 75). While conflicts and discrepancies persist in relation to the framing of these events as being expansive in terms of their trans-inclusiveness (Podmore 2016: 75–76), as well as the very use of the word 'dyke' which may be considered offensive by some LBTQ+ women (Ghaziani and Fine 2008: 62–63), Dyke Marches continue to create alternative political and public spaces to advance political claims made by LBTQ+ women beyond the confines of homopatriarchal[25] structures (Esparza 2017: 150) that exist even within the LGBTQIA+ movement itself.

A similar process to Dyke Marches has been initiated with the creation of trans-centred Pride Events, very often called Trans Pride or Trans Marches (*Marchas Trans* in Spanish). Historically, the inclusion of trans people in mainstream Pride Events has been poor (Ghaziani 2008; McFarland Bruce 2016), despite their centrality in the unfolding of the Stonewall Riots in the North American context (see Chapter 1). To remedy this marginalization, trans activists have increasingly resorted to organizing their own events, both in the Global North and in the Global South. In the context of the Global South, Trans Marches are particularly popular in Latin America, in countries such as Colombia, Brazil, Argentina, to name a few (de Fatima Tranquilin-Silva 2020; Restrepo 2020; Mambrín 2024). Additionally, although Hijra subjectivities cannot fully be subsumed under the banner of Western 'trans' identities, a 'Hijra Pride' has been organized in Bangladesh since 2014 (Hossain 2017). Trans Marches tend to be political (or more politicized) than mainstream Pride Events, with an explicit outlook to fight heterocispatriarchal societal structures.

In a landscape in which Pride Events are working on becoming more trans-inclusive, however, a worrying (although minoritarian in scale) development is constituted by the transphobic attacks on growing efforts to make Pride Events trans-inclusive from so-called 'Trans Exclusionary Radical Feminists' (TERFS) (Hines 2019; Williams 2020; Scheffer 2021). These developments, which should be combatted from within LGBTQIA+ communities themselves, are a reminder that the politics of Pride Events is not static, and that Pride Events can often become exclusionary towards individuals who do not seem to 'fit' with an assimilationist, neoliberal, homonationalist agenda. LGBTQIA+ communities should be wary (and vigilant!) of the ways in which constructive forms of disagreement, confrontation, and 'infighting' could morph into forms of homophobic, transphobic, and racist exclusions.

Pride Events are sites of joy, celebration, and collective elaboration of identities and subjectivities. At the same time, as the chapter has sought to show, these events are also crucial sites of conflict, tensions, and negotiation of meanings and strategies. The global proliferation of Pride Events is a multidimensional phenomenon that is developing along three main axes: Pride Events happening in the Global North/Global South, Pride Events organized in both urban/rural contexts, as well as the exciting differences between mainstream/alternative Pride Events. These global and local trajectories and transformations of Pride Events from 'one' to 'many', show the social and political potential that these gatherings possess in helping local LGBTQIA+ communities around the world to find and articulate their own authentic voices, beyond the need to feel indebted to the historical legacy of the Stonewall Riots.

Notes

1. For a thorough engagement with questions of English linguistic hegemonic, linguistic pluralism, and decentring academic production in English as the privileged source of knowledge acquisition, please see the discussion in the Introduction of this book.
2. For specific emplacements of these divisions, see McLean (2023), Conway (2024), and McCartan (2024), to cite a few.
3. Contrary to some commentators who see institutionalization as a negative aspect of the growth and success of LGBTQIA+ activism, Joseph (2010: 12) perceives this process as a form of 'organizational growth and survival'. For Joseph (2010: 18), the creation of a formal structure that oversees organizing Pride Events does not necessarily lead to deradicalization, as the establishment of bureaucratic rules to follow can be used to protect the most vulnerable individuals within the community.
4. On a similar note, Piña (2022) has also highlighted the incongruence between the 'globalizing' agenda of initiatives such as the 2020 Online Global Pride (organized during the COVID-19 pandemic that saw most Pride Events worldwide being cancelled), and the performative inclusion of BLM (Black Lives Matter) activists in the festivities.
5. For a consideration on the concept of 'atmospheres of violence' towards queer people (with a particular focus on transphobic violence in the US), consult Stanley (2021).
6. There are obviously big differences existing between rural settings and other settings that can be considered 'urban' but on a smaller scale. For a more extensive consideration of these issues, please look at the work of Forstie (2020) on researching LGBTQ communities in 'small cities'.
7. Please note that the references offered here do not do justice to the vast existing North American and Australian literature on rural LGBTQIA+ life.
8. There is a wealth of research on Pride Events, both in urban and non-urban centres, coming from Central and Latin America in both Spanish and Portuguese languages. For some reading suggestions, please consult the reference list at the end of this book.
9. For examples on the connection between Pride Events and homonationalist discourses, see Greensmith and Giwa (2013) for the case of Canada, Ammaturo (2016a) for Italy and the UK, and Woori (2018) for the case of South Korea.
10. In the case of Italy (Ammaturo 2023: 7) gastronomic traditions relating predominantly to food are weaved into the symbolism and/or narrative of Pride Events (see Sorrento Pride, Bari Pride, Apulia Pride, to name a few) to foster belonging into the local cultural imaginary.
11. In the context of the UK (Ammaturo 2023: 9) narratives of belonging are fostered through the reimagining of local heritage and/or history, such as Gaelic heritage in the Hebrides Pride, and the association with key figures of British (imperial) history, such as Admiral Horatio Nelson in the case of King's Lynn and West Norfolk Pride.
12. Another interesting study relating to Pride Events in peripheral locations in Mexico is represented by the work by López Sánchez and Rodríguez Domínguez (2023), who have carried out a thorough analysis of Pride Events organized in four different peripheral locations across the country (Toluca, Silao de la Victoria, Querétaro, and

13. Valladolid), highlighting the micro-politics of each of these locations when it comes to the organization, participation, and performance of local *Marchas del Orgullo*.
14. For an analysis of Pride Events in peripheral/rural locations in Argentina, please see Bernieri Ponce and Larreche (2021).
15. For a broader, and more articulated, discussion about Pride Events and 'eco-sensibilities', as well as environmental sustainability policies at Pride Events, please see Chapter 8 of this book.
16. In her work on Pride Events in Brighton, Browne (2007: 63) speaks of 'emotional geographies', highlighting the importance of emotions in the context of space.
17. See also Durkheim's idea of 'collective effervescence' a sort of status of shared emotional connection between participants that can be used people's behaviour in participating to Pride Events (Day 2022).
18. Ghaziani's (2008: 5) focus is on patterns of infighting between LGBTQIA+ activists in the US who were seeking to organize different of the 'Lesbian and Gay March on Washington since 1979 to 2000. While the findings cannot be generalized across so many different global contexts, and specific forms of infighting will always emerge in specific circumstances, the general issues of *strategy* and *identity* represent good umbrella terms to capture the main reasons why conflicts and infighting within social movements may emerge in general terms.
19. In 1972, on the occasion of Los Angeles Pride, Del Whan, a lesbian activist expressed her disappointment at the ongoing restrictions imposed by organizers of the events on displays of expression: 'This is a liberationist parade. Some gay people stand in the way of gay liberation, and it's unfortunate. Many times they are more obstructive than the heterosexuals' (McFarland Bruce 2016: 81).
20. Homophile politics tends to be associated in the US with the work of one of the first established secret associations representing gay men, the 'Mattachine Society', created in Los Angeles in 1950.
21. Peterson et al (2018b: 11) have suggested that the rise of what they call 'equality normalization discourse' has been accompanied by a growth in magnitude of Pride Events.
22. Please note that this is not an exhaustive list of locations where 'Alternative Pride Events' exist or are organized.
23. Please note the existence of events that centre bisexual/pansexual subjectivities and identities, and events that centre disability activism (such as Disability Pride) and identities that are also LGBTQIA+ inclusive.
24. See, for instance, Matebeni's (2017: 27) discussion of how Black lesbian South African activist Beverly Ditsie challenged white organizers of the first Pride Event in Johannesburg in 1990 by pointing out the absence of 'women of colour' (her words) from the official line-up of speakers at the event.
25. In this respect, see the growing scholarship on South Africa by authors such as Matebeni (2017), Mbasalaki (2022), McLean (2023), and Conway (2023, 2024).
26. Esparza (2017: 150) defines 'homopatriarchy' as: 'a process in which gay and bisexual men embrace or legitimate some of the adverse ramifications associated with patriarchy in return for reaping some of its benefits. The discourse of homopatriarchy accentuates and fortifies male positions of power within cultural, familial, and national arrangements'.

PART II

Exploring the 'Kaleidoscope Modernities' of Pride Events

4

Free to Protest and Celebrate? Exploring Human Rights Issues at Pride Events

The recognition of the rights of LGBTQIA+ (lesbian, gay, bisexual, transgender, queer, intersex, asexual, plus) persons around the world represents an ongoing issue that affects communities and individual lives, both in private and in public. Transphobia, homophobia, criminalization, discrimination, violence, and harassment are still, unfortunately, common experiences for LGBTQIA+ persons across different latitudes, although they are experienced in vastly different ways depending on the legal, political, social, and cultural contexts across countries. At the same time, while we may be tempted to divide countries around the world in terms of 'gainers' and 'losers' in relation to their recognition of LGBTQIA+ rights, researchers are showing that in the last few years, even in countries where the general perception was that 'the fight had been won', particularly in the Global North (Browne and Nash 2014), backsliding of human rights and anti-LGBTQIA+ legislation seems to be growing, not least because of the rise of so-called 'anti-gender movements' (Sosa 2021; Ayoub and Stoeckl 2024; O'Dwyer 2024). The rising transphobia in the UK (Armitage 2020; Pearce et al 2020; Horton 2022), or the recently homo/transphobic legislation adopted by several states of the US[1] (Jones 2023), and the back-rolling of DEI (Diversity, Equity, and Inclusion) initiatives by President Trump at the outset of his new mandate (Ellis 2025), demonstrate the need to keep our undivided attention on violations that affect so deeply the lives of millions of people and entire communities worldwide.

Since their inception, and well beyond the horizon of the 1969 Stonewall Riots and the Western-Eurocentric matrix of contemporary Pride Events, organizers and participants to these gatherings around the world have considered the vindication of human rights as one of their main (sometimes central) messages, and have expressed their concerns and outrage through chanting, shouting slogans, parading banners, singing songs, engaging in direct action, and other forms of performances of protest.

At the same time, while human rights language and discourses seem to be ubiquitous features of the ways in which LGBTQIA+ people take to the streets during Pride Events, they should not be taken for granted; but should be problematized in relation to the role that these discourses play during these demonstrations, how they are specific to the social, political, and legal context in which they are expressed, what reactions they engender in the crowds or from the authorities, as well as how they are embedded in a transnational network of human rights advocacy and politics that sometimes becomes attached to homonationalist (Puar 2007) notions of 'virtuosity' or 'inadequacy' of specific countries.

Acknowledging these challenges that potentially place human rights as the possible cornerstone of so-called 'civilizational approaches' to LGBTQIA+ rights, the chapter highlights the complexity and non-linearity of human rights achievements in relation to Pride Events, particularly in relation to the need to constantly fight organized opposition, hostility, as well as attacks in local settings. Building on the patterns emerging from the interviews, the chapter explores the potential and pitfalls that the mobilization of human rights discourses during Pride Events present. This is achieved by looking at the ways in which human rights issues are defined, articulated, and promoted during the events themselves; the relationship between Pride organizers and authorities (governmental actors and the police) in their management support (or lack thereof) of Pride Events; as well as processes of collaboration existing between activists at the national level with international or supranational actors of different kinds (non-governmental organizations (NGOs), governments, ambassadors) in the articulation, promotion, and safeguarding of LGBTQIA+ rights, highlighting the production of a linear narrative of 'progression' towards a form of LGBTQIA+ 'modernity'.

We've got a right to take the streets: visibility and human rights at Pride Events

As has already been discussed in the previous chapters, Pride Events are polysemic and hold different meanings for people who participate in and/or organize them. Recent research carried out in eight different countries[2] has mapped at least 13[3] non-mutually exclusive types of motives that push people to participate in Pride Events, ranging from the desire to protest and fight for rights and/or tolerance, to wanting to celebrate and have fun, to meet friends and members of organizations and experience a sense of community (Wahlström 2018: 195). While this categorization offers a fascinating and needed insight into the multiple reasons why individuals participate in Pride Events, these 'motives' can be brought back to the often-conflicting ideas that Pride Events should either be seen as a 'protest' or a 'celebration' (McFarland Bruce 2016: 21).

As the pendulum between celebration and protest swings, human rights represent one of the main 'discursive frames' that is expressed and conveyed during Pride Events (Bennett 2017: 349). Several Pride organizers interviewed use extensively the language of human rights, particularly when explaining what the meaning of Pride Events for them is, and in relation to how they conceptualize their activism. Martín, a Pride organizer from Colombia, comments:

> I think that there, in the establishment of marches, we see the birth of the possibility to revendicate rights and visibility for the LGBT population, as well as [the possibility] of constructing one's identity through this space. I don't think that any right that we have today would have been possible if we had not chosen one day per year to become visible. [Freely translated from Spanish[i]]

For some Pride organizers, these events are inextricably linked to demands of justice for LGBTQIA+ people that are enacted by taking the streets and by occupying the (hetero)normative space (Browne 2007), even if it is for only one day per year. The question of visibility (Engebretsen 2015; Edenborg 2020) becomes central to the articulation of a politics of LGBTQIA+ justice, despite the dangers that this visibility may bring with it. This is well articulated in the reflections offered by Gjon, a Kosovar activist and Pride organizer, who reflects on the opportunities and possible dangers of inhabiting the public space for one day with a Pride Event, particularly thinking about whether participants should venture outside of the 'designated square' (Sheshi Skënderbej, Skanderbeg Square) in Pristina (Isufi 2021) where the event was being held in 2021:

> So not having LGBTI people daring to go outside the square and trying to invade all the city, that was quite the panicking. ... We changed that last year. We went beyond the square a little bit by walking. ... The Square does not bring so much visibility with isolated random people. But when you go into the city, then you may see students, and you will see people that are stuck in traffic, and so on. I think that brings more visibility. And it also gives the impression that not necessarily

---

[i] See the original quote in Spanish: '*Yo creo que allí, en el nacimiento de las marchas, nace la posibilidad de reivindicación de derechos y de visibilización de la población LGTBI, como así de ir construyendo también identidad a través de ese espacio. No creo que ningún derecho que tenemos hoy día fuese posible si nosotres no escogiéramos una vez al año para visibilizar*'.

only the square you can use it as a public space. You have the right to feel free to go around the city and be yourself. (Gjon, Kosovo)

However, not all activists interviewed think that visibility, particularly in physical terms as being present in the streets, is accessible to everyone in the same way. Suraj, a Pride organizer from Bangladesh, addresses this issue, highlighting how questions of education, social class, and caste (Dutta 2018; Upadhyay and Bakshi 2020) may impact LGBTQIA+ people's decision to be visible both at Pride Events and beyond:

> After 2016, almost all the visible LGBTQ activists fled out of the country, many of them still living in the UK. But the problem is it divided the narrative of visibility within the LGBTQ community. We have elitist class system within the LGBTQ groups up here. So those who are Western educated are from the rich background and possibly don't have any issues in their life, then their sexuality or identity doesn't matter in their family. They are very much reluctant [about it]. They say, 'No, we don't need this'.
>
> But on the other hand, those who are from the very rural area, every day, they said this is our identity. If we if we hide it, if we just, you know, make our self in in the closet, what will happen? I would die in the closet. ... Because if you if you don't have money, if you don't have power, if you don't have education, you do whatever you want. People don't care. But if you have an education, if you have a such a position people really care about, you also think about it because career progression, societal status is much more important than your sexual and gender identity. (Suraj, Bangladesh)

Visibility in public space for LGBTQIA+ persons should never be taken for granted, as it may often come at a high price for activists and lay participants (Richie 2010; Stella 2013; Engebretsen 2015; Edenborg 2020). At the same time, visibility in the articulation of LGBTQIA+ human rights claims can also offer glimpses of hope, particularly for younger generations who may need points of reference within the LGBTQIA+ community. The experience of Jennifer, a trans woman, and organizer of one of the Trans Pride Events created in the UK, highlights the importance of articulating human rights through a politics of trans visibility that is not just aimed at raising awareness for the public, but is also directed to members within the trans community:

> [H]ow impactful Pride can be as a, you know, providing a source of community for people. That's one of the big focuses of Trans Pride, you know. We're here to help people connect, to give people a day

which they've never had before. Every single event, someone comes up to me and tearfully thanks us for putting on this event, because it's the first time in their life that they've met another child in person or, you know, the first time they've ever been out as the real them. [You see] older trans people who, you know, transitioned decades ago and see the new generation, the kids that are coming up, and get blown away by it.

While most of the Pride organizers express an awareness of the need of centring human rights issues for trans people during their events, the reality is that these gatherings still predominantly cater for a cisgender (and predominantly male) majority of participants, leaving trans activists often choosing to create or participate in Alternative Pride Events, such as Trans Pride, where their priorities can be showcased and advocated (McCarthy 2020; McCartan and Nash 2023).

Despite these ongoing issues relating to the inclusiveness of Pride Events, human rights discourses remain at the forefront of the framing that Pride organizers offer in relation to both the meaning of these events and the justification for their organization. Pride organizers expressed a sustained and strong sense of urgency in relation to the importance of LGBTQIA+ visibility and building critical mass in the public articulation of their rights claims at Pride Events, particularly in the aftermath of the isolation experienced during the COVID-19 pandemic in 2020–2021. As the next section will show, this urgency is expressed in practice by the variety of human rights issues that are articulated during Pride Events.

What are we fighting for? Articulating grievances and human rights issues at Pride Events

Historically, grievances expressed by gay, white, cisgender men during Pride Events have received more attention compared to the issues raised by LBTQ women, trans people, and racialized LGBTQIA+ people (Ghaziani 2008; Mc Farland Bruce 2016; Matebeni 2017: 27). While work still needs to be done to make sure Pride Events become truly inclusive of many different marginalized groups across varying intersectional positionings (racialized people and communities, LBTQ+ women, trans and non-binary people, asexual people, disabled people, working-class people, indigenous people, Roma people), human rights issues continue to play a prominent role during Pride Events, although they may sometimes appear to be cloaked more in celebratory forms of expression, than visible forms of protest and contestation.

In relation to this research, the main human rights issues that are addressed during these gatherings, that have been mentioned by Pride organizers during this research, predominantly pertain to three areas: (1) rights relating to personal safety of LGBTQIA+ persons and the fight against transphobia and homophobia; (2) the rights of trans people, particularly in relation to the recognition of legal personhood, gender recognition, access to healthcare, and inclusion in society; (3) rights relating to relationships between people of the same sex, as well as parenting rights for LGBTQIA+ people and couples. This wide range of issues raised by activists confirms Bennett's (2017: 349) argument on the importance of human rights as one of the main 'discursive frames' deployed during Pride Events.

In relation to violence towards LGBTQIA+ people and communities that is motivated by hate, prejudice, and discrimination, we observe that this phenomenon remains unfortunately widespread, with the growth of 'Global Transphobia' (Plakhotnik and Mayerchyk 2023a: 97) as one of the most worrisome recent developments in the last few years. COVID-19, in this regard, seems to have enhanced the experiences of many individuals who were left isolated from their communities, often having to live with homo/transphobic relatives and/or flatmates (Fish et al 2020), or experiencing violence and harassment online (Rivers et al 2023). This has been also suggested by many interviewees, across different countries (South Africa, Mexico, Colombia, US, UK) who have reported how, during the pandemic, they have undertaken activities to curb these feelings of isolation for LGBTQIA+ members of their local communities, mostly by organizing online activities.

Another important discourse emerging from the interviews, is the role that responses to homo/transphobic violence existing in local settings, rather than abstract conceptualizations of cross-border queer solidarity, play as a sort of 'catalyst' or motivating factors for either organizing the event itself, or for fostering a sense of purpose among participants.

Liam, a Pride organizer from the UK, recalls the motivation to establish a Pride Event in the city:

> Liverpool was a city without a Pride in the UK, and we came from quite horrific murders. I saw Michael Causer,[4] a young guy who was killed for his identity. And very quickly after that there was a series of assaults within the gay community. We really came from a bit of a kind of community uproar, but also, it was about time we stood up and we all did so.

This echoes a similar narrative put forward by Connor, from Ireland, who also recalls how the murder of a gay man named Declan Flynn (O'Dowd 2022) in 1982, by a group of young people whose sentence was suspended because they came from 'good families', acted as the flame that ignited the creation of the first Pride Event in Dublin in 1983.

Another episode of violence, this time in the US, is also cited by Raymond, an organizer of an Alternative Pride Event, as the spark that has revived his activism after years of disillusion in so-called 'mainstream' Pride Events in New York City:

> The only reason I started going again [to Pride] was because I was one of the founding members of *Gays Against Guns*, which formed after the Pulse[5] massacre in 2016. That happened two weeks before Pride that year. And so, we met right after it, and we pulled ourselves together. We created *Gays Against Guns* and we marched, you know, at the head of the Parade of 2016. That was the only reason that brought me back.

Raymond's activism in 'Gays Against Guns' (Neate 2017), signals the importance of building intersectional alliances or awareness during Pride Events (Paul 2019; Schimanski and Treharne 2019). In this regard, some of the participants, particularly from Mexico, South Africa, Kosovo, Colombia, and the US, show a particularly strong sensibility in relation to conceptualization of a framework of fighting against homo/transphobic violence that also encompasses anti-racist and anti-misogynist concerns, particularly in relation to *feminicidios* in Latin America (Guerrero et al 2022), and in relation to the death of George Floyd, a Black man who was killed in the US by Minneapolis police in May 2020, and whose death has created resonance for the concerns raised by the Black Lives Matter movement worldwide. This point speaks to the previously discussed patterns of cross-mobilization or exclusion of specific segments of LGBTQIA+ communities worldwide, particularly in relation to questions of racism and transphobia.

Building on this need for an intersectional understanding of human rights issues at Pride, one further prominent theme that emerges from the empirical data is the perception that the rights of trans people, across different continents, are either inexistent, inconsistent, stagnating or, on the opposite side of the spectrum, in contexts in which guarantees and protections have been granted in the past, that they are imperilled and at risk of being eroded, although the issues faced by trans people across different geographical locations vary enormously.

Paul, an activist from Taiwan, describes the ongoing efforts of his organization to bring transgender visibility to the front of activities for Pride Events in the country:

> For 2022 and 2023, we have a plan. We want to empower activists to understand transgender issues more. We will also do like some surveys and focus groups to understand the living situation for transgender people in Taiwan more, and to organize a workshop to share this. ...

> People don't really understand what 'transgender' means. We need to continue to share their stories and their situation to the general public.

Activists from Bangladesh and India also highlight the vulnerability of trans people in the respective countries, commenting on the intersection between social and economic status and discrimination within society (Konduru and Hangsing 2018). Similar points are raised in the context of Mexico and Latin America, and South Africa, where Pride organizers comment on the compound effects experienced by trans people who are also sex workers (*trabajadores sexuales*), and experience high levels of violence (Koné 2016; Evens et al 2019).

On the other hand, in contexts such as the US and the UK, Pride organizers express their worries about the growing levels of transphobia in society, despite the relatively high degree of legal codification of the rights of trans people. Activists emphasize the need to address transphobia through Pride Events, such as in the case of Jennifer, a trans activist from the UK, who explains:

> Activism is awful, you know, and you're aware of all the awful things. And that's why I say that Trans Pride has been the thing that has saved me, giving me a positive thing to concentrate. And what we create is, is genuinely life changing for some people. I see people on Twitter, calling out [transphobia], you know, that kind of activism. I've done that before and I find it so exhausting, but Trans Pride creates something that's so positive. That's what my activism is. It keeps me happy. It makes me feel like I've really made a difference.

This sentiment is also echoed by Raymond, from the US, who talks about a specific case that motivates his activism in the Alternative Pride Events context in New York City:

> [trigger warning: mention of sexual violence]
>
> We're dealing with the fact that a trans woman, Latee Brockington,[6] has been held at Rikers [Prison] for almost two years on and off, without a trial so far, and been raped three times because they refused to put her in gender appropriate general facility. So, you know, you know, that's what that's what a Pride march must be about.

Issues relating to the healthcare needs of trans people (Pearce 2018) across different countries were also discussed by interviewees during the research. As the data were collected towards the end of the 2020–2021 COVID-19 pandemic, Pride organizers were very attuned to the experiences of trans people in their respective communities when it came, particularly, to access to gender-affirming healthcare by both general practitioners, and specialized services (Jarrett et al 2021; Kidd et al 2021). This was also shared by one of the organizers, Felix, a trans man from Denmark, who discussed how he experienced first-hand delays in receiving his gender-affirming surgery during the pandemic.

A further issue that is featured during Pride Events and is mentioned by organizers in the context of this research, is that of the recognition of same-sex relationships and parenting rights for same-sex couples. These themes feature quite prominently in international LGBTQIA+ activism, as well constituting one of the major human rights issues that are addressed during Pride Events, with important variabilities across countries relating to the existence of criminalizing measures against same-sex sexual contact, which may foreclose entirely the recognition of LGBTQIA+ subjectivities and relationships. Ahmad, from Lebanon, addresses the importance of working with authorities, to address the existence of criminalizing measures on homosexuality in the country: 'The first step to this is to ensure that people are not treated like criminals, like rapists, because we are criminalizing them for simply loving whom they love and another adult who's consenting to this relationship, and the sexual practice that happens in the privacy of home?'

In another context where homosexuality is illegal, Bangladesh, Pride organizer Suraj also discusses how, in 2020, during the COVID-19 pandemic, he helped to organize an online Pride Event which showcased artists' work (including reciting poetry from Bengali poet Rabindranath Tagore), as well as giving visibility to same-sex Bangladeshi intimacies:

> We showcased one gay Bangladeshi couple who was also a friend of that man who was assassinated [Pride organizer Xulhas Mannan[7]]. They are living in Canada. They are living in their own life as a as a couple. We asked them to do a cooking [demonstration] for us. They were doing that to portray how a family can be. How Bengali gay partners can marry and being a family and make the household work and everything.

Suraj's example offers a glimpse into what Duggan (2012) calls 'homonormativity' as a strategy to tame sexual difference to make it 'acceptable' or 'palatable' for heteronormative societies. In this regard, Pride Events can represent key sites of 'normalization' of LGBTQIA+ identities, relationships, and families (Ammaturo 2016a; Taylor 2016; Kenttamaa Squires 2019). Another example of this comes from Italian activists interviewed for this research who express their disappointment deriving from the approval of the so-called 2016 'Cirinnà Law'[8] (Law 20 May 2016, n. 76) which recognized same-sex unions (but not marriage), and did not give any possibility for either single[9] LGBTQIA+ individuals or same-sex couples to adopt children, including so-called 'step-parent adoption' (Donà 2021). One Italian Pride organizer, Xeni, sees Pride as the opportunity to counter the limiting effects of the 2016 'Cirinnà Law', and advocate for the rights of same-sex couples and parents.

Albeit in a more subtle way, homonormative tendencies in Pride Events are also manifested through many activists' comments on the need to make Pride Events a 'safe space' for everyone, including families. While this desire of inclusivity certainly corresponds to an intention of building allyship and normalizing the existence of same-sex families, some commentators also read it as a move to 'sanitize' Pride Events and desexualize them, particularly the presence of drag queens (see the impact of anti-drag legislation in the US; Russell 2023), or the participation of members of 'kinky' communities (Ng 2017; Greenberg 2023).

Opposition and oppression: Pride Events and freedom of expression and assembly in the shadow of COVID-19

One of the most relevant and apparent ways in which the 'discursive frame of human rights' appears in the context of Pride Events is that relating to freedom of expression, assembly and association[10] in relation to the possibility of organizing Pride Events in specific national contexts. Globally, LGBTQIA+ persons are often prevented from freely expressing their opinions, identities, and experiences in public, as well as freely forming and officially registering LGBTQIA+ associations and organizing public events (like Pride Events), or other forms of gatherings for their communities (Polsdofer 2013; Ammaturo 2016a; Muedini 2018; Slootmaeckers 2023). Even when Pride Events are allowed, clashes and incidents can tarnish the enjoyment of these rights, and create dangers for participants, particularly if official authorities, such as the police, do not intervene to prevent violence and harassment (Ammaturo 2016b; Plakhotnik 2022; Slootmaeckers 2023). As will be discussed in Chapter 5, the relationship between Pride organizers, Pride participants, and the police is fraught and charged with tension and, in some cases, overt hostility, because of racism and historical criminalization of LGBTQIA+ people by the police (Russell 2019; Girardi 2022).

Organizing a Pride Event is almost impossible in countries that criminalize homosexuality and/or trans identities, given the tangible possibility of being arrested by the police, and/or being subjected to violence by the general public (see Chapter 2). A similar situation is also experienced by countries in which homosexuality and/or trans identities are not criminalized per se, but in which laws that limit freedom of expression, freedom of assembly and association have been voted, with two notable examples being Russia (Kondakov 2020; Buyantueva 2023) and Turkey (Muedini 2018; Kilic

2023). In some cases, furthermore, Pride Events may not be consistently organized, sometimes because of financial or other logistical issues (Outright International 2023: 11–12).

In countries where Pride Events are organized, opposition is not uncommon and, in some cases, police presence is either insufficient, ineffective, or openly neglectful. Several activists discuss formal and informal examples of opposition to the organization of Pride Events, including curtailments to their rights to freedom of expression, assembly, and association. Janko, a Pride organizer from Serbia, where difficulties in organizing Pride Events have been documented since the (banned) edition,[11] in 2009, up to 2022, when Europride festivities in Belgrade were violently brought to a halt by far-right counter-protesters (Gavranovič 2023), discusses several instances in which hostility has been expressed, both online and offline, about their events. One instance, which illustrates how Pride Events become 'hyper-contextualized' in local settings (Ammaturo 2023), shows the extent to which religious and far-right protesters would go to interfere with LGBTQIA+ persons' enjoyment of their right to freedom of expression:

> One of the drag queens in 2018[12] [Dita von Bill] wore traditional Serbian clothes, and she danced on the truck. She went through such a brutal campaign by the pro-government right-wing media and by some right-wing conservative parties, that even the parties sued her for breaking traditional morals and public morals and religious feelings. She even went to court. I mean, it wasn't successful, of course, for them, but she had to go to court with them. (Janko, Serbia)

In the context of South Korea, Pride organizers have had to contend with particularly virulent opposition from Christian opponents, as well as the inaction of the police when Pride participants were faced with this open hostility. This is the experience recalled by Kyu-won, one of the organizers of Seoul Pride:

> In 2014, we saw a lot of homophobia [from] conservative Christians. They are so violent. They can speak louder or hit other people. They even threw some poo.[13] In 2014, we confronted this homophobia to try to prohibit our Pride Parade. We confronted [them] for six hours. And police officers didn't do anything. Just stood around us and remain idle. So finally, we could march around 10 pm. Because of the homophobia, from 2015, we moved our location to Seoul Plaza, which is front of the City Hall, and because Seoul Plaza is so big, so many people came to our Pride Parade, [but] also many homophobes were coming, so well, too many people were coming!

Both Janko's and Kyu-won's experiences show how difficult and challenging the organization and participation in Pride Events can be, particularly if police forces are unable or unwilling to offer meaningful protection to LGBTQIA+ persons. Opposition to Pride Events, however, is not just framed in religious terms. Some activists, from South Korea, the UK, and Kosovo, have reported opposition to Pride Events from so-called 'TERFs' (Trans Exclusionary Radical Feminists), some of whom identify as lesbian women, who have tried to oppose or sabotage Pride Events because of their respect and inclusion of trans people. A couple of examples illuminate the issues faced by activists:

> [trigger warning: explicit sexual and transphobic language]
> There's a movement at the moment where the TERFs are saying that lesbians aren't welcome at Pride, which is absolute cr*p. However, if you come to Pride with a banner that says trans women have penises, I'm going to tell you to f*** off. Simple. (Larry, UK)

> [We have a] radical feminist problem in South Korea. It started from 2016, when many women identified themselves as feminist due to the #MeToo movement. But after that, around 2017, radical feminist groups started to grow explosively, and they started to attack the transgender community. (Kyu-won, South Korea)

These examples are in line with other cases of 'disruption', such as the case of the infamous TERFs' incursion at the beginning of the 2018 Pride in London (Dommu 2018), where they were eventually allowed to open the parade, distributing transphobic leaflets, amid the confusion and rage of the crowds. Episodes like these do not just point to the existence of possible legitimate differences of opinion between different groups within the LGBTQIA+ community but represent a worrying symptom of a hatred-based and exclusionary drive to erase trans people not only from Pride Events, but more largely from the very histories of LGBTQIA+ communities worldwide, as also discussed in the first part of this book.

The COVID-19 pandemic of 2020 and 2021 has exacerbated some of the challenges connected to the possibility (often fragile and tenuous) for LGBTQIA+ persons to enjoy their right to freedom of expression and freedom of assembly and association. In a way, the events unfolding during the COVID-19 pandemic, and the resulting compression and restrictions to human rights experienced by many, have exposed the vulnerability of these social movements, which rely on visibility to effect social change and raise awareness, as well as requiring protection and legitimation from authorities to protest peacefully and safely. The pandemic has led to restrictions or compressions to human rights entitlements that have occurred for individuals in different spheres of their lives (Tzevelekos and Dzehtsiarou, 2020; Elshobake 2022; Sun et al 2022). Freedom of expression (Kalitenko et al 2021), as well as freedom of assembly and association (Bethke and Wolff 2020), seem to have been crucially affected by the measures adopted during the pandemic, with clear implications for restrictions to the enjoyment of these freedoms by LGBTQIA+ persons.

Activists in Serbia and Germany have reported how far-right protesters have queried the right of LGBTQIA+ activists to organize Pride Events during the COVID-19 pandemic (although most Pride Events were officially cancelled, and those that went ahead followed official guidance). Janko, from Serbia, for instance, discusses how conspiracy theories started to circulate about the fact that the easing of restrictions was planned in concert with LGBTQIA+ to 'show a good picture to the EU about allowing Pride to happen'.

The impossibility of freely gathering for Pride Events worldwide during the pandemic, also enhanced feelings of isolation for LGBTQIA+ persons (Gonzalez et al 2021), who felt deprived of the visibility that they needed to openly counter homo/transphobia. Tina, a Pride organizer from the US, discusses the challenges experienced in Oregon:

> When we had to cancel the in-person Pride in 2020, my very first concern was what would it mean for us not to be so visible at that time on public? We had the whole Black Lives Matter movement happening, which completely kicked up the Patriot Prayer Proud Boys. The Pacific Northwest is a huge neo-Nazi breeding ground. All these things happened when we didn't have our power numbers, we didn't have our visibility, we were isolated, and we were physically and mentally and emotionally threatened. And a whole bunch of people not able to have that together peace that Pride brings. It's really hard for people.

Several participants share Tina's sentiment, particularly in their worry about losing momentum or ground, especially when they live in contexts where homo/transphobia physically threatened the security of individuals. As of 2025, Pride Events have resumed in a post-pandemic world. However, the experience of the COVID-19 outbreak shows the importance of nurturing spaces of freedom of expression, assembly, and association that can become easily sacrificed in times in which 'exceptional measures', or a 'state of emergency' can be declared. In a world in which the taken-for-grantedness of LGBTQIA+ rights starts to crumble, it is possible to see how another global 'crisis', such as the one experienced with the COVID-19 pandemic, can further erode civil, social, and economic rights, particularly for the most vulnerable or marginalized among us.

As a measure to counter the restrictions and bypass isolation and marginalization, the multiplication of online avenues for the expression of LGBTQIA+ subjectivities and human rights claims worldwide during the COVID-19 pandemic, has been cited by participants, as a key tool to foster community cohesion, as well as establishing transnational networks of solidarity and reach some segments of the LGBTQIA+ community (Ammaturo and Burchiellaro 2021), especially younger people, who needed support during times in which they could not see anyone looking like them in the empty streets of cities, towns, and villages across the world. While the world of online media, and particularly social media, seems to represent a fertile terrain for homo/transphobic abuse, as well as racism, sexism, and ableism, these spaces can also act as alternative fora for the expression of belonging and solidarity, especially when physical spaces become foreclosed or seem to be too dangerous to inhabit.

LGBTQIA+ rights through the prism of modernity: international politics, Pride Events, and homonationalism

Human rights discourses and language are crucial tools used in the transmission of a global discourse on sexual and gender 'modernity'. As has been discussed in Chapter 2, LGBTQIA+ rights have become a sort of 'litmus test' of the alleged modernity of specific countries (Ammaturo 2016b; Klapeer 2018; Slootmaeckers 2023), particularly outside of the context of the Global North (Rahman 2014b; Rao 2020), but also within some 'peripheries' within the Global North itself, such as in post-Communist Eastern Europe and the Balkans (Kulpa and Mizielinska 2016; Navickaitė 2014; Ammaturo 2016b; Slootmaeckers 2023). Pride Events represent a tangible strategy through which adherence to processes of 'modernization' can be articulated. This does not necessarily mean that Pride organizers explicitly adopt such framing when organizing Pride Events in their specific contexts or consider this the primary goal of their initiatives. However, Pride Events have been connected to processes of 'Europeanization' (Ayoub 2013; Ammaturo 2016b; Vasilev 2016; Slootmaeckers 2023), as well as tied to development initiatives, such as in the case of Uganda (Svensson and Strand 2024).

The multiplication of Pride Events around the world has been taken as an illustration of how societies become more open, progressive, and inclusive of LGBTQIA+ persons. When it comes to Pride Events, there is 'safety in numbers' (Peterson et al 2018b: 124; InterPride 2017: 10), as the size of these events can help communities to build the necessary critical mass to advance rights claims, raise awareness, and counter homo/transphobia. Yet, the growth of Pride Events is not necessarily a neutral process, as bigger events require bigger organizational apparatuses, lead to the increasing professionalization of organizers, and create bigger financial burdens (for a more in-depth discussion, see Chapters 5 and 6). The growth of Pride Events can also hide tensions and contradictions that brew from within, particularly around participation of actors who are not considered to be 'organic' to the community, such as big corporations (Ammaturo 2016a; Conway 2023) who may engage in 'pinkwashing' of their brands or industrial practices (DeGagne 2020). Furthermore, as discussed in relation to the emergence of the concept of 'Kaleidoscope Modernity', the recognition of LGBTQIA+ rights may be contradictory, tenuous, or subjected to constant challenges from the part of both political and non-political actors, thus undermining the presumption that gains in the field of human rights teleologically determine an ascension to a stable form of 'progress' or 'modernity'.

Most participants in this research have reflected on the growth of their respective events, considering it as an overwhelmingly positive development. As previously discussed, however, visibility may be a double-edged sword for LGBTQIA+ communities (Engebretsen 2015; Edenborg 2020), especially in contexts where homo/transphobia and/or criminalization are rife. Discourses advanced by Pride organizers in this research about their events getting 'bigger and better', however, are not only significant as a sign of success of local activism but acquire a different meaning if seen in conjunction with the emerging theme in this research relating to the comparison of one's own organized Pride Event to other, bigger and more established, gatherings, especially in other countries. This discourse of comparison is quite widespread among the interviewees, as illustrated by the following examples:

> I was thinking that it is going to be the fourth year [of Pride] and that when I look at other organizations and other countries, for example, in London it's the 50th anniversary [in 2022]. And I'm just thinking, when are we going to get there? In 45 years, of course! But it's such a shame that really the building takes so many years. (Jana and Tereza, Czechia)

> Our focus is more on building self-capacity, building confidence, building awareness, because outside of China, in the West, LGBT movements are already 40 or 50 years. But in China, you can see by this year we are only entering [our] 14th year. So very, very young. Relatively everything in China grows exponentially, like the economy. But we are unsure about culture, and we are unsure about our human rights. It will be something exponential that we can achieve in 30 years. Even so, we are just halfway through. (Andrew, China)

Both Jana and Tereza from Czechia, and Andrew from China, conceptualize their respective organizations, or LGBTQIA+ activism in their country more broadly, as having to catch up with the 'established' movements in the West/Western Europe that have been active for 40 or 50 years. Particularly interesting is the narrative of progress, the teleological 'mission' of getting there, even if it takes 45 (Jana and Tereza) or 30 years (Andrew).

At the same time, comparisons are not just carried out in relation to the West, but they can also be articulated at the regional level, comparing one's own achievement to those of neighbouring countries in the region. This is the case for activists from South Africa, China, and Colombia, but also Kosovo, as illustrated by the following example:

> If we compare, for example, the first year [of Pride] with last year, we didn't have so many LGBTI the first people who participated. Mainly it was people from organizations and allies. Every year more and more LGBTI youth and people are participating. I mean that's amazing. ... Knowing the fact that Kosovo in 2015, and 2018, from the reports from researchers from Civil Rights Defenders and from the World Bank, was ranked as the most homophobic country in Western Balkans. (Gjon, Kosovo)

Last, Pride organizers' comparisons with other countries are also articulated by activists in the Global North, who compare their situation to that of countries predominantly located in the Global South (but also in Eastern Europe), where the rights of LGBTQIA+ persons are either at risk or are not recognized, in part or in full. While it is undeniable that these differences exist and jeopardize the safety, dignity, and flourishing of LGBTQIA+ people across the world, this type of comparison risks fostering a sense of 'saviourism' when it comes to Pride organizers from the Global North, who may come to think that they can intervene/address, or offer 'training' or solutions to LGBTQIA+ activists from the Global South, which some of the answers by some interviewees seem to suggest.

One illustration of these 'saviourist temptations' by actors from the Global North in relation to Pride Events in either Eastern Europe and/or the Global South, is represented by the existence of patterns of support, collaboration, and financing from governmental actors, with the most visible illustration of this form of intervention being represented by the actions of ambassadors and other representatives of national governments abroad (Gurok 2022). Embassies are increasingly becoming central in the way in which they articulate a specific form of sexual modernity that is LGBTQIA+ inclusive to be promoted beyond the national borders, and a form of homonationalism (Puar 2007). One recent example in this regard, has been the decision by many US embassies in Muslim-majority countries to fly rainbow flags, such as in the case of Saudi Arabia, United Arab

Emirates, and Kosovo (Kochi 2024), although this initiative has recently been halted by the arrival of President Trump to the White House, in January 2025.

In some cases, the presence of embassies at Pride Events seems to be institutionalized, as is the case of South Korea (see also Chapter 2). In fact, local Pride organizer Kyu-won claims that around 30 per cent of the booths present during the Pride Parade in Seoul are organized by either corporations or embassies, which could prompt reflections about these two different types of 'pinkwashing'. Always in the context of Asia, in China, Pride organizers have faced the hostility of the government (Liang 2023), leading to the cancellation of Pride Events in Shanghai since 2021, but they have been collaborating with several consulates of Western countries to organize an LGBTQIA+ Film Festival that proves to be very successful (Andrew, China).

More broadly, collaboration with international actors, be they governmental or not, can attract opposition and accusations of being 'in the pocket' of foreign actors, with Pride organizers having to navigate these accusations often levelled against them in the press. Several Pride organizers have mentioned finding themselves in this conundrum relating to the accusation of 'importing Pride' from the West (or Global North more broadly). Suraj, from Bangladesh, discusses how Pride organizers faced a decision to create an online streamed version of Pride that was in line with 'moderate values' that would not upset Bangladeshi viewers, but still allowed LGBTQIA+ people to broadcast their stories, rather than having an 'LGBT Pride Rally', or a 'Rainbow Rally'. Another case of this negotiation between the global and the local politics of Pride Events, to counter claims of foreign interference, is represented by the reflections offered by Gjon, from Kosovo, who discusses the importance of being visible in Kosovo as LGBTQIA+, and doing so while speaking and singing in Albanian:[14]

> We are not here because the international community is paying us to say that we are here because there is this mindset that before the war [in Kosovo] we didn't exist. But after the war the international community brought us here, and they are paying us just to say that I'm transgender, or gay, or bisexual. Speaking Albanian, going in the media as an LGBTI person, having a Pride Parade and singing in Albanian through the main squares, I think that's quite powerful for us as activists.

Marcel, a Pride organizer from Slovakia, offers an interesting reflection on the opportunity of helping to organize Pride Events in places in which one is not undertaking forms of activism directly, hence risking 'importing' Pride in contexts in which either participants are not 'ready', or not enough work has been done with local communities:

> You can't have people from very far away importing Pride or colonizing your city with Pride. I want to go and organize Pride [events] somewhere else, but I look for local people, they develop them, I train them, I support them, but it's their own job [to create the Pride Event]. And either there are people there to do that or not. It's okay. The time is not right for that.

This sentiment is also shared by Craig, a Pride organizer from San Diego who discusses collaboration with Mexican counterparts who organize the *Marcha del Orgullo LGBTI* in Tijuana:

> We were very sensitive to not be the big, big *gringo* [emphasis added] from the North who comes down and tells [activists] how to do things. We come and listen and say we have resources, and we have ways to assist you if you need it. If not, we're here just to be your support.

These experiences by different activists, which obviously do not offer a comprehensive picture of a global situation that is extremely heterogeneous, are nonetheless useful in offering a snapshot of the challenges that activists face in relation to their patterns of collaboration with other activists, institutional actors, and NGOs. As Pride Events become increasingly identified as giving access to a sort of 'sexual and gender modernity', Pride organizers may be under pressure to offer and organize similar events in their local contexts.

Similarly, Pride organizers (or governmental actors) in countries in which these events are more 'institutionalized', may be tempted to offer support and assistance to activists whose movements are relatively more recent, by deploying a patronizing, homonationalist, and neocolonialist approach. As shown through these examples, Pride organizers interviewed, are aware of the difficulties of navigating these two issues and constantly engage in processes of negotiation to offer the best representation and visibility to their respective local LGBTQIA+ communities in ways that are meaningful, culturally sensitive, and empowering.

As Chapter 5 will discuss, LGBTQIA+ organizers, as well as the public, entertain a problematic relationship with the police and the armed forces. However, their presence at Pride Events is often heralded as a demonstration of 'modernization' of relevant countries and inclusiveness (Ammaturo 2016b). At the same time, however, this sort of 'militarization' of Pride Events buys into homonationalist (Puar 2007) narratives about 'good queer subjects' as opposed to 'bad homophobic individuals or communities'. While homo/transphobia should obviously not be underestimated, the inclusion of the police or the army during Pride Events shows how nationalist strands of LGBTQIA+ representation can divide communities and further marginalize those who do not fit within the mould of 'respectability' and alleged 'good citizenship'.

A good illustration of the nexus between LGBTQIA+ rights and nationalism is represented by the inclusion of LGBTQIA+ soldiers at the 2024 Pride Event in Kyiv, Ukraine, while the 500 people who were allowed to participate in the march only managed to take a few steps on the pavement before they were ushered down into the metro to make them safe from far-right counter-protesters who also took the streets (Mackenzie 2024). The march, however, was spearheaded by LGBTQIA+ soldiers who had fought against Russian invasion, holding a banner with the faces of all the other deceased LGBTQIA+ soldiers during the war. As scholars working on Kyiv Pride have argued (Plakhotnik 2022; Shevtsova 2023), there is a penetration of nationalist discourses in the context of these events, which is seen as being problematic by many. One example is offered by Günther, a Pride organizer from Germany, who comments on the efforts to show solidarity for the war in Ukraine during Pride in 2022:

> The first truck in the parade is always the Pride Comité Organization truck and we will give this completely as a stage to speakers from LGBT Ukraine organizations. And we will not put their colours or flags on the truck because we think this is a takeover which is not fair. You shouldn't do that with national flags, but we will still support their community.

In light of the ongoing struggles to make LGBTQIA+ movements as inclusive as possible, and fighting against racism and xenophobia, the 'militarization' of Pride Events should remain a concern for Pride organizers, as it risks segmenting and alienating the most vulnerable sections of the communities, and those who are mostly targeted by repressive state force, such as illegalized migrants, racialized persons and communities, trans persons, Roma persons, as well as sex workers and drug users. These challenges are ongoing across several countries, where especially the presence of the police at Pride Events remains contested, as Chapter 5 will discuss.

Notes

[1] Human Rights Campaign has noted that, as of 30 May 2023, legislators across the US had introduced a total of 520 anti-LGBTQIA+ Bills, with 74 of them being enacted into law. These provisions targeted trans people in sports, healthcare provision for trans people, education on LGBTQIA+ issues, bans of drag performers, among other issues. For more information, please see Human Rights Campaign (2023).

[2] The eight countries in question are Czechia, Italy, Poland, the Netherlands, Sweden, Switzerland, the UK, and Mexico.

[3] Wahlström (2018: 195) lists the following 13 motives to participate at Pride Events: (1) Protest or fight for rights and/or tolerance; (2) because of one's conviction or duty;

(3) for visibility or to display one's identity or pride; (4) to express or articulate a minority identity; (5) because of tradition or convenience; (6) to show support; (7) to represent a group or an organization; (8) to meet friends or co-members of an organization; (9) to celebrate; (10) to commemorate; (11) for entertainment or fun; (12) to experience a feeling of community; (13) for one's curiosity.

4   See Pidd (2008).
5   See Zambelich and Hurt (2016).
6   See Riedel (2022).
7   See Lavers (2016).
8   Legge 20 maggio 2016, n. 76, *Regolamentazione delle unioni civili tra persone dello stesso sesso e disciplina delle convivenze*. (16G00082) (GU Serie Generale n.118 del 21-05-2016), Italy. Available at: www.gazzettaufficiale.it/eli/id/2016/05/21/16G00082/sg, last accessed 4 July 2024.
9   In Italy, single-parent adoption is forbidden, apart from very specific circumstances. For more information, see Tuo (2015: 360).
10 See, for instance, the Universal Declaration of Human Rights (Arts 17, 19, and 20), the International Covenant on Civil and Political Rights (Arts 19, 21, and 22), the African Charter on Human and People's Rights (Arts 9, 10, and 11), the American Convention on Human Rights (Arts 13, 15, and 16), as well as the European Convention on Human Rights (Arts 10 and 11), and the European Charter of Fundamental Rights and Freedoms (Arts 11 and 12).
11 The first attempt to organize a Pride Event in Serbia dates back to 2001, but it was small and came under heavy attack from counter-protesters. After that, it took several years for the Serbian LGBTQIA+ community to consider organizing a new event, in 2009, which, unfortunately, was banned by the authorities. The first successful and peaceful Pride Event was eventually held in the country in 2014.
12 For further information on this case, please see Poff (2022).
13 For more information in English see Duffy (2014). For more information on this episode in Korean, see Gu (2023).
14 Please note here the political context of Kosovo, particularly in the aftermath of the 1998–1999 Kosovo war between Serbia and the Kosovar Separatist militia called the 'Kosovo Liberation Army' which led to the independence of the country from Serbia.

5

Back to Grassroots? Conflicts and Tensions in Community-building at Pride Events

What does it mean to create a sense of community during and through Pride Events? What do these 'communities' look like, and what happens when people do not see themselves represented or included in them? These are some of the questions that Pride organizers must confront when creating events for the local LGBTQIA+ (lesbian, gay, bisexual, transgender, queer, intersex, asexual, plus) communities. As Pride Events multiply in number and grow in size around the world, Pride organizers face ever-greater pressures to deliver events that are representative, inclusive, but at the same time that are financially viable, and are organized professionally. As has been mentioned already, the tension between the conceptualization of Pride Events as either a 'celebration' or 'protest' (McFarland Bruce 2016: 21) strongly shapes both organizers' and participants' expectations relating to the characteristics that specific events should possess. Furthermore, activists have historically oscillated (and continue to do so) between strategies that either focus on 'single-issue pragmatic politics' (narrowly focusing on rights for LGBTQIA+ people) or embrace a 'multi-issue radical politics' (considering intersectional entanglements with issues such as 'race' or class, to name a few) (Ghaziani 2008: 8).

The existence of these different perceptions and expectations regarding the role, characteristics, and strategies of Pride Events, leads to the emergence of tensions and conflicts in relation to their organization, management, and participation, as discussed in Chapter 3. These conflicts or tensions may arise among activists themselves or can occur between organizers and local members of LGBTQIA+ communities. While they may present themselves with great variability, depending on the specific geographic context in which Pride Events are organized, and the level of institutionalization of Pride Events in the social, political, and legal fabric of a specific country (Joseph 2010; Podmore 2016; Ammaturo 2023), there are some themes that become recurrent in the analysis of these frictions or fractures, particularly from an empirical perspective, as evidenced by several of the conversations with Pride organizers collected in the context of this research.

This chapter centres the empirical data obtained from the 60 interviews to explore three main axes alongside which tensions and conflicts relating to Pride Events may arise. First, it considers tensions relating to the professionalization of Pride Events (Greer 2012; Butterfield 2016). As Pride Events grow and multiply across different locations, the demands on activists also increase, requiring organizational and logistical structures that ensure a professional delivery of these events. This process of 'professionalization', however, may have unexpected consequences, particularly in relation to feelings of belonging or alienation that members of local LGBTQIA+ communities may experience when Pride Events do not seem to be representative, inclusive, and/or connected to local challenges experienced in their daily life.

Second, the chapter explores the growing divide between urban and rural/peripheral settings in relation to the inclusion of LGBTQIA+ people in Pride Events. Increasingly, Pride Events organized in both rural and peripheral areas challenge the metronormative politics (Halberstam 2005; Ammaturo 2023) that underpin the organization of these gatherings and help to draw new geographies of LGBTQIA+ mobilization that either eschew or resize the importance of the city for these events.

Third, this chapter contains an analysis of the ongoing controversies relating to the professional role of the police at Pride Events, as well as the inclusion of police personnel in the context of Pride Parades and/or festivities (Holmes 2021). Police participation, both in the form of provision of security and protection during Pride Events, as well as in relation to participation of contingents and/or police and armed forces personnel within marches and parades, remains strongly contested and often creates rifts within local LGBTQIA+ communities.

Last, coming back to the three tensions previously outlined, the chapter adopts a more holistic approach to the question relating to the growth of Alternative Pride Events which have been rapidly multiplying in the Global North but have also increasingly been organized across different locales around the Global South (Conway 2024). Beyond the architecture of this chapter, a fourth axis, namely that relating to the increased commercialization and corporatization of Pride Events (Johnston 2007b; Enguix 2009; Ammaturo 2016a; Taylor 2016; Conway 2024), which is tightly connected to the issue of the 'professionalization' of Pride Events, will be analysed separately in Chapter 6, as it requires a separate discussion, given its global significance and magnitude.

Who is Pride for? Professionalisation, community-building, and belonging at Pride Events

The worldwide success of Pride Events, the ever-growing pressures to become 'better and bigger', as well as their symbolic status as the 'hallmark' of sexual and gender modernity at a global scale, all create unspeakable pressures for Pride organizers. Squeezed between the expectations of participants, the possible opposition from antagonistic forces, legal and bureaucratic requirements from both national and local authorities, as well as the pressures of market economy and soaring organizational costs, Pride organizers must possess a complex understanding of their social, cultural, legal, and political environments, the local communities, as well as the strategies that will yield the best success for their events.

Today, a growing number of Pride Events are run 'professionally' through organizations that employ paid staff working all year long on the organization of these events. Notable examples in this regard are organizations that promote big Pride Events in global metropoles, such as 'Pride in London' in the United Kingdom, 'Heritage of Pride – NYC Pride' in the US, or 'Sydney Gay and Lesbian Mardi Gras' in Australia. At the same time, events that continue to be organized at the grassroots level, by volunteers and members of local LGBTQIA+ communities, can also become 'professionalized' if the organizational demands, combined with the specific success of the event, become sufficient to require full-time attention from the organizers.

This process of 'professionalization of Pride Events', whereby the 'do-it-yourself' element of Pride Events subsides in favour of the deployment of either specialist professionals or trained-up volunteers, follows the broader imprint of the process of 'professionalization of LGBT activism' discussed by scholars. While this type of activism creates new connections and opens options to change institutions, it can also foreclose other avenues of activism, particularly those connected to grassroots politics (Butterfield 2016: 24). On a similar note, Paternotte (2016: 390–391) speaks of 'NGOization of LGBT activism' in relation to the process of professionalization of ILGA-Europe and highlights how this process is often needed because the initial skills of 'first generation activists' are insufficient to address the 'policy environment'. This process of professionalization of LGBTQIA+ activism talking, and the subsequent emergence of an elite of LGBTQIA+ professionals, has also been considered to be participating in the creation of a category of 'career queers' (Rodriguez 2018).

Several activists in this research discuss their backgrounds, career trajectories, and motivations, particularly when answering questions relating to the meaning of Pride Events for them. Many of them disclose how they have started as volunteers for a previous Pride/LGBTQIA+ organization, or the one they are currently working for, and/or have acquired previous relevant professional experience in other jobs such as curating, marketing, communications, event-management, to name a few. Some participants see the process of 'professionalization' as an asset that can be put at the service of their respective communities. This is the case of George, from the UK:

> If you want the charity to be effective and successful, you need to get people who are good at running successful organizations. And the same applies to Pride. Of course, 99 per cent of Prides are run entirely by volunteers. ... We don't have professionalized every Pride yet to the point at which we make sure people are capable of doing the job. ... And so that's why we don't necessarily communicate well. We don't necessarily bring in the right sponsors, and it just creates an overall problem.

George's position can be described to be pragmatic in terms of 'delivering' Pride effectively and professionally. On the other hand, the process of 'professionalization' of LGBTQIA+ activism and/or Pride Events is often considered to lead to the detachment from more grassroots elements of activism and mobilization (Ward 2003; Butterfield 2016). This issue represents a worry for some activists interviewed who, instead, place the political and militant element of Pride activism above any other professional skills that individuals may possess or have gathered through their experience, highlighting the need to remain close to the 'grassroots' strata of LGBTQIA+ activism. Such is, for instance, the perspective shared by Martín from Colombia:

> Together we managed to build something politically, and that's the fact that the march is not monopolized by the elites. What we avoided is that elites are those who speak, [whether it is] the economic one, the elite of the State, or the academic elite. On the contrary, it is the social bases (*bases sociales*), from where they come from, and from where they move, that hold a space of enjoyment of speech. [Freely translated from Spanish[i]]

A similar feeling is shared by Felipe, an activist from Spain, who also reflects on the demands of a growing Pride Events organizational apparatus, and

---

[i] See the original quote in Spanish: '*Y logramos juntes poder construir políticamente algo y que es la manera en que la marcha no es monopolizada por élites. Sí, lo que evitábamos es que la élite sea la que hable, sea la élite económica, la élite del Estado o las élites académicas, sino que sean esas bases sociales de donde estén y donde se muevan, que tengan un espacio de disfrute de discursos.*'

the desire to maintain the grassroots origin of the initiative: 'Even though [the march] has been growing and getting bigger and, as you say, it's been institutionalizing and professionalizing, the activist component (*componente reivindicativa*[1]) continues to be one of the most important pillars' [freely translated from Spanish[ii]].

As these quotes show, and as also evidenced by numerous other reflections by participants, Pride organizers are acutely aware of the sometimes-conflicting demands between putting together ever-more impressive events and embracing human rights claims relating to gender and sexuality. This echoes the work by Joseph (2010: 36) who has studied four different Pride organizations in the context of the US and has suggested that activists often found themselves amid conflict and were forced to ask themselves the question of whether they were 'simply an event-planning organization or … a civil rights organization'. In this regard, the approach by some scholars to the study of Pride Events as 'events' that can be 'managed' (Lockett and Lewis 2022; Vorobjovas-Pinta and Pearce 2024) points to the fact that Pride Events may be seen as a leisure or lifestyle opportunity, rather than a gathering with socio-political significance, along the lines of what Taylor (2016) has called the 'festivalization of Pride' (see Chapter 6). This approach to Pride Events as raising questions of identity for the organization is also connected with perceptions around organizers' own values, such as in the case of Larry, from the UK:

> I think integrity is a massive thing, the integrity of the people who organize the Prides and the values and ethics that they hold. I set this up to charity because obviously I went through a lot of really bad things in my life drug addiction, alcohol addiction about HIV for years, and I nearly died. And I set this charity up because it was my idea was nobody should ever have to go what I went through on their own.

In broader terms, the question of the 'professionalization' of Pride Events, raises more far-reaching issues about the relationship between 'grassroots' communities and the organizational apparatus of the events (López Sánchez and Rodríguez Domínguez 2023; McCartan and Nash 2023). In this regard, the theme of 'community' was quite central in most of the conversations with activists. Jana, from Czechia, for instance,

---

[ii] See the original quote in Spanish: '*A pesar de que ha ido creciendo y haciéndose más grande y se ha ido, lo que se dice, institucionalizando, es decir, profesionalizando, la componente reivindicativa sigue siendo una de las pilares fundamentales.*'

discusses her motivation to be a Pride organizer as a way to represent her own community:

> I always said, it's me making our ancestors proud. For me, it's continuing the battles that they started. It's really a protest for me. It's not a parade for me. It's really going and screaming and fighting and really empowering the community around us because it is still happening that people think that they are alone in the community.

Similarly to the feeling of responsibility expressed by Jana, many other activists discuss how they perceive a sense of accountability towards their local communities. This is the case, for instance for Marcus, from the US who discusses how COVID-19 and the demands raised by the Black Lives Matter Movement in 2020, in the aftermath of the death of George Floyd, pushed his organization in Washington DC to do some 'soul-searching' in relation to how they were underserving particularly the Black members of their LGBTQIA+ communities (Piña 2022). A similar sense of responsibility and accountability is also palpable in the thoughts shared by Lance, from Canada, who discussed how local Pride Events need to be used to support communities that are marginalized and underserved locally, such as Indigenous/Two Spirit[2] individuals in the country (Depelteau and Giroux 2015).

Although research on Pride Events often tends to focus only on 'the day of the event' (Joseph 2010: 9), service to the community is seen as especially important beyond the context of the Pride Event itself. Many pride organizers, in fact, are active with their organization in their respective communities throughout the year, with structured forms of support, such as counselling services, outreach, mutual aid, health and sexual services, migration support, and other forms of community-based activism. When other forms of welfare, state assistance, or care crumbled or disappeared, mutual aid (Pleyers 2020; Spade 2020) became an important feature of activism for many Pride organizers during the COVID-19 pandemic of 2020–2021, when many organizations were confronted with the heightened financial, social, and medical vulnerability of many members of their local LGBTQIA+ communities. Many Pride organizers recall how they have diverted resources destined for the organization of Pride Events (which were for the most part cancelled during those two years) to buy food parcels, food vouchers, and provide other forms of mutual aid assistance for members of their local communities, particularly individuals from marginalized groups such as trans people (Konnoth 2020), elderly people (Hafford-Letchfield et al 2022), and/or disabled people (Croft and Fraser 2022). These examples show the need to go beyond the perception of a Pride Event as 'one-off' event that pops up in the landscapes of cities, towns, and villages where it is organized without significant ties to local communities. Pride Events may happen in more organic, haphazard, diffused ways across a longer period of time, especially when engaging with communities who may be bearing the brunt of social isolation during the longest part of the year. Contextually to their multifariousness, Pride organizers highlight the embeddedness of their respective organizations in the local LGBTQIA+ communities, in various guises.

Following from discussions on community, a relevant theme emerging from conversations with Pride organizers relates to the mythology of the 1969 Stonewall Riots. As has been discussed in Chapter 1, this mythology represents an important framing for Pride Events worldwide, despite its specific historical situatedness and epistemological value in explaining diverse forms of LGBTQIA+ organizing in different contexts. Activists taking part in this research often mention 'Stonewall' as reference to an understanding of Pride Events at the service of the community, sometimes in nostalgic or mythologized terms. A good illustration of this 'mythologization' of Stonewall is represented by the comments by Neal, from the US:

> My hope is that the younger folks can join with the older[3] folks, people who are old enough to remember Stonewall and the Gay Liberation, as it was referred to in our country, because maybe some people become too lackadaisical on taking things for granted. It's a real problem, and that's our concern.

However, activists are also profoundly aware of the specific histories of their respective Pride Events, particularly when their organization stems from histories of homo/transphobic violence, as was the case for the examples discussed in Chapter 4 by Liam, from the UK, and Connor, from Ireland. One interesting example of this embeddedness of Pride Events in local LGBTQIA+ histories is offered by Pavel, from Mexico:

> I don't agree with holding Pride on June 28th. I believe that for Mexico itself the most appropriate date to remember this LGBT movement is the 17th of November, because on the 17th of November the famous 'Ball of the 41' (*El Baile de los 41*)[4] took place in Mexico City. That was the first time that the Federal Government of Mexico intervened against the LGBT community, in 1901. Therefore, I think that in Mexico this activism, this fight for freedom of sexual diversity is much older than Stonewall. I think that for me and for Mexicans this date of 17th November should be more important of that of June. [Freely translated from Spanish[iii]]

[iii] See original quote in Spanish: '*Yo no soy muy de acuerdo hacerlo en junio para el 28 porque yo creo que para México tal cual a la fecha más adecuada para recordar este el movimiento LGBT es el 18 de noviembre, porque 18 de noviembre estuvo en Ciudad de México el famoso baile de los 41. Con eso estuvo por primera vez que interviene el gobierno federal o gobierno de México contra*

Pavel's perspective offers a glimpse into an understanding of Pride activism that tries to broaden the repertoire of histories and legacies that are honoured beyond the US-centred horizon of the 1969 Stonewall Riots. This effort to 'localize' or 'hyperlocalize' Pride Events (Ammaturo 2023) offers an opportunity to reconfigure the concept of 'tradition' beyond heteronormative confines, thus offering a local genealogy of queer histories that is mindful of local LGBTQIA+ communities' struggles, episodes of discrimination and/or violence, but also instances of local resistance.

Proud in the countryside: queering rural and peripheral spaces through Pride Events

The previous section has considered the issue of the 'return to grassroots' for many Pride organizations whose activities and/or volunteers have become 'professionalized'. In the current ever-changing landscape of growing popularity of Pride Events on a global scale, as attested by data from organizations such as InterPride (2017) or OutRight International (2023), one interesting development, as also discussed in Chapter 3, is the growth of Pride Events organized in peripheral and rural settings. Research on these events remains relatively limited compared to that dedicated to big urban centres. However, there is a growing body of literature, both in English and Spanish, that considers specific configurations of Pride Events in various geographical locations around the world (Shah 2015; Ammaturo 2019, 2023; Barreto 2020; Bernieri Ponce and Larreche 2021; Lewis and Vorobjovas-Pinta 2021; Conner and Okamura 2022; Lockett and Lewis 2022; López Sánchez and Rodríguez Domínguez 2023).

While the reasons behind the decision to organize Pride Events in peripheral and/or rural locales remains largely unexplored in the context of academic research, possibly because of a longstanding 'metronormative bias' (Halberstam 2005) and more should be done to explore motivations, strategies, and obstacles encountered in this regard, conversations with Pride organizers in the context of this project point to different elements. Significantly, many Pride organizers talk about awareness-raising and sensitization of the local population on LGBTQIA+ issues which can be achieved by bringing a Pride Event to the convenience of their doorstep. Such is, for instance, an example discussed by Beinta, a local Pride organizer from the geographically remote context of the Faroe Islands (Denmark)

---

un grupo de la comunidad LGBT, el año 1901. Entonces yo creo que en México este activismo, esta lucha por la libertad de la diversidad sexual es muchísimo más larga que Stonewall. Yo siento que para mí y para los mexicanos debería estar en la fecha de noviembre muchísimo más importante que la junio'.

where, during the COVID-19 pandemic in 2020, she helped organize a Pride Event that took place with cars driving across the islands, including through the so-called 'Bible Belt' of the Islands, an area of the north-east including centres such as Eysturoy, Klaksvík, and Norðoyggjar (Hákun 2018):

> We would go up in one side of the fjord and we went all the way round and down the tunnel again into our town. Then we drove around Tórshavn [the capital] and ended back into Tórshavn. ... People would be discussing LGBT issues and they said that they were much more likely to stand up for themselves knowing that we were coming [to their area]. Suddenly we were visible, and they weren't afraid. We could just see that we were needed in that area as well. (Beinta, Faroe Islands)

Some Pride Events in rural or peripheral contexts are also organized in an 'itinerant' way with examples of rotating events in different townships in the region of Ekurhuleni, in South Africa, as discussed by local activist Sabe; 'rainbow flag-raising' ceremonies held in different villages in the Simcoe County of Canada, as explained by activists Adam, Jax, and Louie; or 'pop-up' events in some towns and villages in Puglia, southern Italy, as recounted by Fulvio. In fact, geographical remoteness or peripheral status, for many interviewees, often becomes synonymous with isolation or lack of opportunities for socialization and/or representation for local members of LGBTQIA+ communities. These initiatives are seen as countering these feelings of isolation and offer visibility and representation.

At the same time, some Pride organizers working in peripheral and/or rural settings, adopt a more critical approach to the necessity of creating these events in geographically marginal(ized) areas. Some of these accounts seem to adopt a metronormative critique (Halberstam 2005; Ammaturo 2019, 2023; Duckett 2021) of the presumption that Pride Events should be the preserve of big urban centres. Chris, a Pride organizer from the UK, comments on the local Pride in the city of Oldham, near Manchester:

> This [Pride] is for local people. It showcases the local talent and the local need. It gives an opportunity to local businesses and the Council to participate and show that they are inclusive themselves. And quite a few people who are in Oldham wouldn't want to go to the big celebrations where there were hundreds and hundreds of people. ... Also, the style of Manchester Pride the last few years has been very commercial. I think it was £70 or £80 for tickets to attend, and they had the big names, Ariana Grande and others, who would be on the stage. People weren't interested in that. They wanted local community and to find local resources.

In southern Italy, Fulvio reflects on the conflicts arising from different factions of local Pride organizers and LGBTQIA+ associations who expressed different views on whether organizing small Pride Events made sense:

> When we organized the first Puglia Pride, we created it with the idea to have a regional Pride, only one Pride Event, every year in a different city, so that people could be concentrated [in one spot]. However, the [COVID-19] pandemic made us realize that many people would not travel, would never be able to travel ... for economic reasons, for many other reasons. So, what's the problem if we organize a Pride that brings only 50 people? Are we cheapening the meaning of the word 'Pride'? Who cares! [Freely translated from Italian[iv]]

The point raised by Fulvio seems to contest the embedded idea, that has been discussed in Chapter 3, that Pride Events inevitably need to become 'bigger and better' year on year (Joseph 2010: 2). In fact, the relatively small numbers of participants in some peripheral or rural Pride Events may seem irrelevant or insufficient to create that crucial 'critical mass' required to shift public opinion, and influence policymakers and/or legislators. At the same time, however, it would be limiting to think that small Pride Events cannot catalyse local LGBTQIA+ people. As reported by a few participants, who are mostly Pride organizers from small Pride Events, once an event is established, expectations about attendance are often exceeded. This is the experience reported, for instance, by Felix from Denmark, Rose from the UK, and Patricia from New Zealand, who comments as follows:

> The very first event, we did a walk because I didn't like for it to be a march. I didn't want anyone to have any reason to be negative, like 'all these people are marching, it's angry'. I just wanted to be able to have like a nice walk around, and 250 people turned out for that. I was just like 'Holy shit! This is insane'. And the more I talked to them, the more I talked to people in the community, the more people were just coming out literally of the woodwork, of the closet, to be like 'Yeah, we're here!' It soon turned out to be quite a massive community within the community.

[iv] See original quote in Italian: '*Quando creammo insieme il primo Puglia Pride, lo creammo proprio con l'idea di averne uno regionale, uno solo regionale, ogni anno in una città diversa; e che le persone potessero tutte concentrarsi. Però la pandemia ci ha fatto capire quanto ci siano persone che comunque non si spostano, ma non potranno mai ... per problemi economici, per problemi di tante cose. Qual è il problema se noi organizziamo un Pride che ci porta anche solo 50 persone? Bruciamo il concetto della parola 'pride'? Ma chi se ne frega!*'

Preconceptions about numbers of participants and the possibility of building critical mass during small Pride Events are also combined with an existing strong metronormative bias that tends to consider rural or peripheral areas as being inherently 'backward' when it comes to LGBTQIA+ rights or issues (Gray 2009; Kazyak 2011; Ammaturo 2019). The organization of Pride Events in rural and/or peripheral settings, however, may help disrupt this entrenched metronormative narrative. While several Pride organizers from rural or peripheral contexts taking part in this research consistently adopt a comparative framework between their events and bigger ones organized in bigger cities, some of them express a particular sense of localized satisfaction (or pride) about local achievements. Catalina, a Pride organizer from the Mexican region of Cohauila, in the north-east of the country, expresses poignantly this feeling of local achievement:

> Cohauila has spearheaded many of the improvements of the rights here in Mexico. For instance, we are always behind Mexico City, and this is very important. We should not feel less [worthy]. Ok, we are behind Mexico City, but it's Mexico City, it's the capital of the Republic, and yet we are always behind them, improving all the issues regarding laws for all the community. We are the vanguard, we came second in the acceptance towards people who can get married, in education. To this day there are still states in the Mexican Republic that still do not accept egalitarian marriage. [Freely translated from Spanish[v]]

Additionally, many Pride organizers from smaller cities, towns, or villages, compared to their more urban counterparts, tend to emphasize in their comments the role of building relations and trust with either/or local administrations and local (heterosexual) allies. This aspect is in line with broader findings relating to research on rural queer life that posits that, compared to LGBTQIA+ activists working in more urban settings with denser queer networks and stronger organizational infrastructures, those in rural and/or peripheral contexts have to strategically build alliances with unexpected allies (Marple 2005: 73; Ammaturo 2019: 89), in order to

---

[v] See the original quote in Spanish: '*Cohauila ha sido punta de lanza en muchas de los avances de los derechos de aquí de México. Por así decirlo, siempre estamos detrás de la Ciudad de México y eso es muy importante. No deberíamos de sentirnos un poquito menos. Bueno, vamos detrás de la Ciudad de México, pero es la Ciudad de México, es la capital de la República y aun así siempre estamos detrás de ellos, en mejorando todas las cuestiones de leyes para toda la comunidad. Estamos en punta de lanza, hemos ido a los segundos en la aceptación hacia las personas que se puedan casar, a la educación, cosas que todavía hasta el día de hoy hay estados aquí en la República Mexicana que todavía no aceptan el matrimonio igualitario.*'

compensate for the lack of queer network and activism 'density' proper of urban locales.

The question of rurality or peripherality of Pride Events constitutes an element of tension within the context of Pride organizing, particularly when understood through the framework of metronormativity (Halberstam 2005), whereby LGBTQIA+ experiences and activities undertaken in urban contexts are implicitly considered more advanced, complete, and/or effective compared to those of more peripheral and/or rural contexts. While organizers of big Pride Events report offering logistical or organizational support to smaller groups to 'train them up' in the organization of their own local events, some Pride organizers from small cities or towns lament a lack of attention, particularly in economic terms, to the interests, priorities, and needs of LGBTQIA+ communities beyond the confines of the big metropolitan centres, as will be discussed in Chapter 6 in relation to financial issues, sponsorships, and funding problems experienced by Pride organizers.

All cops are banned: Pride Events and controversies around police presence and participation

While homonormative (Duggan 2012) and homonationalist (Puar 2007) discourses appear to be ubiquitous in the ways in which 'respectable' sexual citizenship is framed in contemporary liberal LGBTQIA+ activism and human rights narratives (Ammaturo 2016b; Richardson 2016), there is some resistance that is expressed, particularly in queer circles, in relation to the role of military, carceral, and policing institutions (Puar 2007; Russell 2019; Spade and Belkin 2021). In the context of the prevention and punishment of hate-motivated crimes or discrimination towards LGBTQIA+ persons, the police, the punishment and carceral apparatus, as well as the military, are increasingly considered to be allies in fighting homo/transphobia (Russell 2019: 2). However, for others, these same institutions are the source itself of violence, harassment, discrimination, hate speech, and hate crime and, therefore, they are difficult to trust (Miles-Johnson 2013; Cavalcanti et al 2018; Girardi 2022). Particularly important, in this regard, is the distrust often held towards these institutions by LGBTQIA+ racialized persons, who disproportionately experience police and military violence (Owen et al 2018; Babu 2022), as well as trans people in general (Blum 2019: 30). Police presence at Pride Events, furthermore, can be particularly stressful and threatening for LGBTQIA+ people whose migration status may be precarious, illegalized, or regulated by temporary conditions of approval (Luibhéid 2023: 1884). Moreover, if we broaden our geographical horizon, military and police institutions often promote homonationalist agendas abroad on behalf of Western countries (Puar 2007), promising to 'save [brown] gays' (Bracke 2012: 247) from their respective homophobic governments.

Pride Events are important, and to some extent central, sites where these tensions over police and military participation are experienced and become evident. While LGBTQIA+ organizers and participants may seek police support and intervention in order to be able to enjoy their freedom of expression, assembly, and association safely and without incidents from counter-protesters, particularly those from religious and/or far-right groups; on the other hand, there can be reluctance to proactively seek police and/or military participation to Pride Events, given the long legacy of violence and harassment of LGBTQIA+ people both in public and private spaces (Gossett et al 2011; Blum 2019; Goldberg et al 2019). Russell (2019: 8), on this subject, has used the expression 'carceral pride' to describe this phenomenon:

> By using the term 'carceral', I intend to capture diffuse logics and practices of securitisation, governance, and containment that are readily expressed through state policing and punishment (Moran et al. 2018). While queer activists have frequently exposed and challenged the violence of policing and law, there are also ways in which LGBT rights campaigns have buttressed these systems.

Issues relating to the presence of the police and/or the military during Pride Events can be regrouped under two categories: first, police presence that is 'required' and/or 'requested' to ensure the safety of participants and protect 'public order'; second, the inclusion of police and armed forces contingents within the groups officially participating in Pride Marches and Parades. Both forms of participation come under scrutiny from members of the local LGBTQIA+ communities. In the former case, policing of Pride Events may not be done appropriately, effectively, or may reproduce homo/transphobic dynamics (Amnesty International 2021; Bliszczyk 2024). In some cases, police inertia and inaction in the face of incidents may put participants at risk, such as in the widely documented case of Pride Events in Serbia (Irvine and Irvine 2017; Ejdus and Božović 2019).

In relation to the participation of contingents of police and/or military forces during the marches or parades themselves, this move is seen as an attempt to build a respectable, homonormative, and homonationalist picture of the 'good' queer citizen (Ammaturo 2016b: 28; Giwa et al 2021: 8; Plakhotnik and Mayerchyk 2023b: 38), as well as to 'pinkwash' the history of policing against LGBTQIA+ communities (Holmes 2021: 1341). This structured presence at Pride Events, however, further marginalizes and ostracizes segments of LGBTQIA+ communities that have been disproportionately at the receiving end of police harassment, violence, and discrimination (Luibhéid 2023). One interesting case, in this regard, as also mentioned in Chapter 4, is the militarization of Pride Events in

Kyiv, Ukraine, starting from the post-Maidan Era, with veterans almost receiving preferential treatment over non-military participants to Kyiv Pride (Plakhotnik and Mayerchyk 2023b: 38).

Pride organizers widely comment on police involvement during Pride Events, both in relation to the question of the actual policing of the events, and from the perspective of structured organization of police personnel during the marches and/or parades. Some activists report quite good relations with police forces who, in their experience, enable and ensure that these events happen safely for participants and onlookers alike. Arjun, a Pride organizer from the Indian State of Gujarat, explains, for instance, how after initial hesitancy to allow the first Pride Event to take place in the city of Gandhinagar in 2020 (*The Indian Express* 2021), the police helped to ensure the safety of all participants, particularly from potential counter-protesters:

> [In 2020] [t]here was another movement going on [the 2020 Farmers' Protests[5]], because there were some laws which were passed by the government about which many people were not happy. There were protests in many parts of the cities. That was one of the reasons why we were not given permission for a very long time. There were rumours that the same thing was going to happen to our Pride parade. We told the police people 'we're not involved with those groups', but at the same time, it is now your responsibility to look after people's safety. They did help to an extent. Overall, people loved it being the first Pride parade, even though they were not expecting that this was going to be a really big thing.

A positive relation with the police, which is also developed through acting as a point of reference for LGBTQIA+ people who have encounters with the police, is also discussed by Sabe, from South Africa:

> We do have a police presence. Because when you organize a Pride, you have to meet with the police, for safety, even the traffic police. Our relationship is good because they know about the organization. When people experience challenges at the police station, they come to [our] organization. Then you go and help them. You know, if there's discrimination, if the police do not want to attend to your case, if they put you in the wrong cell. We are very involved when it comes to that. But as I said, it is different police for different subregions. So, we have to sensitize more police stations around our region.

However, Gjon from Kosovo, discusses a more pragmatic strategy that involves police protection in relation to possible threat to Pride participants.

Gjon seems to suggest that the presence of foreign ambassadors at the events may prompt a better response from the police, and may act as a deterrent for counter-protesters who may want to physically threaten or harass participants:

> The first question [the police asks] is if the ambassadors will be there. Of course, they play that card, and we always say that, yes, we have the US ambassador, the EU ambassador. And based on that, they do the strategy. So, people are aware that we do have international support. They don't dare to do something publicly or because they know that if someone will be hurt, especially from international community, then there will be huge consequences.

On the other hand, there are negative experiences that are reported by some activists, particularly in relation to instances in which policing has been overly aggressive, hostile, or neglectful towards LGBTQIA+ persons taking part in the events. Kyu-won, from South Korea, previously mentioned in Chapter 4, discusses, for instance, the police's lack of intervention during the 2014 Seoul Pride Festival when conservative Christians had started to throw excrement at Pride participants, who were prevented from safely carrying out their event until 10 pm. In some cases, where there is institutionalized hostility towards LGBTQIA+ persons, but not necessarily criminalization of homosexuality per se, Pride organizers interviewed have encountered interference by the police to prevent or halt the organization of their events. These cases are reported, for instance, from activists from China and Lebanon.

At the same time, while one may be tempted to think that these negative experiences would mostly be confined to countries where homosexuality is criminalized or where hostility towards LGBTQIA+ people in social, cultural, and political settings is considered or perceived to be high, examples offered by participants to this research also come from countries in which, allegedly, LGBTQIA+ persons enjoy legal protections. In some cases, these negative experiences are not the result of a particular action by officers but can be attributed to the existence of a latent 'hostile environment' (Bowling and Westenra 2020), particularly for groups who are already marginalized and disproportionately targeted by the police, such as with 'stop and search' or 'stop and frisk' actions. Kieran, from the UK and who is part of the organization 'Traveller[6] Pride', discusses this problem: 'The bigger [Pride] gets, you are then required to have police, and that's the problem for certain groups, us included. Those guys hate the police and with good reason. So, you know, I would like to see an alternative.'

Raymond, who helps to organize an Alternative Pride Event in New York City, describes a similar situation of distrust and unsafety felt particularly by Black and migrant LGBTQIA+ persons during the Heritage of Pride March (the mainstream Pride Event) in the city:

> We held Town Hall [meetings] focusing on the overwhelming presence of police in the Heritage of Pride March, because it's not just the officers marching in uniform, but [also] corrections officers, and parole officers, the NYPD marching band, and these big Homeland Security vehicles, and Homeland Security people with semiautomatic military-style weapons, ostensibly to protect us. All of that had been building up for years, and made more and more members of our community feel unsafe, particularly Black people, particularly immigrant people, especially under Trump.

Calls to ban police presence at Pride Events (Lamusse 2016; DeGagne 2020; Holmes 2021) are something that some Pride organizers interviewed have had to contend with. Most times, protests concern the presence of uniformed and armed police in a professional capacity during the parades. Individual members of the police forces and/or armed forces are normally considered to be allowed to march, if they do not represent their organization (Holmes 2019: 4–5). Alex, a Pride organizer from a Southern State in the US, describes the process whereby his Pride organization arrived at the decision to prevent uniformed police from participating at Pride, fuelled, in particular, by the racist murder of George Floyd in May 2020:

> One of the things we did in June of 2020, at the height of the George Floyd protests in the US, is that we responded to community concerns about the presence of law enforcement agencies. In our event, we cannot control the presence of police officers in their capacity to provide public safety. Our city requires that they are there. But what we did, was to create a new policy that precluded the participation of any law enforcement agency in our parade or having a vendor booth at our festival. That was received warmly by the community who had been asking for us to make that change. And we're going to, we'll keep looking at different ways that we can be more intentional and more inclusive.

Controversies and tensions around police participation at Pride Events discussed in this section highlight the existence of different perceptions of the role that the police and the armed forces can or should play during these gatherings. While some activists emphasize how police protection or support can provide their movement and event with legitimacy vis-à-vis potentially hostile opponents, other Pride organizers are more sceptical of the usefulness of their intervention, either for its current or historical involvement in suppressing, harassing, or discriminating against local LGBTQIA+ communities. In light of these discrepancies, together with many other contentious issues, such as anti-capitalist claims, anti-transphobic initiatives, and calls to decentre whiteness from Pride Events, there is an increasing move from some activists and Pride participants to organize alternative events, and/or to forsake their participation in mainstream Pride Events, as will be discussed in the remainder of this chapter.

Another Pride is possible: The rise of Alternative Pride Events

Considering the tensions and divisions discussed in this chapter so far, it is easy to see how opinions on how to best organize Pride Events may diverge between activists and participants. These differences in opinion were present from the birth of the so-called 'modern LGBT movement', both in the Global North (Bravmann 1995; Ghaziani 2008; Armstrong 2002; Duberman 2019; Quéré 2022), as well as in the Global South (Belmont and Ferreira 2020; Caro Romero 2020). Furthermore, in their current global, as well as localized, configurations, Pride Events are far from being homogeneous in terms of their participation, identities, social and political positionings, and orientations. Raymond, from the US, who helps to organize an Alternative Pride Event in New York, comments on the idea of a seemingly homogeneous LGBTQIA+ community:

> One of the things that we feel had gotten lost inherent in the Heritage of Pride Parade [mainstream Pride Event in NYC] over the over the years post-Giuliani[7] and post 9/11 was that that's folks referred to the gay community, the LGBTQ community, as a singular. And that's never been the case. We are multiple communities. And the thing about Pride is it allows us for that one day to come together as a as a single community, for all these communities to come together as one.

All the activists interviewed for this research are organizers of mainstream Pride Events, apart from five: Jennifer, a Trans Pride organizer who helped to create 'Trans Pride Brighton' in the UK; two Italian activists, Agnese and Federico, who are part of the organization of Alternative Pride Events in two different cities in northern Italy ('Marciona Milano' in Milan and 'Free-K' Pride in Turin); Raymond, from the US, who has helped in the creation of 'Reclaim Pride' in New York City; and Jason, who is also from the US, and is part of the network of activists who have created and promoted 'Global Black Pride'.

As has been described in depth in Chapter 3, Pride organizers, and participants in general, tend to find themselves at odds with each other on broad issues of *strategy* and *identity* (Ghaziani 2008: 5). These two crucial issues, which lead to infighting, conflicts, and sometimes real fractures, predominantly centre around these two key questions: (1) *what* Pride Events should be for (*strategy*); (2) *who* Pride Events should be for (*identity*). On the one hand, Alternative Pride Events that are organized position themselves in opposition to the perception that mainstream Pride Events have become too institutionalized, detached from radical politics, and/or commodified. These Pride Events often adopt an anti-capitalist, anti-militarist framing to send their message during the events. Such was, for instance, the very inspiration for counter-Pride Events organized under the banner of 'Gay Shame' in various cities across the US, as well as in some European cities, from 1999 to 2013 (Halperin and Traub 2009; Taylor 2016). Jana, who organizes a Pride Event in Czechia, comments on the need to have Alternative Pride Events that do not centre corporatization and capitalism:

> I was going to Alt Pride, because Prague Pride was not right for me because they have a lot of sponsors. For example, there was ExxonMobil. ... They were focusing on topics that most Prides don't focus on. For me it was very nice that from a young age I could talk about those topics. ... Big Prides, that have a long history, I completely understand why they do things the way they do, because they are the older generation who is not as against the system as we are.

Alternative Pride organizers have a clear idea that the 'topics' that Jana was referring to need to be centred in their platforms. This is, for instance, the description that Federico, from Italy, makes in relation to the 'Free-K Pride' in Turin:

> Fundamentally, it's an antagonist Pride, anti-racist, anti-sexist, anti-speciesist[8] (*anti-specista*) that has also started, since last year, to have particular distrust in organizations that support Israel's 'pinkwashing'. In this regard, since last year, we have strengthened the connection with Palestine. For this reason, it is also an anti-militarist Pride, and beyond any kind of imperialism. [Freely translated from Italian[vi]]

Many Alternative Pride Events share this type of platform that addresses several political issues that are interrelated and often remain marginalized during mainstream Pride Events. One of these issues is, for instance, discussed in the documentary *Pride Denied* (Chisholm 2016), in which director Kami

---

[vi] See original quote in Italian: '*Fondamentalmente è un Pride antagonista, antirazzista, antisessista, antispecista, che dall'anno scorso guarda anche con un certo occhio di non riguardo le associazioni pro-pinkwashing di Israele quindi diciamo che in un certo senso dall'anno scorso si è consolidata la rete con la Palestina. Quindi è un Pride anche antimilitarista, al di fuori di ogni imperialismo*'.

Chisholm shows the historical conflicts arising over the inclusion of pro-Palestine groups within the mainstream Pride Event in Toronto, as well as during the 2014 World Pride. Issues relating to Israeli's 'pinkwashing' and human rights violations in Palestine remain one of the most divisive points between mainstream and Alternative Pride organizers, particularly after the Hamas attacks of 7 October 2023 when around 1,200 people were killed and 250 were taken hostage, and the subsequent military response by Israel that has displaced most of the two million strong population of the Gaza Strip, and Israel is currently under investigation for violations to the 1948 'Genocide Convention'[9] by the International Court of Justice (ICJ) and the International Criminal Court (ICC). In the summer of 2024, many Pride Events in the US, as well as in Europe, and across the world, have seen contingents and/or protest groups, participating in the celebrations, displaying signs that read 'No Pride in Genocide', trying to draw attention to the humanitarian situation in Gaza, and asking for a ceasefire and the end of the occupation (Offenhartz 2024).

On the other hand, for some, Pride Events are not fully inclusive of all intersectional identities and positionings of LGBTQIA+ persons within local communities. This is, for instance, reflected in the thoughts offered by a couple of interviewees:

> A lot of Black organizers, you know, don't feel comfortable in mixed or predominantly white spaces. I personally have a background that allows me to do that comfortably, but I respect other folks who don't. So, you have to you have to be mindful of that. (Raymond, US)

> Trans Pride Started in 2013, as a result of the feeling within the community. Brighton Pride wasn't safe for trans people, because it attracts a lot of cisgender straight people, and there were a lot of reports of visible trans people being harassed. ... There was about half a dozen of us who organized the first year and we expected like 300 to 500 people, and we got 800. It was a huge success and it's kind of gone from there. (Jennifer, UK)

Hence, Alternative Pride Events that offer focused platforms for specific groups (Dyke Marches, Black Pride, Latino Pride, Trans Pride, Bisexual Pride, to name a few), create opportunities to centre often marginalized segments of the communities, create a sense of belonging and pride, as well as focusing attention on specific challenges faced by these groups, such as racism, transphobia, or xenophobia (McFarland Bruce 2016: 200; Kenttamaa Squires 2019). Prejudice and discrimination within LGBTQIA+ communities themselves, in fact, is not that uncommon. For instance, Gjon from Kosovo reflects on existing prejudices within the LGBTQIA+

community that leaves some groups, in this case Roma LGBTQIA+ persons, feeling unwelcome:

> When it comes to LGBT Albanians[10] towards LGBTI Roma, people do have a different approach and I think that's very sad because is coming from a community that is constantly pressured, and then doing the same thing. ... But we have Roma people that come [to Pride] and we have people that are included in our offices from the Roma community. ... But unfortunately, it's not united within the community. I think that's what is missing, just to have an understanding that people can have different backgrounds, but that should not be an issue.

George from the UK, who has experience of organizing Pride Events at the national, regional, and international levels, weighs in on the rise and importance of this phenomenon of 'Alternative Pride Events', arguing that heightened awareness of social injustices may be the fuel that is enabling the multiplication of this type of mobilizations:

> I don't agree with the Reclaim Pride movement on 90 per cent of what they say, but I can see [where] that feeling is coming from: [the fact that] we want Pride to be about human rights on our streets, diversity, equality, LGBT equality. I just don't necessarily agree with where they're going. I think it's not just about LGBTI. It's about a groundswell of feeling that ... we've had enough collectively of how things are, and we want to change it. And so that's why more people are becoming activists across all social issues.

Günther from Germany is also sceptical about the proliferation of Alternative Pride Events, which he sees as weakening the fight for a common cause:

> I wish that we wouldn't separate in the LGBT community so much. To make one Trans Pride, one Gay Pride, you know? Let's come back all together again, as it used to be, under one big rainbow flag and march together for our rights, and not everyone separated. At the moment, I see a big separation by every little group, and I think we're only getting their visibility if we are one united group.

The splintering of Pride Events, the emergence of various forms of conflicts and antagonism, as Günther may seem to suggest, could be interpreted as a sign of weakness on the part of local LGBTQIA+ communities, or as the symptom of an inability to agree on a common platform and shared values to be represented during these public-facing events. However, as has been previously mentioned, LGBTQIA+ communities are far less homogeneous than they are often assumed to be, subsuming different political sensibilities, lived experiences, and 'prognostic framing' (Benford and Snow 2000) on how to solve relevant problems faced by individuals and groups. For these reasons, all Pride organizers, within the context of what we could consider the 'Kaleidoscope Modernities' of Pride Events, have to grapple, and often manage, these existing tensions and conflicts that may brew within the context of so-called 'mainstream Pride Events', or may spill over to lead to the creation of 'Alternative Pride Events' which, sometimes, may be in direct opposition to the more established events.

Building on this analysis, and expanding it further, one big area of disagreement between Pride organizers that has still not been explored in the book is the question relating to the commercialization and corporatization of Pride Events (Johnston 2007b; Enguix 2009; Joseph 2010; Ammaturo 2016a; Taylor 2016) which is welcomed by some as a way to strengthen and grow Pride Events, while for others it is perceived as a form of 'selling out' (Joseph 2010: 211). Chapter 6 will delve into these debates and show the complexity of navigating between acquiring economic resources to finance the organization of Pride Events and maintaining an anti-capitalist stance while serving grassroots LGBTQIA+ communities.

Notes

[1] Here it is interesting to note how, during the interviews, activists from hispanophone, francophone, and italophone backgrounds, respectively, often use the terms *reivindicación*, *revendication*, or *rivendicazione* to discuss their activism, which translates into English as *revendication*, but is not widely used in anglophone contexts, as it is borrowed from the French language. Its meaning refers to an act of restoration or restitution (see Cromwell 2015: 1172, note 42), thus implying a pre-existing claim or right that has been stripped from the individual or legal subject.

[2] Please note, as Davis (2019) explores, that the term 'Two Spirit' is not universally agreed with by Indigenous activists and individuals and that the term itself may designate a wide plurality of experiences in relation to gender and sexuality, even within the same tribe.

[3] An interesting theme that cannot be explored in this book for lack of adequate space relates to generational differences in relation to Pride Events. Many organizers discuss how younger and older cohorts often have different expectations, modalities of participation, and priorities when it comes to Pride Events, and that sometimes it is hard to bridge each group's perspective of the other.

[4] The 'Ball of the 41' (*El Baile de los 41*) is an episode in Mexican queer history during which, on 17 November 1901, the Mexican police raided a private house where a lavish party was taking place and arrested 41 men, half of whom were dressed as women (Irwin 2000).

[5] For details on the 2020 Farmers' Protests across India, please see: BBC News 2021.

[6] For a specific discussion of the experiences of LGBTQIA+ persons from Romani and Traveller communities, see the work of Fremlova (2022).

[7] Referring to the years during which Rudolph Giuliani was Mayor of New York City, from 1994 to 2001.

[8] Anti-speciesism is a philosophical approach that assigns equal importance to all species and does not consider humans to be a superior species in relation to others. For more information, please see Weitzenfeld and Joy (2014).

9. UN Convention on the Prevention and Punishment of the Crime of Genocide, available at: www.un.org/en/genocideprevention/documents/atrocity-crimes/Doc.1_Convention%20on%20the%20Prevention%20and%20Punishment%20of%20the%20Crime%20of%20Genocide.pdf, last accessed 19 July 2024.
10. Here Gjon is referring to the Albanian ethnic group that is part of the multi-ethnic make up of Kosovo.

6

A Necessary Evil? Funding, Sponsorship, and the Commodification and Corporatization of Pride Events

In 1982, Dennis Altman (1982: 20–21) offered an interesting reflection on the entanglement between gay identities and capitalism: 'No other minority has depended so heavily on commercial enterprises to define itself: while the role of movement papers, dances and organisations has been significant, it has been overshadowed, especially for gay men, by the commercial world.'

While Altman was referring to the growth, particularly during the late 1970s and early 1980s, of a dedicated niche in the market that could cater to the needs of particularly (white[1]) gay men, such as bars, clubs, saunas, and other commercial spaces and products, this argument can also be applied to Pride Events as, increasingly, capitalistic logics permeate the organization of these events at the global level. This issue becomes particularly significant when Pride Events become 'institutionalized', starting to attract ever-bigger crowds (see Chapters 3 and 5), thus raising questions relating to logistics, funding, sponsorship, and 'event-management' (Lockett and Lewis 2022).

This chapter discusses the complex challenges faced by Pride organizers when addressing this seeming opposition between commodification and corporatization of Pride Events as opposed to a return to 'grassroots politics' (see Chapter 5). The chapter critically appraises the complexity of financial and economic challenges for Pride organizers within global capitalistic structures, and offers an opportunity to reflect on the opportunities and dangers that are intrinsic to the aligning of LGBTQIA+ (lesbian, gay, bisexual, transgender, queer, intersex, asexual, plus) activism with corporate and commodifying strategies.

In a world where identities become marketable, capitalism plays an important role in shaping particularly, but not exclusively, gay subjectivities. Capitalism creates sexual citizens (in this case gay – or LGBTQIA+) who are in pursuit of what he terms a 'commodified self', whose expressions of citizenship (and societal acceptability and inclusion) are manifested through the pursuit of private satisfaction and acquisition of style (Evans 2013). Sexuality, as well as gender, appear imbricated in capitalistic structures through which they are expressed in appropriate or convenient forms that pave the way to societal inclusion. Capitalism, and the rise of waged labour, have contributed to open spaces for the emergence of 'modern' gay identities (D'Emilio 2007).

Nation-based, or context-specific explanations, however, appear to be insufficient to charter the complexities of the interrelationships between gender, sexuality, and capitalism. For this reason, therefore, it is important to adopt a broader horizon of analysis, as Rao (2015a: 48) does through the conceptualization of 'Global Homocapitalism' as a way of 'repackaging queer normativity in recognizably local idioms which those outside this class can identify or aspire to inhabit'. In light of previous discussions in this book about the ways in which Pride Events function as 'modernizing events', both within the Global North and the Global South, it is possible to see how Pride Events can play a key role in the potential conveyance, or transmission, of these aspirational principles of (global) queer inclusion.

In this regard, while it would certainly be a cynical exaggeration to argue that Pride Events map neatly onto Evans' (2013) or Rao's (2015a) arguments about an interpenetration between sexuality (and gender) and capitalism; it is inevitable to ask how the growing and ever-successful apparatus of the organization of Pride Events at the global level, despite its multiple local(ized) configurations already discussed in this book, shapes, regiments, and – sometimes – constrains our ability to truly imagine grassroots and community-driven politics, especially in the context of persisting societal homo/transphobia across the world. In other words, the question can be framed as follows: how do we disentangle global capitalistic pressures to commodify and package LGBTQIA+ identities and activisms in palatable and commercially intelligible ways, from the existence and affirmation of empowering and authentic expressions of LGBTQIA+ rage, thirst for social justice, and affirmation of individual and communal identities and experiences?

In the last three decades, scholarly analyses (Chasin 2000; Rao 2015a; Pedroni 2016; Rumens 2017; Rodriguez 2018; Bengry 2020; Burchiellaro 2023) on the commodification of LGBTQIA+ subjectivities, identities, and activisms, have multiplied on a global scale, and have offered much-needed critiques of the ways in which capitalism has seeped into, colonized, and phagocytized the lives of LGBTQIA+ persons in ways that often appear innocuous, supportive, and celebratory. Contextually, a growing body of scholarship explores the role of Pride Events as key sites of commodification and corporatization of LGBTQIA+ identities, in both the Global North

(Johnston 2007; Markwell and Waitt 2009; Ammaturo 2016a; Taylor 2016; Enguix 2017; Domínguez Ruiz 2019), and the Global South (Kuriakose and Alex 2018; Lamond 2018; Matebeni 2017; Conway 2022, 2024; Mbasalaki 2022). Although practices of commodification and corporatization are far from being homogeneous across the globe, as the literature just cited inevitably shows, there always seems to be a tension between an understanding of Pride Events as marketable, mediatizable, commodifiable events, and a conceptualization that emphasizes the political and emancipatory root of these events (Domínguez Ruiz 2019: 2). These tensions are present in the context of the current research where Pride organizers must navigate the complex reality of Pride Events as inextricably embedded and intertwined with capitalist structures of marketing, branding, pinkwashing, and global circuits of leisure and tourism.

The chapter first looks at the processes of commodification and corporatization of Pride Events as experienced by the interviewees in their specific geographical, social, and political contexts. This section shows the heterogeneity of organizers' experiences and challenges faced, and how they make sense of the use of corporate funding. Second, the chapter explores the difficulties in navigating different opportunities to accept corporate funding and/or choose or seek public sponsorship, including the mobilization of professional skills, and the existence of networks of support between organizers of bigger and smaller Pride Events. Third, the discussion continues with a consideration on how Pride organizers conceptualize and make sense of opposition to the commodification and corporatization of these gatherings, as well as how they respond to critiques levied by participants in this regard. Last, the chapter reflects on how the arrival of a 'crisis', namely the COVID-19 pandemic of 2020 and 2021, has dramatically reshaped the choices made by Pride organizers, altered their operations, impacted their stream of funding, and, in some cases limited the opportunities to recover and start again to organize events in a post-pandemic landscape.

Victims of their own success? The commodification and corporatization of Pride Events between corporate and public funding

Social justice issues have enormous appeal on corporate actors: from the rise of feminist messaging and endorsements in the aftermath of the #MeToo Movement (Bennett 2024), to the expression of support for the Black Lives Matter Movement (BLM) (Banet-Weiser and Glatt 2023), to the unstoppable ascendance of 'corporate environmentalism' (Bowen 2014), corporations have found endless ways to connect their reputation to the support of 'progressive' causes. LGBTQIA+ social justice issues are not foreign to this process. The exponential rise of the so-called 'commercialisation of social causes' (Stronach 2014: 570) calls into question the possible positive or negative effects on activism of these practices. Social movements themselves, for instance, have been influenced by this phenomenon through the rise of the 'trademarking of social change' (Stronach 2014: 569). As an example, it can be observed, that many Pride organizations around the world have registered a 'trademark' which gives them exclusivity of use of the specific 'brand' for their events, much like a real corporation.

Despite the limits concerning the idea that Pride Events are homogeneous phenomena, which has been discussed in Chapter 3, the concept of 'cultural anchors' of Pride Events offered by Ghaziani and Baldassarri (2011: 197) can be useful to understand why Pride Events are so easily commodifiable. In their 'standard' or 'paradigmatic' form, in fact, Pride Events present at least three 'cultural anchors': 'coming out scripts', 'parade format', 'rainbow iconography' (Ghaziani and Baldassarri 2011: 197). These 'cultural anchors' are not just useful for members of LGBTQIA+ communities to foster common belonging and a sense of togetherness, but they also represent powerful tools for corporate actors: first, 'coming out scripts' can be adopted through the process of 'coming out' (branding) as an inclusive brand or company; second, corporate sponsors can 'show up' and materially occupy queer spaces, such as the parade, with groups of employees belonging to LGBTQIA+ affinity groups; last, corporations can easily adopt a rainbow iconography in their products, logos, and advertising, to signal their LGBTQIA+-friendliness.

On the other hand, as Pride Events grow bigger and bigger, organizers are also faced with growing pressures to create events that cater for ever-larger crowds, with better-than-ever line-ups and programmes, and with security measures that ensure protection for all participants (Conway 2024: 5). These pressures may lead to the search for substantial amounts of funding that can often only be secured through corporate, rather than public, sponsorship. Hence, corporate support represents an enticing opportunity, one that does not just provide material or financial capital to organizers but may also confer a form of 'symbolic capital' in terms of legitimacy and social acceptance (Joseph 2010: 29–31). The presence of sponsors and brands is often also seen as a way for LGBTQIA+ people to appropriate mainstream commercial symbols through practices of resistance (Kates and Belk 2001; Joseph 2010).

Before proceeding further with this discussion, the terms used in this chapter need to be briefly explained. 'Corporatization' and 'commodification' (of Pride Events) refer to two different, but interrelated phenomena. The former addresses the ways in which activist practices become regulated and exercised through mechanisms proper of businesses and corporations, as well as becoming co-opted (partially or fully) by the agendas and the priorities of corporate sponsors. Some visible illustrations in the ways in which Pride Events become 'corporatized' are represented, for instance, by the decision taken by the organizers of the 2015 Pride in London to allow Barclays Bank to lead the parade, instead of the community-led group 'Lesbians and Gays Support the Miners (LGSM)' (Peterson and Wahlström 2018: 157); or the request, accepted by organizers, by condom producer 'Trojan' to have exclusivity of distribution during the 2014 World Pride in Toronto, as discussed in the documentary *Pride Denied* (Chisholm 2016). The 'corporatization' of Pride Events can have important consequences on the possibility of organizing for imagining alternative queer futures, as Burchiellaro (2023: 3) argues:

> The process of incorporation by which an otherwise radical leadership is channelled into corporations and local government has meant, among many things, the loss of experience, the loss of imagination and, ultimately, the loss of a genuine transformative vision for challenging structural inequalities in favour of a more de-politicised advancement of individual careers and the strategic interests of the institutions to which these individuals are ultimately accountable.

The second phenomenon – commodification – relates more closely to the way in which Pride Events themselves become 'commodities', branded happenings, that can acquire marketizable value, generate commercial clout, attract investors, as well as tourists and travellers. In relation to the issue of commodification, for instance, Taylor (2016: 33) speaks of Pride Events has having often become 'festivalized spectacles of Otherness in the marketing of cities and commodities'. Pride Events, in fact, are often mentioned by cities to attract cosmopolitan crowds (Puar 2002; Rushbrook 2002; Bell and Binnie 2004; Dixon 2024). Puar (2002: 123) for instance, has described the 2000 World Pride held in Rome (the first ever edition of this event), as an 'exquisite example of "selling liberation"'. These decisions to put corporate interest, or profitability, over concerns of grassroots groups and communities, both 'corporatization' and 'commodification', shape, albeit to different degrees depending on the specific context, the ways in which Pride Events are organized, and can lead to the emergence of conflicts and dissent within LGBTQIA+ communities (Taylor 2016: 35–36; Peterson and Wahlström 2018: 157).

Pride organizers interviewed adopt different positions in relation to the use and search for corporate funding and sponsorship. Some of them welcome corporate sponsors and funding as a lifeline to fund activities that, otherwise, they would not be able to offer to local LGBTQIA+ communities. This is the case of Craig, a Pride organizer from the US who, despite acknowledging that his organization has tried to reduce its reliance on corporate sponsorship (as of May 2022, it was down from 90 per cent of total financing to 70 per cent), is still very enthusiastic about the work they can achieve through the obtention of these corporate resources:

> We use the money we raise at our festival to do these programmes year-round, but we also give back. In 2019, the last year we had a large festival [before the COVID-19 pandemic], we gave back over $200,000 in grants to LGBT-serving organizations. They could apply for a grant. We're going to give it back to the community, so they can work to enhance LGBT serving trans people, youth, seniors, border [relations with Mexico], bilingual [groups]. We've also funded some groups in a group in Bulgaria, a group in Ghana, and a group in Malaysia. I think I feel proud to be part of the group.

James, a Pride organizer from New Zealand, appears to be more critical, as he thinks that corporations' donations to Pride Events are not as substantial as they could possibly be:

> People just assume that it [Pride] happens for free. It doesn't. It's really expensive. And without money, we can't make these events happen. ... The amount of money we're talking about is so small for corporates. The amount of money we get from our main sponsors would be the same as printing a billboard. You are not talking about big spending, people! Just round it up, even if it seems frivolous. It creates spaces and it gets activism going, because without money there is nothing actually happening.

James' comment seems to imply the existence of an inextricable link between corporate sponsorship and the possibility of embarking on activism in the first place. The establishment of this relationship echoes the analysis offered by Schulman (cited in Conway 2024: 5), for whom Pride organizers have now adopted this 'gentrifying' mentality (see also Burchiellaro 2023), whereby the need for corporate funding to create big Pride Events is almost a given, and leads to a limiting of the imaginaries of LGBTQIA+ activism.

In other cases, Pride organizers have expressed a more nuanced approach to accepting corporate donations which is based on ethical considerations about 'what type' of sponsors are/should be involved. One example of this approach is offered by George, from the UK:

> I think if a corporate sponsor wants to pay, that's good for me. But Prides need to be better than they are, and better than they have been recently, at the ethics and sponsorship. You know, there are some Prides sponsored by BAE Systems,[2] who manufacture warheads and

weapons, that are sold to [Saudi Arabia³]. I mean that they should be nowhere near Pride, nowhere near any human rights movement. So, I think we have to be better at the ethics.

George's comment shows the conundrum experienced by Pride organizers who want to accept corporate sponsors but know that some partnerships may tarnish the reputation of their organizations. One case in point that will be analysed in Chapter 8, is the question of corporate sponsors that engage in greenwashing and/or invest in fossil fuels and are, as such, deemed to be incompatible with Pride Events by some LGBTQIA+ activists.[4]

In this regard, a strategy used to reduce or tame the risk of accepting problematic or unethical sponsors, and to 'screen' them, is represented by the existence of 'background checks' or agreements whereby these sponsors have to actively show their support for LGBTQIA+ causes, rather than just 'passively' donate a specific sum. In the sample of organizers interviewed, there are few of these agreements, coming from countries such as Norway, Ireland, Spain, and Canada. Lance, from Canada, for instance shares his experience in this regard:

> I work very closely with our business partners to make sure that they share our values. We learn about them, they have to complete surveys, and all this kind of stuff. I feel good about the people that we partner with, but I also know that I don't want this just to be a marketing opportunity for them, right? I'm hoping that they're coming because they want to let their employees know that they are a more thoughtful organization.

In some cases, in fact, corporate sponsors pursue different strategies depending on the context in which they operate, such as in the case highlighted by Marisol, a Pride organizer from Mexico:

> Local companies, like Tequila Sauza, have an impressive record at the global level, supporting San Francisco Pride, San Diego Pride, but they do not support Guadalajara Pride. We have this very ambiguous part. The same Mexican companies with a double moral that exists widely and it is quite engrained. [Freely translated from Spanish[i]]

---

[i] See original quote in Spanish: '*Empresas locales como Tequila Sauza que tiene una trayectoria impresionante a nivel mundial, apoya al Pride de San Francisco, el Pride de San Diego, pero no apoya el Pride de Guadalajara. Tenemos esta parte muy ambigua. La mismas empresas mexicana con una doble moral que también existe mucho y está muy arraigado*'.

Some Pride organizers, particularly from Mexico (Catalina) and Colombia (Martín), have suggested the existence of a sort of 'third way' where only local, LGBTQIA+-owned businesses, are allowed to participate in the events, or to perform as entertainment, particularly vis-à-vis the deeply entrenched levels of unemployment and economic deprivation that LGBTQIA+ persons in local communities experience.

Thank you for your donation: navigating the tensions between corporate and public sponsorships

Some Pride organizers express reluctance, ambivalence, or outright opposition to the obtention of financial support through corporate sponsorship (Conway 2024), reflecting on the relationship between capitalism and Pride organizations. Some of the following examples, illustrate the opinions of some of these organizers:

> In the end, all forms of collaboration with the capitalist world, with the corporations, always lead to a strong and serious compromise in the fight for LGBTI people. [Freely translated from Spanish[ii]] (Felipe, Spain)

> You would see like Tower Hamlets[5] Sikh LGBT Society, and you go 'that's exactly what this kind of event is for!', showcasing groups like that and having a wonderful day out. Isn't that cute? And then behind that would be Barclays. … It's weird that they need representation. There's something that really makes my skin crawl about the idea of the people of Barclays just rounding up 50 of their LGBT employees. They don't really even know each other because it's a massive company, and they just kind of bust down the street once a year. (Kieran, UK)

In some specific cases, these reflections are articulated through a direct comparison between the activists' own organization (which minimizes or rejects corporate funding) and those who, instead, make wide use of this form of sponsorship. These examples show the existence of important tensions between activists (Taylor 2016: 35–36; Peterson and Wahlström 2018: 157) who position themselves in relation to their stance on allowing

---

[ii] See original quote in Spanish: '*Al final toda colaboración con con el mundo capitalista, con las empresas, siempre pasa por que haya un compromiso realmente serio y firme en la lucha a favor de las personas LGBTI*'.

or not corporate sponsorship for their events. Jennifer, from the UK, and Federico, from Italy, speak about their positioning:

> We have always been non-corporate. We don't accept donations of money from corporations. We've always been funded through what we call community meetings, which means donations and small grants and funds that we get from different places. It's always been free to enter into the park. That's been really important because at the time Brighton Pride was charging 15 quid for a ticket. And like if you're poor and you're just coming out as gay or trans, you know, like you don't got 15 quid to find your community, you know, you should be able to find it for free. (Jennifer, UK)

> They flaunt how much money they obtained to have a parade with trucks from gay clubs or political parties that talk about the environment and their rainbow flags end up on the stages, as well as on Ikea's, Amazon's or Coca Cola's pins, who also end up being the sponsors. But that leads me to say that all this money is not there in the context of Free-K Pride, and it's not even needed. Our [Free-K Pride] is self-produced, and self-financed and it is not that expensive. So, the question is: all this money and this power that seem necessary, where do they end up? [Freely translated from Italian[iii]] (Federico, Italy)

When Pride organizers decide to focus on obtaining public or competitive funding for their events, however, grant-writing is an activity that becomes a central skill to master. Building on previous discussions on the 'professionalization' of Pride organizers (Greer 2012; Butterfield 2016) in Chapter 5, it appears that the possession of a professional skill such as grant-writing ability is to be considered an asset, and that the lack of possession of this skill may prevent grassroots or cash-strapped organizations, often also run by volunteers, from obtaining the funding they need for their events. This is listed as an important aspect of Pride organization work by many activists, such as from countries like the UK, the US, Czechia, Slovakia, Italy, to name a few.

In some cases, however, when Pride organizations are not officially registered and/or legal in their respective country (perhaps because of the

---

[iii] See original quote in Italian: '*Fanno sfoggio di quanti soldi sono riusciti a prendere per fare una sfilata di carri dei club gay o partiti politici che inneggiano all'ambiente e le bandiere rainbow finiscono tanto quanto sui loro palchi quanto sulle spille dell'Ikea o Amazon e Coca-Cola [che] finiscono per diventare sponsor. Però mi viene da dire che tutto sommato questi soldi che vengono fatti nel caso del Free-K Pride non ci sono e soprattutto non servono, perché il nostro è autoprodotto e autofinanziato, e non costa così tanto. Quindi la domanda è tutti questi soldi e questo potere che sembrano necessari, in realtà dove vanno a finire?*'

criminalization of homosexuality), access to funding through grant-making becomes either limited or impossible. This circumstance has been reported as being a problem by activists in both India and Bangladesh. Suraj, from Bangladesh, explains the challenge in securing funding for the organization:

> Sometimes we apply for additional grant funding because we are not a registered organization in Bangladesh, and we do not have a bank account. So, we always have to look for specific small-scale funding which is flexible and unrestricted, which is very limited; and we also need to depend especially on the LGBTQ funding. This is the primary funding.

The obtention of public funding, however, is also fraught with ambiguities, as it can lead to the enmeshment between politics and LGBTQIA+ activism, that some Pride organizers are keen to eschew or avoid. In some cases, Pride organizers' reliance on public funding is engrained and does not cause frictions. In other cases, organizers want to avoid instrumentalization by public bodies as much as they want to avoid it from corporations or companies who may want to sponsor Pride Events. This is, for instance, the case for Su-Wei, a Pride organizer from Taiwan, who says: 'We don't take any money from the government because we don't want them to think that they can be in charge of anything'. Other organizers, instead, are critical of public funders, particularly local governments, who are perceived to have a duty to step up in terms of supporting their local Pride Events. Tina, from the US, shares her experience in this regard:

> I was managing a city council campaign and, [I asked] this person: 'What do you mean that you don't have Pride on your calendar? How can you not have the largest LGBTQ plus cultural event in the state on your calendars?' [He responded] 'Well, you know, you have to invite us'. I'm like, 'No, that's not we're not going to beg you to come and spend time with us, because we're important enough for you to be here'. Now the city finally even gives us a teensy tad of money. They sponsor in a very small way, but it's something they never used to do. We've now had years where the mayor of the city is standing at the end of the parade route, shaking hands with everybody as they come in.

A similar experience is also discussed by Lucy, from Australia, who describes the competitive nature of getting public funding in the country for different social justice or activist organizations like hers:

> We have a really supportive state government here that spends a lot of time and effort in equality and the LGBTI space, but I think we fall between the gaps because they see us as better funded than a lot of other groups that don't have any funding. Why are we getting so

much less than the next organization who's doing less work than us and has less people coming but isn't queer? I don't think it's blatant homophobia. I think it's a continuation of what was homophobic decisions that were probably made 20 years ago.

Last, differences in the enjoyment of funding exist between big and small Pride Events, including Pride Events organized in rural or peripheral locations. As can be intuitively expected, bigger cities tend to have more resources that allow them to invest in key aspects such as 'visibility, support, and celebration' (McFarland Bruce 2016: 133), whereas small Pride Events may encounter difficulties in securing funding to create their events, although the required amounts may be significantly smaller. Organizers of small Pride Events may feel the pressure from the community to create ever-bigger events, as is implied by one Pride participant interviewed by Formby (2023: 128), who argued that compared to Manchester Pride, small Pride Events feel 'cheap'. Some Pride organizers interviewed for this research, expressed their frustration at the challenges they face compared to bigger Pride Events. One activist from the UK, Rose, who organizes a small Pride Event in a town with 20,000 inhabitants, shares her opinion on this topic:

> If you look at Brighton, you look at London, I think they are fine because they have a framework in place. You know, they are running as … they are Prides, but they're running more like … I don't really want to say business, but in a way they are. They have a structure. … That's really nice, and they are big Prides, but they have the framework, they have the local support from businesses, and all of those types of sponsorships. For smaller ones, that framework just isn't there, and the local support isn't there.

While some organizers of big Pride Events, in countries like the UK, Ireland, and Taiwan, report a good pattern of collaboration with smaller events, some organizers of Pride Events in peripheral or rural areas feel differently. For instance, Chris, from the UK, laments the fact that, in his experience, the organizers of a big Pride Event in his local area have pledged to help and support smaller ones in the neighbouring area, but they have not fully followed through with their commitments. As an alternative, Chris reports that eight different smaller Pride Events joined forces to pool resources, provide mutual training, skills, and talents.

Between a rock and a hard place: exploring Pride organizers' dilemmas regarding funding

Pride Events that have undergone 'corporatization' and 'commodification' are often perceived as being sites of alienation and exclusion (Formby

2023: 111). The lavish display of consumer goods, branded trucks, sleek promotional material, through the presence of corporations, may give the impression that LGBTQIA+ communities are more affluent than is the case (McFarland Bruce 2016: 204), thus marginalizing people who may feel they do not fit with that portrayal of affluence, or 'lifestyle' (Conway 2022). Ticketing, choice of location, the presence of physical barriers, as well other organizational and logistical decisions, may also stifle participation and enhance the existence of a sense of extraneity to the event (Browne 2007; Matebeni 2017; Conway 2022, 2024; Mbasalaki 2022; Formby 2023). Hence, the commodification and corporatization of Pride Events may end up excluding, not necessarily always physically, but also symbolically, the very people who should be celebrated and put at the centre of Pride celebrations.

Pride organizers face intense scrutiny in relation to their decisions to accept corporate funding. Conway (2024: 10) argues that this type of critique, which is relatively widespread in the Global North, is also present in the Global South,[6] but that, in the context of the Global South, these critiques are also accompanied by a 'pragmatic approach to corporate money', especially when there is little or no public support for LGBTQIA+ rights.[7] In line with the observations made by Conway (2024), most (but not all) Pride organizers interviewed who express opposition to the commodification and corporatization of Pride Events are located in the Global North, and particularly in the UK, the US, and in Canada, whereas many of those who are open to considering corporate money are Pride organizers who operate in different contexts in the Global South. However, given the composition of the sample for this research, which has been obtained largely through convenience sampling (Robinson 2014), it is not possible to deduce any meaningful relationship between the data and the hypothesis presented here.

For some of the Pride organizers interviewed, corporate support is not just desirable, but necessary, as it offers opportunities that would not otherwise be available in the organization of Pride Events. These Pride organizers tend to display a mentality of 'working from within' that is seen to represent a way to change structures, in this case corporate, to make them more LGBTQIA+ friendly. Such is, for instance, the experience shared by Alex, from the US:

> Given the reality of the economic system that we live in and given the reality of how fundraising is done in our country, an event of this size cannot operate without corporate support. There's no way that community members could crowd source crowdfund an event of this size. I also recognize that there are legitimate criticisms of how corporations behave and act in the world. However, corporations are also made up of people. … When you see LGBTQ employees of a bank marching in the parade under behind their corporate banner, not that long ago … their opportunities for advancement would have

been limited, or they would have just been fired. ... So, I want to ensure that we're we are always taking into consideration the very real human experiences of all people and people who happen to be employed by a corporation.

Alex's position focuses on the fact that participation in Pride Events of corporate LGBTQIA+ affinity groups can be seen as a tangible way to demonstrate that change can happen even within the realm of the corporate world. For this reason, his position seems to be in line with Joseph's (2010: 341) point, for whom fighting against corporate inclusion at Pride Events feels like a fight 'against Goliath' and should be replaced, instead, by an attempt to 'create cultural change within the corporate sphere'. Dean, a Pride organizer from the UK, also shares this pragmatic approach to the inclusion of corporate sponsors:

My position has always been [that] it's better to have people on the inside, shouting about inequality and bad stuff, than it is shouting from the outside, where they can shut the door and shut the noise out. These organizations are always going to exist. They're not going away. So, let's at least have some insiders in there.

This pragmatism regarding corporate sponsors' participation can be enticing for Pride organizers, particularly when faced with the difficulties of raising funds. Both Lance from Canada, and Dean from the UK, lament that the exclusion of corporate sponsors is not really an option, given how costly events are. Both activists express frustration at critiques received from their respective communities regarding the acceptance of this type of financial support:

I think people who don't organize events underestimate the costs involved, the marketing costs, the security costs, the damn toilets for them to go have a piss so they don't get a £60 fine. Like it's very easy to forget that, when that criticism is levelled at Pride Events, but I think the onus is on a Pride Event to manage that corporate presence, so it doesn't feel trivial or that people are utilizing it to pinkwash. (Dean, UK)

The other thing that frustrates me is our community can be often very hard on folks who partner or sponsor Prides. They're like 'these banks, they're just pink washing'. But at the same time, at least they're helping. We truly do need the funds and we're hard on the banks that are supporting us, but no one is complaining about the banks that aren't giving anything back to the community. What about this other bank that is truly doing nothing that takes, takes, takes, but isn't giving anything back? (Lance, Canada)

Lance's and Dean's comments illustrate how some activists may feel wedged between a 'rock and a hard place', wanting to truly create events for their local communities, which they think should be financed appropriately, but then being faced with criticisms about how these events are created, particularly because of corporate presence. Both statements, moreover, offer an insight into how polarized this 'debate' about corporate inclusion at Pride Events can be, particularly when these corporate sponsors are suspected of participating at these events to 'pinkwash' their reputation (Holmes 2022: 450–451).

Other Pride organizers are more cautious regarding their acceptance and management of corporate sponsors and seem to be more interested in striking a balance between the financial needs of the organization, and the opinions of their local communities. This is the case for several activists from countries such as Malta, Ireland, Taiwan, South Korea, and Mexico. Andre from Malta, for instance, thinks about how his organization compares to big international Pride Events:

> We have to tread very carefully. I am very aware that, for example, international big Prides like London and Manchester, they take on a commercial approach, and they are run by a commercial entity. And then there is criticism and backlash by the LGBTQIA+ community because and all they see is how to get money and make relationships with big corporations. We have to make sure that as Malta Pride we also have to have a balance. ... Having thousands of people in the streets, you need to make sure that you have police security, you have to have ambulances, and this doesn't come for free.

At the same time, some activists have expressed a deep dissatisfaction with the lack of interest of corporate sponsors for their events, particularly in the Global South, following earlier discussions, in this section, about a 'pragmatic approach to corporate money' (Conway 2024: 10). In some cases, as was noted in Chapter 5, Pride organizers also engage in activities of community outreach, mutual aid, migration support, as well as year-round awareness-raising in the local areas. Some activists, particularly in different locations across the Global South, such as Mexico, India, and Bangladesh, highlight the fact that they have often had to use money from their own pockets to fund local initiatives. Pavel, from Mexico, discusses how his activist work to organize a Pride Event in the region of Quintana Roo, has taken a personal toll on him:

> I've been doing it for ten years. There is no support from the community, the municipality or anything, and I don't have that much

money. I spent a lot of money in the last ten years from my purse, from my savings, and I can no longer continue. I'm 60 in a year, I need to go to Europe, I want to see my mom because my mom is sick, and I need to take care of myself because I'm also a little sick. [Freely translated from Spanish[iv]]

Suraj, from Bangladesh, also discusses how some of the expenses have been footed through personal funds, but also suggests that his organization seeks to involve the Bangladeshi diaspora abroad for whom contributions may not be as onerous as for LGBTQIA+ persons living in the country:

> We fund initially by our own pocket, for example, it is our part of our volunteer work. Yeah. So we for example, last month we had the *Xhulaz Mannan Memorial Award of Diversity*, it is named after the activist who actually was assassinated [Xhulaz Mannan – see Chapter 4]. The value [of the award] was around $150. I had to give that because this this time we had no donor. Maybe we establish two foot guards for two transgender people that will cost around $400, so maybe two or three persons will contribute. That will run for six months. This is because $100, for those who are living outside of the country, is not a big issue.

Suraj's and Pavel's examples show how constrained Pride organizers may become where they are committed to serve their local communities and organize Pride Events but struggle financially and organizationally because of lack of structured and steady funding. Beyond anti-capitalistic opposition to the commodification and corporatization of Pride Events, which brings to the surface legitimate, urgent, and necessary problems and issues to be addressed, there is a real problem in relation to how people can enjoy opportunities to collectively organize for social justice issues, such as those related to the identities and experiences of LGBTQIA+ people, in the context of social and institutional structures where capitalism has cannibalized almost every opportunity of socialization, including protests and demonstrations. While, therefore, we should continue to interrogate ourselves about the necessity or opportunity for corporate sponsors to 'exploit' Pride Events to undertake their practices

---

[iv] See original quote in Spanish: '*Yo lo hago diez años. No hay apoyo ni por parte de la comunidad, ni por parte de municipio ni nada, y yo no tengo tanto dinero y gaste mucho dinero en los últimos diez años de mi bolsa, de mis ahorros, que ya no puedo seguir. Tengo 60 en un año, yo necesito ir a Europa, yo quiero ver a mi mamá porque mi mamá ferma y yo necesito cuidarme a mí porque también estoy un poquito enfermo*'.

of 'pinkwashing', we should simultaneously question whether we can imagine forms of social mobilization that totally, or partially, eschew the logics of capitalism.

This question also raises another adjacent issue, highlighted by Luibhéid (2023: 1887), in relation to 'buying into' oppressive structures and institutions (such as the police), which participate in the 'organization' of Pride Events (security, routes, and so on), while representing a real threat, particularly for some communities, such as racialized LGBTQIA+ persons. The recent trend that has seen corporations rolling back their DEI (Diversity, Equality, and Inclusion) policies both in the US and elsewhere (Murray and Bohannon 2025), represents a worrying phenomenon that calls into question whether Pride organizers can effectively continue to trust and count on the support of corporate sponsors, or whether funding gained from corporate giants or other big businesses will start to wane in the years to come, leaving the organization of Pride Events vulnerable to this dramatic fall in resources.

In light of what has been discussed so far, it is possible to argue that the real 'dilemma' that emerges extends beyond the question of whether or not Pride organizers should accept (or seek) corporate funding, but it requires a radical interrogation of what are the structural constraints that capitalism has imposed, and continues to do so in ever-more permeating ways, on our ability to express our political and social dissent to structures of power that oppress various groups, including LGBTQIA+ persons.

Feeling the pinch: exploring the impact of COVID-19 on Pride Events

With its dramatic global impact, and shocking death toll, the 2020–2021 COVID-19 pandemic has not only impacted the right to freedom of expression, association, and assembly for LGBTQIA+ people, but has also taken a financial toll on many Pride organizers around the world, who have often seen their funding streams reducing or, in some cases, completely drying up.

Simultaneously, social movements, including LGBTQIA+ movements, were faced with the need to focus on immediate forms of solidarity towards members of their community (Pleyers 2020: 6), beyond their usual provision. This section explores some of these challenges experienced by various activists, while acknowledging the existence of a heterogeneous landscape relating to the specific ways in which the COVID-19 pandemic has stricken and affected different countries around the world.

Pride organizers were faced with a 'crisis' of unprecedented scale for which they were not prepared, and which has often exacerbated or exposed vulnerabilities that have strongly impacted the opportunity for these activists not only to organize their events as usual, but also to reach out to their local communities through actions and activities that they were normally carrying out all year round. This section gives a glimpse into some of the effects of this 'crisis' and shows how the delicate architecture of Pride Events organization can be crucially (and sometimes even fatally) put to the test in times of turbulence or instability.

The COVID-19 pandemic has increased the challenges for social movements activists, not just in terms of the amount and type of resources that can be mobilized, but also regarding the opportunities available for mobilization (Zajak 2022: 134). For LGBTQIA+ movements, and for Pride organizers specifically, this has not only meant a loss of financial resources, but also a loss of spaces, particularly physical spaces to engage with their local communities. During the COVID-19 pandemic, many groups and organizations turned to digital activism, with most interviewees for this research discussing how they created 'digital Pride Events' for their communities (Cheded and Skandalis 2021; Altay 2022; Kilic 2024). However, the halting of 'normal' operations has had a substantial impact on the operational capacity and motivation of these groups or organizations.

Differences were, of course, registered in relation to the ways in which different countries managed the COVID-19 pandemic. At the global level, for instance, Taiwan was almost instantly applauded for the way it managed the pandemic, leading to a minimized impact for its citizens at the domestic level (see Johns Hopkins Bloomberg School of Public Health 2020). Pride organizer Su-Wei argues that the pandemic did not really impact the organization of Pride Events in Taiwan in 2020, whereas most Pride Events in the world had been cancelled. However, at the regional level, the financial situation of LGBTQIA+ organizations, was much more dramatic, as Arjun, a Pride organizer from India, who also is part of an Asian regional LGBTQIA+ network, has explained:

> Taiwan has been recovering really well. ... This is not the situation with other countries and other organizations. By the end of 2020, I remember especially in Philippines, two organizations were having financial strains. I think one or two members of the organizations lost members due to COVID. ... When I reached out to Vietnam, that was a time when they were going through very tough times, and they had financial strains.

At the same time, although it was expected that social movements would just fade into the shadows during the pandemic, waiting for the right time to make a comeback when restrictions were lifted, the reality is that social movements around the world showed incredible dynamism (Pleyers 2020: 9) and an ability to quickly adapt to difficult circumstances to convey their messages and serve their communities (Pinckney and Rivers 2020; Pleyers

2020: 13; Petitjean 2022: 218; Sajor 2022: 57). Notwithstanding this capacity to channel activism into much-needed forms of alternative support, many organizations or groups have struggled in terms of the financial resources available to them (Waniak-Michalak et al 2022: 174; Warren et al 2024). Many describe how corporations, who in the past had been sponsoring their respective organizations, stopped or drastically diminished their support to Pride Events. These challenges were particularly heightened for Pride organizers in China and South Africa, who very often relied on international corporations for financing their events, as explained by Andrew (China), and Priya (South Africa).

Pride organizers interviewed widely report having faced some forms of financial constraints, with only a couple of big(ger) Pride organizers from the US claiming to have 'healthy reserves'. In other cases, as Cédric, from France, discusses, Pride organizers had to eat into their own savings to weather the drop in funding during the COVID-19 pandemic:

> The first year of COVID we had almost no subsidies. As a result, given that we were no longer doing any activity, we were strongly impacted in terms of subsidies. ... On average it's at least €7–8,000 per year [of organizational costs], plus almost the double [the amount] that we did not receive from public structures, so we're lucky that we had a lot of savings, so of all the money saved, we put it aside. Unfortunately, COVID almost ate up all the savings we had made for a few years. [Freely translated from French[v]]

This lack of funding during the COVID-19 pandemic often left organizations unable to mobilize resources to help the most vulnerable members of their local communities. In this regard, Alejandro, a Pride organizer from Mexico, discusses a particularly upsetting experience during the pandemic:

> Unfortunately, sometimes as associations we do not have enough resources to be able to help all the people we need. It touched us a little ago that a person passed away and their parents did not take charge [of the burial]. She was a trans person, they did not take charge of the burial, and [the friends] did not even know where her parents were. Her trans sisters connected with us and said, 'We wanted to

---

[v] See original quote in French: '*La première année de COVID on n'a quasiment pas eu de subvention. Du coup, étant donné qu'on ne faisait plus d'activité, on a été fortement impacté sur les subventions. ... En moyenne c'est €7–8000 au moins par an, plus quasiment le double qu'on n'a pas eu des structures publiques, donc on a de la chance qu'on avait pas mal d'économies avant, donc de tout l'argent épargné, on le mettait à côté. Malheureusement, le COVID nous a quasiment tout bouffé les économies qu'on avait fait pendant quelques années.*'

give our sister a worthy burial'. For us it was very emotional, very difficult, and very frustrating and that we could not help them. So, I said 'I don't have resources to help you, but I have more social networks. What I can do is help you by creating a campaign'. And so, fortunately, there were people with a very big heart, even giving us $4,000, which was enough for the expenses we faced. [Freely translated from Spanish[vi]]

Similarly to the feelings Alejandro discusses, many other Pride organizers interviewed for this research have expressed similar sentiments of powerlessness in relation to their (in)ability to help members of their community who turned to them during the pandemic. Gjon, from Kosovo, explains the sense of disappointment felt by local LGBTQIA+ organizations when services or support stopped:

It wasn't good before the pandemic. With the pandemic, it got worse because there was also a disappointment for LGBT organizations because they didn't understand what was going on. We couldn't give so much support that was needed explaining to each of them that we do not have funds to support all [their] requests.

Despite citing financial burdens and loss of funding, a few Pride organizers felt that the fact that their activities were reduced or halted meant that they could take some time to think about the way forward for their organization, in terms of mission, structure, and strategies. Jennifer, from the UK, offers an insight into this process for her organization:

I've just seen our financial report for that for [2020] and throughout the whole of the year, we lost about three and a half thousand pounds. So, it really impacted our fundraising ability. But in a way, it was good because it gave us the chance to stop. … Over the pandemic we've kind of changed our funding model, and we've gone for projects and got

---

[vi] See original quote in Spanish: '*Desafortunadamente también nosotros a veces como asociaciones, no contamos con los recursos suficientes para poder ayudar a todas las personas que quisiéramos. Nos tocó hace poco que una persona falleció y los papás no se hicieron cargo. Era una persona trans, no se hicieron cargo del sepelio, ni siquiera sabían dónde estaban sus papás. Entonces fue muy complicado y sus hermanas trans se conectaron con nosotros y nos dijeron queremos darle una sepultura digna a nuestra hermana. Para nosotros fue muy emotivo, muy difícil y muy frustrante el no poder ayudarles. Entonces le digo no tengo yo los recursos para ayudarte, pero tengo mis redes sociales. Lo que yo puedo hacer es ayudarte haciendo una convocatoria, una campaña. Y sí, afortunadamente hubo personas de muy gran corazón, incluso una nos donó 4.000 $, o sea, de golpe, que para los gastos que necesitamos fue bastante.*' (Alejandro, Mexico)

grants from places to pay for these projects which have been building up the base. The structures, the foundation of the charity now are okay.

Another important element relating to the impact of COVID-19 on the resources available to Pride organizers has been in terms of the reduction of 'human resources'. In fact, the constraints created by the pandemic have also impacted the number of people involved in groups or organizations that are delivering Pride Events. This has manifested through the reduction of paid staff working who may have been laid off during the pandemic, because of lack of funding for the organizations. Moreover, these challenges were also present for these organizations or groups that saw a dramatic shrinking in the number of volunteers recruited to create Pride Events. It is true that the pandemic has had a great impact on the delivery of services that were mostly based on voluntary terms (Grotz 2020; Lachance 2021; Luksyte et al 2021). Rose, who organizes a small Pride Event in the UK, shares her experience:

> [COVID] has hit us massively. When we first started Pride, we reached out to get support from people from local community, to then set up and find the directors of our community interest company. We are all volunteers. None of us is paid. We had quite a good number of people with a good cross-section of people that were involved. We're now obviously really trying to get some people off the ground. So this year, 2022, we're finding that we are probably twenty people down, [there is] probably three of us now. We're really struggling to get any and with anybody to help support us. (Rose, UK)

At the same time, for others, the pandemic was also an opportunity to join forces with other volunteers, especially in trying to deliver assistance to members of the LGBTQIA+ community, as Antoine, from France, explains:

> We really immediately established a network with other associations. We have associations that have found work. We were able to network all these people and our volunteers too, with a chain of taking care of each other. There was really this idea of solidarity. It was still able to strengthen links, more on food aid and financial aid. [Freely translated from French[vii]]

[vii] See original quote in French: '*On a vraiment tout de suite mis un réseau avec les autres associations. On a des associations qui ont trouvé du travail. Nous, on a pu mettre en réseau toutes ces personnes et nos bénévoles aussi, avec comme une chaîne de prendre soin des uns des autres. Il y avait vraiment cette idée de solidarité, ça a pu renforcer quand même des liens, plus sur l'aide alimentaire et l'aide financière*'.

The COVID-19 pandemic seems to have exacerbated the financial problems of organizations whose funding was often precarious, whereas the big organizations seem to only have experienced a temporary 'dip' in sponsorships and donations and have been able to bounce back. More in general, from the conversations with activists, it is possible to gauge a real sense of uncertainty and uneasiness about the pressures of finding financial resources to continue to carry out their various activities. This has obviously happened in a landscape in which the COVID-19 pandemic has caused an economic recession (Foroni et al 2022) whose effects are still lingering at the global level. These experiences show the financial and logistical fragilities that Pride organizers can face when creating their events in times of 'crises'. The pandemic only represents an illustration of the fact that Pride Events rely on financial, human, and other resources that can easily wither when the economic landscapes change, thus leaving LGBTQIA+ persons, and Pride organizers more specifically, feeling vulnerable and exposed, and often unable to serve their own communities, despite decades-long activism, or even while balancing healthy books and reserves. In a way, the focus on the effects of the pandemic represent the other side of the coin relating to the challenges of corporatizing Pride Events, as the fragilities of a funding model based on corporate intervention and support can become apparent once a 'crisis' diverts the sponsors' attention to other priorities.

This chapter has addressed the various challenges faced by Pride organizers when deciding how to fund their events, focusing in particular on the dilemmas created on them by growing dynamics of commodification and corporatization of Pride Events. While the growth of Pride Events is considered to be a key element of the very reason to organize Pride Events in terms of impact on society (Joseph 2010: 12), this same growth can often be dependent on the acquisition of corporate sponsorships that enable the multiplication and differentiation of activities, programming, and entertainment to be offered to the community. At the same time, this growth does not come 'for free', as commodification and corporatization of Pride Events are accompanied by a penetration of commercial actors in the very fabric of the events, representing a true form of 'corporate takeover of everyday life' (Bloom and Rhodes 2018: Burchiellaro 2024). Furthermore, the experience of the COVID-19 pandemic also opens a new question: what happens when corporations 'lose interest' in LGBTQIA+ causes, dropping funding that they had, perhaps opportunistically, pledged for Pride Events organizations or groups? Can we rely on corporations to enable individuals to exercise their freedoms in relation to expression, association, and assembly? What are the dangers involved in this enmeshment?

In Chapter 2, the teleological scope of Pride Events as harbingers of modernity was called into question, particularly in relation to neocolonial understandings of sexual and gender modernity that put pressure on social movements around the world, particularly in the Global South, to 'catch up' with the big Pride Events held in metropoles like London, New York City, or Sydney, to name a few. In light of the exponential growth of Pride Events around the world, and the contextual rise of commodification and corporatization of these events, it is crucial to ask whether the future of commodified and corporatized Pride Events, in which Amazon, Coca Cola, or Barclays Bank all have an assigned slot within the parade with corporate floats and groups of employees, in the Global North as well as in the Global South, truly represents a facet of 'modernity' that Pride organizers want to wholeheartedly embrace; or whether we should fundamentally question what it means to be modern if this modernity is acquired through the corporate language of capitalistic 'inclusion' and 'diversity'. In times of branded Pride Events, who is left out of the commodifiable spectacle of Pride Events? Who can afford to embody these identities and occupy these spaces?

If Pride Events become dependent on this type of corporate funding to organize their events, either because municipalities impose hefty costs in terms of security, cleaning, or other administrative expenses; or simply because they work within an institutionalized framework, with paid staff and organisational costs, that requires them to incrementally grow year after year; it can become increasingly difficult for organizers to disentangle themselves from requests advanced from these 'benefactors', who may play a role in taming 'the political radicalness' of some of these events (McFarland Bruce 2016: 122), and/or lead to a de-politicization and growing apathy of participants (Formby 2023: 126). In some cases, global corporations, such as Nestlé, for instance, possess more economic magnitude than specific countries (Patchell and Hayter 2013: 28), and lack any type of political accountability, but can still work as political actors in disguise, influencing economic, political, and social relations at the global level. The rolling back of DEI programmes by corporations may also mean disinvestment in Pride Events for many of these capitalistic giants in the near or more distant future. It should also prompt questions from Pride Events organizers themselves: should these be our allies?

Whether one sees Pride Events more as a celebration or a protest, there is still room to interrogate the opportunity for Pride organizers to align themselves with these economic actors, as the 'takeover' could end up serving these corporate actors more than it serves local LGBTQIA+ communities. This could even lead us to think: if Pride Events are under this unstoppable 'urge' to become 'bigger and better', and to achieve this goal an ever-greater amount of economic resources is needed, should we start to consider how we 'degrow' Pride Events in a financially economic way that takes away power from corporations, who would not be able to exercise such an appeal on activists, and transforms these events into moments of purposeful connection (and celebration) for LGBTQIA+ persons who still encounter shocking levels of homo/transphobia around the world?

Notes

1. As the recent work by Hilderbrand (2023) has discussed, in the context of the US, gay bars have historically mostly catered to white crowds and patrons, often displaying racist attitudes towards Black and Brown customers. As some have observed (Ruez 2017; Patel 2019; Han 2022), these racist and unwelcoming attitudes persist to this day against all members of the LGBTQIA+ community. Other authors (Johnson and Samdahl 2005; Thomas 2024: 34) have also discussed how women were excluded from gay men's bars and how they often encountered misogyny when they were exceptionally allowed in these spaces. Simultaneously, Thomas (2024: 48–49) has pointed out how lesbian bars have also played a role in excluding Black and Brown queer women from these spaces.
2. For more information about BAE Systems' sponsorship of Pride Events, please see Peace Pledge Union (2022).
3. Here the interviewee was factually incorrect, as the original formulation was 'sold to Yemen'. However, after fact-checking, the quote has been changed to reflect the reality, which is that BAE Systems has sold weapons to Saudi Arabia that have been used on attacks on civilians in Yemen. For more information, please see Sabbagh (2020).
4. In this regard, please see the example of the British organization 'Just Stop Oil' that interrupted the 2023 edition of Pride in London to protest against the participation of corporate sponsors that invest in fossil fuels and other polluting practices. See *The Guardian* (2023).
5. Tower Hamlets is one of the boroughs of London.
6. Conway uses the terms 'One-Third World' and 'Two-Thirds World' instead of 'Global North' and 'Global South'.
7. Conway (2024: 11) refers to the existence of these two alternate possibilities as an illustration of what Moreau and Currier (2018) have defined as a 'queer dilemma', namely situations in which activists from the Global South are in a vulnerable position in relation to accepting funding (particularly from the Global North), as this could represent the exercise of homonormative or homonationalist pressures that underlie extant colonial relations.

PART III

No Pride Without Social Justice: Building the Futures of Pride Events

7

Making Space, Creating Place: Disability and the Making of Accessible Pride Events

This chapter centres the participation of disabled and neurodivergent LGBTQIA+ (lesbian, gay, bisexual, transgender, queer, intersex, asexual, plus) persons to Pride Events as an important, yet underestimated, issue. Far from wanting to adopt a tokenistic approach to the inclusion of disabled and neurodivergent people in the most paradigmatic events organized by different LGBTQIA+ communities around the world (does this particular Pride Event 'tick' all the boxes when it comes to accessibility policies?), this chapter seeks to connect previous analyses presented in this book in relation to community-building, conflict, as well as capitalism, with the necessity of rethinking Pride politics through an emancipatory lens, one that privileges the needs of the communities, rather than the desire to grow exponentially and endlessly. The arguments made in this chapter also point to the emergence of new ways of doing Pride politics, characterized by interconnectedness, reciprocity, and radical rethinking of the priorities for the LGBTQIA+ community. Disability liberation, or the liberation from all forms of ableist frameworks, truly has the potential to overhaul current structures of societal organization by putting into question hierarchies relating to gender, sexuality, race, and class, because of its invitation to rethink the very concept of 'inclusion' and 'access'.

Pride Events tend to make the invisible 'visible' for one day, as LGBTQIA+ people inhabit and occupy public spaces temporarily 'queering' them (Browne 2007; Ammaturo 2016a; Valentine 2016). Yet, questions around who can inhabit and occupy these spaces during these events remain pressing and signal the fact that often Pride Events may be far from inclusive for all the various segments of local LGBTQIA+ communities, as has already been discussed in this book (see Chapters 2 and 5). This is often the case for disabled[1] and neurodivergent[2] LGBTQIA+ persons who may encounter challenges in accessing and participating in Pride Events in a way that makes them feel welcome, safe, and represented (Webb 2014; Pieri 2021). From issues relating to lack of infrastructures and inaccessible physical spaces, to the presence of sensorial and environmental factors (noises, crowds) that make participation challenging, to the lack of provisions that facilitate communication (interpreters, captioning, and so on), the inclusion of disabled and neurodivergent LGBTQIA+ persons at Pride Events represents an important issue that often remains unaddressed even within the domain of LGBTQIA+ activism and community organizing (Pieri 2021: 19). At the same time, issues relating to the presence of disabled and neurodivergent LGBTQIA+ persons at Pride Events extend beyond the mere question of 'inclusion', and call into question the normative ableist paradigms of society itself.

While activists have been debating issues of accessibility of disabled and neurodivergent persons at Pride for at least the last two decades, academic attention to issues relating to the experiences of disabled and neurodivergent LGBTQIA+ persons at Pride Events is practically non-existent, apart from a couple of exceptions (Webb 2014; Pieri 2021), both within anglophone academia and beyond. This may potentially signal the existence of a dominant academic ableist framework of analysis when understanding Pride Events, and the intersectional identities of those who take part, one that invisibilizes the experiences of disabled and neurodivergent LGBTQIA+ persons. This book seeks to make an intervention in this sense and centre the question of disability at Pride Events as necessary and urgent in the context of academic research, to 'catch up' with activists' conversations on the ground.

So far, academia has shown relatively more interest in the longstanding (and growing) phenomenon of 'Disability Pride' (Vasey 2004; Clare 2015; Mattlin 2022) which presents commonality with the idea of 'pride' articulated at Pride Events, but centres disability as an identity (and source of pride – and joy!) well beyond the framework of queerness. Given the importance that intersectional thinking and theorizing has on advancing claims and issues of social justice (Laperrière and Lépinard 2016; Broad 2017), it is imperative to develop frameworks that take seriously, analyse, and valorize the experiences of disabled and neurodivergent LGBTQIA+ persons, particularly in light of the global growth of Pride Events around the world that has been previously discussed in this book.

To develop these frameworks that centre the experiences of disabled and neurodivergent LGBTQIA+ persons, academic research needs to adopt a critical approach, one that goes beyond the mere question of tokenistic 'inclusion' within an alleged 'able-bodied' majority. Without discounting the material realities of impairments (and consequently of disabilities), which may present individuals with symptoms such as pain and discomfort, and may require medical and specialist attention, it is important to go beyond the so-called 'medical model of disability' (Iriarte et al 2016: 12) which almost exclusively relegates disability to the domain of the medical field, where doctors and other health professionals are those in charge of 'managing' disabilities and/or intervene to 'improve' disabled and neurodivergent persons' lives (Iriarte et al 2016: 12). This model, which often disempowers disabled and neurodivergent persons, relies on a vision of disability as something that requires 'fixing', to allow the person to get on with their lives and be amalgamated within the folds of society. Rather, an analysis of the experiences of disabled and neurodivergent LGBTQIA+ persons in the context of Pride Events needs to embrace a 'social model of disability', a concept coined by the organization Union for the Physically Impaired Against Segregation (UPIAS) (Goodley 2014), and discussed for the first time in academic circles by British disability scholar and activist Mike Oliver (1990), which considers how individuals with impairments are 'disabled' by social institutions and the environment whose rules and conventions put disabled and neurodivergent persons at systematic disadvantage, thus leading to a form of oppression (Iriarte et al 2016: 17). A social model of disability,[3] therefore, does not place the onus on disabled and neurodivergent persons to find a 'fix' to their situation, so that they can become included within society, but questions the social structures, rules, and conventions that privilege able-bodiedness as a 'default' condition of human existence, whereas this is far from being the truth.

This argument has been developed further by queer theorist Robert McRuer (2008) whose work in the field of *Crip*[4] *Theory*[5] has analysed not only the dynamics of compulsory able-bodiedness, but also how these tend to neatly map onto expectations of compulsory heterosexuality, and how the two work to reproduce each other (McRuer 2008: 2). The 'naturalization' of both heterosexuality and able-bodiedness contributes to the oppression of those who diverge from these canons because their bodies and/or behaviours do not conform to the so-called 'norm'. Crip Theory, therefore, represents a critical development that takes Disability Studies further in their attempt to deconstruct the impact that societal structures play in the discrimination and oppression of disabled and neurodivergent persons. It does so by showing that there is a productive intersection between ableism and homo/transphobia that police, regiment, and exclude bodies that exceed or deviate from the 'normal', whatever the 'normal' may have been constructed to be, beyond the narrow confines of identity-based paradigms.

Building on McRuer's analysis on the mutually constitutive character of heterosexuality and able-bodiedness, as well as on the previously mentioned argument regarding the temporary queering of 'heterosexual' space operated by LGBTQIA+ during Pride Events (Browne 2007; Ammaturo

2016a; Valentine 2016), it can be argued that (physical) space is similarly 'normalized' to be both heterosexual and able-bodied by default. Hence, if Pride Events function to temporarily 'queer' spaces otherwise seen as being inherently heterosexual and heteronormative, by the same token, the presence of disabled and neurodivergent persons in public spaces similarly disrupts the assumption of able-bodiedness as the norm in these same spaces (Kitchin 1998). If we tend to assume that visible queerness and disability are 'exceptions' in the social landscape of public spaces, then Pride Events that make disabled and neurodivergent LGBTQIA+ persons feel welcome can have the important task of disrupting these compounded normative expectations. For a long time, in fact, both disabled and neurodivergent[6] and queer persons were pushed into the private ('out of sight, out of mind') sphere, far from the hetero-able-bodied crowds that shunned them as 'abnormal'. In some cases, both queer and disabled and neurodivergent individuals are still not 'expected' to be in public spaces, with disabled and neurodivergent persons still experiencing important violations in terms of spatial and institutional segregation (Steele 2024), such as so-called 'special education' (Oliver 1985; Holt et al 2019).

This chapter develops across four sections. First, the chapter situates the history, experiences, and activism of disabled and neurodivergent persons in relation to LGBTQIA+ communities that often display ableist attitudes. Second, the discussion moves to an analysis of the empirical data collected for this research, highlighting the experiences of Pride organizers, some of whom are themselves disabled and neurodivergent LGBTQIA+ persons, in creating events where individuals feel truly welcome, particularly in the backdrop of financial challenges and the emergence of the COVID-19 pandemic. Third, the chapter critically addresses the potentialities and pitfalls relating to the rise of technology, and particularly digital technology through streaming and video calling (for example, Zoom, Facetime), in relation to the opportunity of enjoying Pride Events remotely, such as in the case of 'Digital Pride Events' that became popular during the COVID-19 pandemic, when gatherings in real life were cancelled. Last, the analysis focuses on the need to go beyond the question of 'accessibility' that forms the core of Pride organizers' interventions to make Pride Events disability-friendly, to interrogate how a framework of 'disability justice' can transform these gatherings and deliver true representation, engagement, and liberation for disabled and neurodivergent LGBTQIA+ participants. Ultimately, this chapter opens up a conversation about 'who Pride Events are for' beyond the realm of what has already been discussed in this book, pushing us to really question whether Pride Events can help to bring about human emancipation beyond the neoliberal confines within which they are currently neatly squeezed in.

No Pride without us: disabled and neurodivergent LGBTQIA+ persons navigating LGBTQIA+ communities and Pride Events

Impairments and disabilities are lived and experienced by individuals in myriad different ways, depending on personal, societal, cultural, medical, and other factors. As such, disabled and neurodivergent persons represent an extremely heterogeneous group of individuals across geographical contexts (Ingstad 1990; Riddell and Watson 2014), and with interests that may not always easily coincide or align with each other (Iriarte et al 2016: 11; Shakespeare 2017: 4; Egner 2019a). Disability activists tend to align themselves, similarly to LGBTQIA+ activists, and other social movements activists, along lines of either *celebration* or *suppression*[7] of differences (Egner 2019b: 145). This means that, for some activists, disabled and neurodivergent people's inclusion in society represents the zenith of disability equality, whereas others prioritize the questioning of the very ableist nature of societal structures, conventions, and rules in the first place (Egner 2019b: 146). These differences are important, particularly because of the parallel history that disability and queerness present in relation to their respective medicalization and normative regimentation that has led to the marginalization, discrimination, and, in some cases, outright demonization of disabled, neurodivergent, and queer people. Contextually, the advent of capitalism (Finkelstein 1980), and the rise of neoliberal society (McRuer 2008), have contributed to cast disabled, neurodivergent, and queer people as being outside the bounds of 'productive' (heterosexual/ heteronormative[8]) society.

Given this similar genealogy of discrimination and marginalization operated through the hegemony of medical discourses, the conflation of homosexuality with 'illness' or 'disability', and portrayals of disability as being 'queer' (see McRuer 2008), one would expect that a form of solidarity could emerge between different activist groups from the recognition of such similar, albeit obviously differently articulated, patterns of 'othering' that disabled, neurodivergent, and queer people have endured. However, disabled and neurodivergent persons who look for inclusion and recognition within LGBTQIA+ communities often find closed doors and ableist attitudes (Eliason et al 2015; Kempapidis et al 2023: 44). In similar ways, when looking for acceptance as LGBTQIA+ , some individuals also experience homophobia within disabled and neurodivergent activists' circles and communities (Wilson et al 2018; Kempapidis et al 2023: 45). Hence, being positioned at the crossroads between disability and queerness, some disabled and neurodivergent LGBTQIA+ persons may feel disenfranchised and alienated from communities that should represent and welcome them.

In relation to the history of ableism within LGBTQIA+ communities, there is a paucity of research[9] on the topic that shows the importance of bringing to the surface these neglected aspects of LGBTQIA+ history relating to the marginalization of some segments of the communities. The few resources available tell us a story that is far from idyllic. Regina Kunzel (2018), for instance, traces the progressive distancing of LGB[10] activists from Disability Activism in the United States, in their efforts to establish homosexuality as being 'healthy', in direct opposition to the psychiatric medicalization of homosexuality as being a 'mental illness'. The achievement of this objective was marked by the removal of homosexuality as a 'mental illness' by the American Psychiatric Association from the *Diagnostic and Statistic Manual of Mental Disorders* (DSM) in 1973, and it has been considered to simultaneously represent both one of the key founding moments of the gay liberation movement, as well as a moment of 'distancing from disability' (McRuer in Kunzel 2018: np). One illustration of the (anti-disability) attitudes held by some gay American activists, such as Frank Kameny (1965), is discussed by Kunzel (2018: np) who quotes a passage from an article he authored in the magazine *The Ladder* (published by the US lesbian organization The Daughters of Bilitis), in 1965:

> [trigger warning: this quote contains language that people may find offensive]
>
> Properly or improperly, people ARE prejudiced against the mentally ill. Rightly or wrongly, employers will NOT hire them. Morally or immorally, the mentally ill are NOT judged as individuals, but are made pariahs. If we allow the label of sickness to stand, we will then have *two* battles to fight—that to combat prejudice against homosexuals per se, and that to combat prejudice against the mentally ill—and we will be pariahs and outcasts twice over. One such battle is quite enough.

Kameny's quote shows how the association between homosexuality and disability (in this case mental illness) was considered to be detrimental to the liberation of LGB people, and how it was impossible to think about fighting 'two fights' at the same time (today we would call this type of analysis or activism 'intersectional'!). Ultimately, as Kunzel (2018: np) argues, building on McRuer's analysis of the concept of 'compulsory able-bodiedness', the distancing from disability framing and disability activism by LGB activists, was not just an attempt to gain respect and recognition for the dignity of these individuals in their own right and merit, but contributed to create and reinforce the socially constructed boundaries of what we call 'disability' in the first place: 'disability studies scholarship helps us understand health not simply as an assertion of pride over stigma, as it is so often cast in the story of gay liberationist assault on psychiatric authority, but as a project in normativity and exclusion, producing hierarchies of worth and worthiness' (Kunzel 2018: np). This analysis becomes more complicated, of course, once the HIV/AIDS epidemic of the 1980s is added to the picture, as discourses on health/sickness and ableist discourses also contributed to marginalize members of the LGBTQIA+ community that were living with HIV/AIDS (Hrynyk 2021).

In the context of Pride Events, empirical research on the experiences and exclusion of disabled and neurodivergent LGBTQIA+ persons is practically non-existent, with some examples being of an anecdotal nature (Stonewall 2018: 13; Kempapidis et al 2023). One small piece of empirical research, published as an undergraduate dissertation in 2014, has analysed the experiences of disabled and neurodivergent LGBTQIA+ persons at Amsterdam Canal Pride (Webb 2014). Another example of empirical work, this time in the form of a peer-reviewed academic publication, has been offered by Pieri (2021), who has focused on the experiences of chronically ill LGBTQIA+ persons navigating public spaces, including Pride Events. The reach of Webb's and Pieri's work may be limited in terms of how it can be used to gauge the broader experiences of disabled and neurodivergent individuals attending Pride Events across different geographical contexts, but these works certainly need to be praised as, to date, they represent the only examples (to my knowledge) of empirical research that effectively centre the voices of disabled and neurodivergent LGBTQIA+ persons themselves in considering how Pride Events may or may not be inclusive of them.

As has been argued earlier in this chapter, this shocking lack of empirical (and theoretical) work on the experiences of disabled and neurodivergent persons at the largest kind of collective gathering for LGBTQIA+ communities needs to be addressed urgently, to counter the invisibility that disabled and neurodivergent LGBTQIA+ persons still face within their own communities. This is ever-more important if we consider that disabled people have a longstanding history of demonstrating and using public spaces to articulate their demands (Barnartt and Scotch 2001; Barnartt 2008; Bregain 2013; Gill and Schlund-Vials 2016). At the same time, disabled and neurodivergent persons who rely on the external provision of care from professionals and/or members of their family or friends, may experience further problems relating to homophobic attitudes (McCann et al 2016) when trying to access Pride Events. Hence, addressing the lack of inclusion at Pride Events for disabled LGBTQIA+ persons represents, simultaneously, both an issue of queer justice and an issue of disability justice that are interwoven with other grounds of oppression and discrimination, such as race, social class, gender, and, in some cases, age.

Making Pride accessible: strategies, challenges, and opportunities for Pride organizers

As has already been mentioned in this chapter, there can be several obstacles or limitations in disabled and neurodivergent persons' access to Pride Events that make participation difficult or not enjoyable. Some Pride Events, especially those that attract big crowds in large urban centres, can be particularly challenging for disabled and neurodivergent persons, because of long routes, lack of enough accessible toilet facilities, big crowds, and loud noises, as well as logistical issues relating to transport and reaching the areas where the celebrations are held (Pieri 2021: 19–20). If academia has culpably not caught up with the need to explore the experiences of disabled and neurodivergent LGBTQIA+ persons in accessing Pride Events, disabled and neurodivergent individuals have started to be increasingly vocal about their needs and the shortcomings of the planning of Pride Events that leaves them out, particularly through online opinion pieces, articles, talks, and other forms of public engagement across different national contexts, in both the Global North[11] and the Global South.[12]

Pride organizers, in turn, are increasingly starting to adopt accessibility measures that make Pride Events more inclusive, such as choosing routes that are accessible, mobility support during the events by providing buses or vans, training volunteers and disability stewards, enhanced provision of sanitary services along the route, areas where individuals can decompress, rest, or break away from the crowds, as well as sign language interpreting during speeches and performances, and close-captioning. In this regard, many websites of Pride Events organizations currently dedicate specific sections to their 'accessibility policies'. At the same time, even when formal commitments exist on paper, accessibility practices may fall short or be disregarded. Pieri (2021: 19), for instance, recalls how efforts by the only Italian LGBT Disability group to make the route for Bologna Pride accessible in 2017 failed for lack of commitment from the organizers:

> In Italy, in 2017, a long negotiation was carried out by Gruppo Jump, the only Italian organisation for LGBTQA+ disabled and neurodivergent people, and the organisations involved in the Bologna Pride Parade. It was actually the very first time that accessibility was discussed as a non-negotiable requirement to organise the parade. Negotiations lasted months in order to find the best route that would accommodate all types of mobility. However, only a few weeks before the parade, the organising committee opted for a route that was only partially accessible but had the economic advantage of passing by some of the cafés which had sponsored the event. As a consequence, Gruppo Jump dissociated itself from the organising committee and did

not participate in the parade. However, as a matter of fact, this event did not lead to any significant national protest.

Hence, while improvements have been made, and disabled and neurodivergent people are increasingly consulted on their priorities and needs in relation to the organization of parades, marches, and demonstrations, much remains to be done in order to offer accessibility as a 'gift', but to create empowering public spaces where disabled and neurodivergent LGBTQIA+ persons feel not just accommodated or tolerated but fully welcomed.

In the context of this research, the question of making Pride Events accessible has been addressed by a few of the interviewees, some of whom also self-identified as being disabled and neurodivergent, or as having a disability. For some, making Pride Events accessible is a way to ensure that the event mirrors the community that it caters for, as Craig, from the US, explains:

> It's all about making people feel welcome. We work really hard to make sure Pride looks like the people that come through the gate. Not like white muscled boys, as much as I like to look at white muscled boys. That's not who we are. We're white old men. … And we are young people and old people, and we're people in wheelchairs. And we're people who are blind and deaf. … I want everyone to come to Pride and feel welcome and feel that this is their Pride.

Some Pride organizers feel that they still have a long way to go in order to make their events accessible to disabled and neurodivergent LGBTQIA+ persons. Marcel, from Slovakia, for instance, admits that, as of 2022, his organization had not put a lot of thinking into the provisions that could help disabled and neurodivergent people access Pride Events, citing lack of 'input' from the community, and that more work was needed in relation to this issue:

> In general [in relation to] accessibility, we tried to have the events in wheelchair accessible places, but this is really something that we haven't had that much request from the community. I have to admit that we have to look into also, for example, sign language interpretation or stuff like that. In the past we were approaching some sign language interpreters, and they were not willing to … I don't know … or we didn't have the funding, or they were not willing to do that. But yeah, that's one of the challenges for us to next year.

Marcel's comment on the lack of 'request' from the community goes to show how, in some cases, accessibility measures may be perceived as 'optional', rather than as a 'default' feature of programming and organization (Martens

2019). On the other hand, some activists, such as Lance, from Canada, express a strong interest in accessibility issues that takes centre-stage in the planning of their events:

> I'm really quite passionate about accessibility [and] my team is taking the time to think about how we make sure that folks with accessibility needs are supported. If you put that thought into it, you're covering everyone, you know? Everyone benefits from us having an accessible festival. So that's what accessibility is all about for us.

Some Pride organizers interviewed have already entered sustained conversations with either disabled and neurodivergent participants (through feedback), and/or organizations for disabled and neurodivergent LGBTQIA+ persons, to adopt and implement measures that can effectively improve the experiences of disabled and neurodivergent persons. One such approach has been expressed by Jennifer, who organizes a Trans Pride Event in the UK:

> So, in 2021 the general feedback was that we didn't we didn't do too well on accessibility, but everything else was great. ... So that's why in 2021 we went big on the accessibility and spent a lot of money. And literally there was not a single complaint. Everybody loved it. People thought it was accessible, it was inclusive, it was diverse.

Economic pressures for organizers are quite widespread, as also Jennifer's point about 'spending money' shows. Improving accessibility is an expensive feat and one that may prove challenging for organizers who are working with limited budgets, as discussed in Chapter 6.

In relation to partnerships with disabled activists, Amalie, from Norway, also reflects on the relationship between the organizers of the country's biggest Pride Event, and disabled activists who are offering their own perspectives and advice on how to make Pride Events accessible:

> We're working with one of the organizations for disabled people, one of the biggest in Norway. [They] just moved into the offices under us. So, we're going to have like meetings with them and just sit there with maps of the parks and let them point out what we should do.

When Pride organizers are themselves disabled and neurodivergent, their perspective on disability and accessibility requirements at Pride Events may be coming from their own awareness of things that able-bodied people may 'take for granted', as Emma, a disabled Pride organizer from the UK, explains:

> I think you see it differently, you know, because you could face some problems and, you know, things that used to be taken for granted that you did automatically, you have to think about [them] consciously. So, for example, you know, it might be a [that I need to use] a handrail, but then, maybe I can't get to that handrail due to … people. I have to think about safety, you know, fires. Can [people] get out of the building? You sort of risk assess all the time, don't you? But I also want to be visible.

One issue that has been raised by a number of Pride organizers in relation to disability at Pride Events has been the role of the COVID-19 pandemic in bringing to the surface the realities of members of the LGBTQIA+ community, such as disabled and neurodivergent persons, who had been traditionally forgotten and/or left behind (den Houting 2020; Lebrasseur et al 2021; Schormans et al 2021). Amalie, from Norway, reflects on this newly found awareness in relation to the needs of disabled and neurodivergent LGBTQIA+ persons who cannot attend Pride Events in person:

> We're constantly working on making everything more accessible for everyone. One of the things we learned in 2020 and 2021 were that those people who don't want to come to the park felt included [through online Pride Events] because it was available online, and because they're not out there to their families. But there are also people who can't come because maybe they have anxiety or they're sick or disabled and neurodivergent. So, we're going to continue with that.

For some organizers, this awareness came from the acknowledgement that members of their own communities (sometimes at the intersection of disability and old age) were disproportionately suffering from the isolating effects of the pandemic and needed some forms of contact and interaction with other LGBTQIA+ persons, perhaps through attendance at Pride Events, either in real life or online. When discussing accessibility requirements or measures, Pride organizers mention the intersection between old age and disability as one of the issues that they try to tackle:

> You do get a lot of older people but, you know, there are limitations. In terms of the parade, it can feel very long if you're 75 years of age. So, what we try and do with the parade is [to have] one or two accessibility vehicles so older people, and obviously some disabled and neurodivergent people that have mobility issues, can go on these buses and they can be in the parade while sitting down. (Connor, Ireland)

These measures that acknowledge the intersection between impairments, disability, and old age can be effective in addressing the marginalization that older LGBTQIA+ persons may face at Pride Events, especially when they are big, dynamic, and fast-paced.

The data presented in this section, which offers a snapshot of some of the experiences of Pride organizers interviewed for this research, point to the importance of addressing accessibility requirements at Pride Events not as an 'afterthought' or as an 'optional' element of event planning, but as a key measure for gauging how representative, inclusive, and empowering the Pride Event in question is for everyone attending. Disabled and neurodivergent LGBTQIA+ persons may not feel welcome at Pride Events if accessibility needs to be 'demanded' but may feel empowered and comfortable attending if they are either consulted on what measures would work best, and/or are informed of what arrangements have already been put into place. As has been previously mentioned, disabled and neurodivergent persons have very diverse needs, priorities, and requests when it comes to accessibility, so this issue cannot be thought of as requiring a 'one-off' intervention that addresses accessibility requirements once and for all, but needs to be considered as an ongoing process where disabled and neurodivergent LGBTQIA+ persons need to be at the centre of planning, decision-making, and monitoring, according to the well-known principle of disability activism that recites 'nothing about us, without us' (Waldschmidt et al 2015).

Pride Events, technology, and accessibility: between inclusion and technoableism

As has already been discussed, making Pride Events 'accessible' for disabled and neurodivergent LGBTQIA+ persons may, in some cases, represent a challenge for Pride organizers, as this process requires engagement with individuals and/or groups that are routinely left out of decisions about their own wellbeing and welfare, as well as the enacting of intentional interventions, and allocation of economic resources to execute accessibility plans. Moreover, disabled and neurodivergent LGBTQIA+ persons have been excluded, and continue to be excluded, not just in the context of Pride Events, but also in other circumstances, such as in accessing LGBTQIA+ bars, clubs, saunas, and other venues for socialization, dating, flirting, and sexual experiences (Martino 2020; Kempapidis et al 2023; Overton and Hepple 2022). The discussion about accessibility, therefore, extends well beyond the question of making Pride Events accessible, but surely finds in the topic of Pride Events one of the privileged sites where social change can be brought about. As has been previously discussed, disabled and neurodivergent activists have always occupied public space to raise their demands and denounce the discrimination that they encounter on a daily basis (Barnartt and Scotch

2001; Barnartt 2008; Bregain 2013; Gill and Schlund-Vials 2016) and they should feel welcome at Pride Events.

At the same time, beyond physical locations, spaces are also opening online, where disability activism can take new forms and have a broad reach. Haller (2017), for instance, has argued that the advent of social media has reinvigorated disability activism, as disabled and neurodivergent groups and individuals can undertake outreach activities, connecting with other advocates and other disabled persons, as well as developing online activist platforms. Haller (2017: 306) embraces Nelson's (2000) argument for whom the advent of the Internet has become a 'liberating technology' for disabled and neurodivergent persons. In this regard, several scholars have also explored how the Internet, and in some cases social media more specifically, can represent virtual sites where disabled and neurodivergent persons can articulate their subjectivities, discuss their priorities, and find friends and allies (Ellis and Kent 2016; Trevisan 2016; Gubermann 2023). However, others recognize that virtual spaces can also harbour forms of exclusion or present obstacles that prevent disabled and neurodivergent individuals and/or activists from engaging and can further foster marginalization from society (Kent 2019; Bitman 2023).

The emergence of the COVID-19 pandemic in the first trimester of 2020 has represented a sobering reality for many, showing the need for continued and sustained advocacy for the rights of disabled persons, both online and offline. As governments around the world ineptly scrambled to find effective containment strategies for the virus, as well as working on a cure that would prevent death and long-lasting debilitation, disabled and neurodivergent persons paid a disproportionate price in terms of mortality rates (Bosworth et al 2021; Weaver 2024), often accompanied by attitudes of 'expendability' of disabled lives (Kendall et al 2020; Andrews et al 2021). As networks of formal and informal support also started to vanish, many disabled and neurodivergent persons experienced isolation and marginalization (Schormans et al 2021; Shakespeare et al 2022).

As can be imagined, the effects of this shrinking web of social support were also experienced by disabled and neurodivergent LGBTQIA+ persons, who may have felt the compounded effects of marginalization as being both disabled and LGBTQIA+, especially if living in contexts where their sexual orientation and/or gender identity are not respected by family members, carers, and other members of their close circles. With the cancellation of Pride Events worldwide due to the COVID-19 pandemic, opportunities for disabled LGBTQIA+ persons to feel included and part of the community were reduced even further. Against this backdrop, Pride organizers in 2020 started to create online events, often described as 'Digital Pride Events' to obviate the cancellation of 'in-real-life' gatherings. These events, the biggest of which has been the '2020 Global Pride', a 26-hour-long event streamed on YouTube on 27 June 2020, co-organized by Europride and Interpride, offered the opportunity to individuals to celebrate Pride remotely, regardless of whether they were disabled or not.

While everyone benefitted from the creation of these 'Digital Pride Events' in times of forced social isolation due to the pandemic, conversations started to happen in relation to the benefits for disabled and neurodivergent LGBTQIA+ persons, and individuals who could access Pride Events online while not being 'out' or needing to risk being outed by attending these events (Leary 2020; Wareham 2020). Particularly in relation to disabled LGBTQIA+ persons, 'Digital Pride Events' could provide a sense of belonging to the LGBTQIA+ community, even for those who were not able to participate in person to these events before the pandemic. In the context of this research, for instance, several Pride organizers interviewed have discussed how the pandemic has disproportionately affected disabled and neurodivergent LGBTQIA+ persons, together with trans persons, more than any other segments of the community, and how the creation of 'Digital Pride Events' has been perceived as a way to both alleviate feelings of exclusion, as well as making Pride Events more inclusive in general. Adam, Jax, and Louie from Canada, for instance, discuss the feedback they have received in 2020 after creating online Pride Events:

> I've heard feedback from disabled people within the community who have asked as restrictions lessen, and we have more in-person events, to make sure that we still have virtual events. ... For people who might be immunocompromised and don't want to leave the house and don't want to put themselves at that risk, having virtual events and making sure that we have an online presence and a way that they can attend with not in-person, is a really important thing that we need to continue [to do], to make sure that those needs are being met.

On a similar note, Kieran from the UK, also shares some feedback received about online events organized by him for LGBTQIA+ Travellers and Roma people during the COVID-19 pandemic:

> I dug my heels about Zoom hangouts and I really didn't want to do them. But the times we have done them, that's been really nice, I enjoyed them. And there's a couple of people on one of the group chats who are just like 'Well, no way in my current condition, you know, my disability, [that] I'm going to be able to engage in any outside stuff'.

These examples by Kieran, Adam, Jax, and Louie are only some instances in which disabled and neurodivergent LGBTQIA+ persons have expressed to Pride organizers their enjoyment of the provision of online digital events by Pride organizations during the pandemic, particularly during 2020 and 2021. At the same time, however, Digital Pride Events may have been configured as temporary measures aimed at filling the gap left by the lack of 'in-real-life' events, so their organization (or the inclusion of livestreamed contents) after the pandemic has certainly fizzled out, leaving many disabled and neurodivergent LGBTQIA+ persons wondering whether that effort at making Pride Events more accessible was mostly accidental, rather than intentional.

Another issue to consider also relates to the role of so-called 'Technoableism' (Shew 2023) on the lives of disabled persons. Shew (2023: 8), a disability advocate and scholar, describes 'Technoableism' as:

> a belief in the power of technology that considers the elimination of disability as a good thing, something we should strive for. It's a classic form of ableism – bias against disabled people, bias in favor of non-disabled ways of life. Technoableism is the use of technologies to reassert those biases, often under the guise of empowerment.

Following Shew's argument on 'Technoableism', it can be argued that the growing role of digital technologies, such as the creation of 'Digital Pride Events' to make disabled and neurodivergent persons feel more 'included' within society, may also harbour problematic aspects, as technology becomes a way to 'solve a problem', rather than a truly empowering tool for disabled and neurodivergent persons themselves. While, on the one hand, the exponential growth of streaming and online calling during the COVID-19 pandemic has opened up opportunities for some disabled and neurodivergent persons to engage and participate in fora from which they have been traditionally excluded because of lack of infrastructure, accessibility, and/or funding and financial resources; making things 'accessible' online may, in some cases, represent a way to avoid answering key questions about how we make 'in-real-life' participation for disabled and neurodivergent persons a reality, rather than an option that can be overruled by streaming an event online.

In this regard, Shakespeare et al (2022) have researched the effects of the pandemic on disabled persons and have also looked at how the use of technology could be detrimental, rather than beneficial, for the inclusion of disabled and neurodivergent persons in society. In particular, one quote by Ashley, one of the 69 disabled persons they have interviewed for their research, shows the ambiguous role that technology can play:

> What worries me is that I don't want that, after this crisis is over, for people to say, oh, well actually we don't need to make that meeting

accessible, because disabled people, you can Zoom it, or WebEx it, or Teams it. And that really worries me that you know, actually this whole online connectivity will lead to more isolation. Not less. Of course it is wonderful, for some people it is absolutely fantastic and brilliant, but I don't want it to be the only thing. (Shakespeare et al, 2022: 111)

As has been previously mentioned in this chapter, disabled and neurodivergent persons have been marginalized and shunned by society for a very long time, and in some cases are still experiencing these forms of societal segregation (Steele 2024). While the growth of communication technologies and social media can offer opportunities for interaction and participation, and foster inclusion, they can also, in some cases, represent a low-hanging fruit that simulates inclusion without having to act on the structural barriers that prevent disabled and neurodivergent persons from participating in Pride Events in person. This point does not mean that Pride organizers act in bad faith, or are ill-intentioned, as this process has more to do with societal perception of technology as a way 'to solve the problem of disability', as Shew (2023: 8–9) argues, rather than individual attitudes towards disabled persons:

Sometimes technology is seen as redeeming our lives: nondisabled people believe – and expect us to believe – that technology will 'solve' the problem of our disability and save us, or those like us, in the future. Yet these expectations often don't match out circumstances. They confine us. When people assume that one device will 'fix' us, they don't pay attention to the host of other concerns around disability technology – the bad planning and design, the need for constant maintenance, the problem of money …, and the staggering lack of social support for disability accommodation. These are all forms of ableism.

The growing number of events, including Pride Events, that are currently live streamed or posted online, therefore, cannot be the only 'improvement' offered to disabled and neurodivergent LGBTQIA+ persons in relation to the organization of Pride Events. If Pride Events in real life continue to function through ableist paradigms in relation to the management of crowds, the creation of infrastructures, the provision of specific services, the streaming of these events will not be a truly accessible practice, but a way to further confine disabled and neurodivergent LGBTQIA+ persons in their own homes, while praising the miracles that technology can offer us in terms of creating a 'boundless' society. Furthermore, the digitalization of Pride Events cannot represent the panacea that it might appear to be, as different disabled and neurodivergent persons may experience a 'digital divide' (Spanakis et al 2021; Cho and Kim 2022) and may not have the skills (and in some cases the privacy and the safety) to access LGBTQIA+ content. Furthermore, as disabled and neurodivergent persons are disproportionately affected by poverty and economic deprivation (Brucker 2020), they may lack the economic resources to access the technology needed to participate in these remote events. Hence, while technology can be an ally in reaching populations and groups that may feel isolated and not included within LGBTQIA+ communities, concomitant efforts need to be made by organizers, and society at large, to make sure that substantial resources, efforts, and actions are put into place to move from performative inclusion of disabled and neurodivergent persons to true and emancipatory participation in social life.

Beyond accessibility: implementing and promoting disability justice at Pride Events

Historically, Pride Events have not always been welcoming to disabled and neurodivergent LGBTQIA+ persons, and, in many cases, they continue to be organized following ableist canons regarding who can participate and what kind of participation is encouraged or welcomed. Navigating a cordoned-off city with mobility impairments can be a nightmare for many; sensory overload and lack of spaces where people can rest and decompress can be stressful experiences for some; lack of provision of sign language interpretation or close-captioning during speeches or entertainment can make people who participate feel alienated from the celebrations of the day (Pieri 2021). This does not necessarily mean that individual Pride organizers deliberately decide to discriminate against disabled and neurodivergent persons who want to take part. Ableism is so pervasive in our societies that it may go undetected for most, thus leaving disabled and neurodivergent persons having to articulate their demands, hoping that they will be actioned.

Accessibility represents a growing priority for Pride organizers who want to make a difference for disabled and neurodivergent members of their communities, particularly in a context where Pride Events need to be seen and scrutinized through the lens of intersectionality and multiple layers of oppression and marginalization. At the same time, however, making Pride Events psycho-physically and architecturally accessible does not necessarily mean that these spaces become automatically welcoming for disabled and neurodivergent persons. Ableism, in fact, is experienced by disabled and neurodivergent persons in many ways (Nario-Redmond 2019), and Pride participants' attitudes towards disabled and neurodivergent LGBTQIA+ persons are as important as the provision of ramps, accessible toilets, and sign language interpreters by the organizers. Anecdotally, disabled and neurodivergent persons have reported episodes of hostility towards them at Pride Events by other participants (Stonewall 2018: 13; Kempapidis et al

2023), an issue that is surely much bigger than the few episodes mentioned in the literature. For this reason, when thinking about welcoming disabled and neurodivergent persons at Pride Events, accessibility cannot be thought of as a 'tick box' exercise, whereby the presence of particular measures that enable psychological and physical wellbeing for disabled and neurodivergent participants during the event is seen as the 'end goal'. On the contrary, these measures need to be coupled by creating a truly welcoming environment during Pride Events where ableism and discrimination are actively discouraged, combatted, and prevented.

Furthermore, the question of accessibility at Pride Events needs to be seen not as a 'concession' from able-bodied crowds to disabled and neurodivergent LGBTQIA+ persons, but as a rethinking of both the history and purpose, as well as the role, that Pride Events play in the context of society. In this regard, the words of Brown disabled scholar and activist Leah Lakshmi Piepzna-Samarasinha (2019: 60) offer the opportunity to reread the events that happened at the Stonewall Inn in New York in June 1969:

> I still wonder: If we see Stonewall through a disability justice lens, and we know many of the instigators of it were Mad and trauma surviving, can we also claim this moment of queer and trans rebellion as a Mad and disability justice space? ... Many Stonewall warriors live(d) CPTSD then from surviving constant transmisogynist violence, rape, abuse, and shunning. This is a disabled trans knowledge too. If we look for disability in the Stonewall Rebellion, might it mean that we stop forgetting disability, thinking of it as a forever footnote or afterthought? Might it mean that we have more queer disabled wordhouses, tools, strategies, ways of imagining how we fight now, for the future that tastes like free than we need?

Piepzna-Samarasinha (2019) argues that we should stop treating disability as a 'footnote' or as an 'afterthought' in the history of the Stonewall Riots, and consider the role of disability, madness, and trauma in the making of such an iconic and mythologized 'founding moment' (see Chapter 1) for the history of LGBTQIA+ communities, both in the US and around the world. This suggestion decentres the dominant ableist narrative around the Stonewall Riots and opens up the possibility of reimagining our queer histories through the contribution of disabled and neurodivergent activists and laypersons that have been invisibilized or marginalized, both in the US, but also well beyond that specific geographical horizon. As such, this suggestion by Piepzna-Samarasinha (2019) does not just ask us to engage with accessibility as a practice that addresses ableist canons in the organization of Pride Events but leads us to interrogate the very concept of 'disability justice' as a practice and an approach that should be central to the organization of Pride Events more in general.

As a concept, in fact, 'disability justice' encapsulates a broader liberatory and emancipatory framework for disabled persons than the concept of 'accessibility'. Without wanting to cynically underestimate or criticize efforts to make Pride Events accessible, or the concept of accessibility more in general in achieving the inclusion of disabled and neurodivergent persons within society, there is broader scope for asking for disabled liberation from oppressing ableist structures that make disabled persons' participation a 'concession' rather than a given in society. Pride Events can be crucial sites where these requests can be made, and actions can be put into practice. Similarly to approaches discussed in earlier chapters of this book that tried to show the intersections between racism, colonialism, classism, sexism, transphobia, and homophobia in the ways in which individuals are excluded from Pride Events across different geographical contexts, the concept of 'disability justice' refutes the premise of single-issue advocacy, as explained by disabled activist Sins Invalid (2016: 13–14):

> Disability Justice activists, organizers, and cultural workers understand that able-bodied supremacy has been formed in relation to other systems of domination and exploitation. The histories of white supremacy and ableism are inextricably entwined, both forged in the crucible of colonial conquest and capitalist domination. One cannot look at the history of US slavery, the stealing of indigenous lands, and US imperialism without seeing the way that white supremacy leverages ableism to create a subjugated 'other' that is deemed less worthy/abled/smart/capable. A single-issue civil rights framework is not enough to comprehend the full extent of ableism and how it operates in society.

Invalid's (2016) words echo many of the other intersectional frameworks offered by activists who have sought to centre intersectional practices in the organization of Pride Events. Can we truly think of Pride Events as places where social justice can be imagined, demanded, and created, if we adopt a single-issue approach to the rights of LGBTQIA+ persons? The concept of disability justice proves that there is a crucial entanglement between systems of domination that very often use accusations of sickness, illness, and inability to create marginalizable and, in some cases, 'expendable' others, beyond the existence of tangible and real impairments. Rather than wanting to distance ourselves from LGBTQIA+ persons who were pathologized in the past, and continue to be so in many contexts (see, for instance, the ongoing pathologization of trans persons), we should embrace the knowledge that processes of disablement by society are deployed as repressive measures that seek to dehumanize and delegitimize the existence of individuals who defy the hetero-able-normative canons, rather than 'neutral' acknowledgements of the existence of impairments for individuals.

In times when Pride Events exponentially grow and multiply, attracting ever-bigger crowds of people across the world, the risk is that we lose sight of who needs to be represented the most and for what reasons. This exponential growth and success of Pride Events, and its rampant capitalistic morphing into mega-events, risks obliterating the importance of constructing a movement centred around the experiences of individuals who are dealing with multiple forms of societal oppression, where ableist discrimination may be one of them. Hence, disability justice should be part of the ethos of Pride Events as a way to acknowledge the common, and intersecting, lineages of oppression and discrimination experienced through compulsory able-bodiedness and compulsory heterosexuality (McRuer 2008) by LGBTQIA+ persons in various guises, as well as the historical commonality in terms of fighting for access to public spaces that both movements have sought to achieve. For some, such as Piepzna-Samarasinha (2019: 17), disability justice represents the pinnacle of queer liberation, as explained in the quote that follows:

> When I think of what the past twenty-five years of queer movement work have gifted me with, one of the first and biggest blessings is the queer gift of disability justice. Created by disabled and neurodivergent, mostly queer and trans Black, Brown, and poor white disabled and neurodivergent people out of our body/minds deepest knowledges and needs, to describe a movement framework that centred disabled and neurodivergent queer and trans, Black and Brown knowledge, lineages, desires, and demands, grounded in intersectionality, anti-capitalism, leadership of the most impacted, sustainability, and building collective access and cross-disability solidarity. (Piepzna-Samarasinha 2019: 17)

As has already been discussed in several chapters of this book, Pride Events are polysemic and represent moments of queer joy, celebration, anger, protest, and affirmation of one's identity and imagining of better futures. Disability Justice should play a key role in this process of reimagining a society freed from discrimination against LGBTQIA+ persons not just because of their sexual orientation and/or gender identity, but also in relation to the intersection of myriad characteristics and positionalities that often lock individuals out of feeling part of a big LGBTQIA+ community. Despite the debate, sometimes heated, about whether Pride Events are about celebration or protest (McFarland Bruce 2016: 21), making Pride Events truly inclusive should always include intersectional conversations that centre the most marginalized segments of the community, rather than reproducing capitalistic and neoliberal ideas that 'festivalize' (Taylor 2016) a movement born out of the desire to change society for the better for LGBTQIA+

persons. Disability Justice requires boldness in thinking about a future where making Pride Events accessible does not just guarantee the physical presence of disabled and neurodivergent persons in a temporarily 'queered' public space, but fosters the idea of changing the very perception of what it means to be embodied and queer in such normative spaces, despite the constricting character of hetero-able-normativity.

Notes

1. The term preferred here is 'disabled' as it emphasizes how disability can be considered (or thought of) as a source of identity. The expression 'persons with disabilities' is also often used (and preferred) by some activists. The rationale for these different usages can be explored more in depth by referring to Galvin (2003), Mkhize (2015), and Żychowska-Skiba (2023).
2. The word 'neurodivergent' is disaggregated from 'disabled' as neurodivergent individuals may not always identify as 'disabled' (Egner 2019b; Shmulsky et al 2021).
3. Please also note that the Social Model of Disability has also been criticized for not sufficiently taking into account the 'material' aspect of impairment and its impact on individuals' lives (Iriarte et al 2016: 17).
4. Please note that the word 'crip' represent an attempt by some disabled activists to reclaim the derogatory term 'cripple' in a way that is similar to how LGBTQIA+ persons have reclaimed the equally derogatory term 'queer' (Shew 2023: 30).
5. For an analysis of the origins of Crip Theory, please see McRuer and Cassabaum (2021).
6. To know more about the history of societal segregation of disabled and neurodivergent people and its historical and cultural contexts, please see Finkelstein (1980), Barnes and Oliver (1993), and Hanes et al (2018).
7. See Bernstein (1997) for more on this concept.
8. In this regard, please also refer to discussions regarding the compulsory sterilization of disabled and neurodivergent people across different countries as both a form of eugenics, as well as a biopolitical effort to dictate which lives are 'reproduceable' (Goodrow 2018: Withers 2024).
9. Efforts made in the context of this project to research relevant literature in English, French, and Spanish have returned very few results, and all of them were in English and related to the contexts of either the UK or the US.
10. It is worth noting, as Kunzel (2018: np) does, that the depathologization of homosexuality in the DSM was partly achieved at the expense of the further pathologization of gender non-normativity (or 'gender identity disorder', as it was then described in terms of diagnosis).
11. For some contributions, please see: Brownworth (2019), Vargas (2019), Ishak (2021), Jones (2021), Coi and Hernández-Morales (2022). These contributions are mentioned in Kynn et al (2023: np) and they are not exhaustive. For a recent discussion in the context of the UK, please see Gauci (2024).
12. See, for instance, discussions happening in countries such as Argentina (*Pagina12* 2021), India (Mad in Asia Pacific 2021), and Mexico (IMETAC 2024).

8

Pride on Tow? Environmental Sustainability and Queer Eco-Criticism at Pride Events

So far, this book has discussed how Pride Events are complex and multilayered and are interconnected with several issues beyond the narrow confines of LGBTQIA+ (lesbian, gay, bisexual, transgender, queer, intersex, asexual, plus) rights, such as racism, the legacy of colonialism and imperialism, capitalism and its impact on social movements, the role of policing in contemporary societies, as well as disability justice, to name a few. Effectively, these gatherings represent a social and political microcosm, shedding light on the struggles and challenges experienced by the various LGBTQIA+ communities around the world. Sometimes, Pride Events also bring to the surface the tensions and contradictions experienced by LGBTQIA+ communities, particularly in relation to issues such as discrimination, commercialization, and connivence with oppressive structures, such as the police forces.

This chapter addresses the concept of environmental sustainability in the context of Pride Events, interrogating its importance and limits. The increasing number of Pride Events around the world, as well as the growth of some of these gatherings from hundreds of thousands of participants to crowds that exceed a million people in the streets, as has been discussed in Chapter 3, require a reflection on both the environmental impact that these events may have, as well as on Pride organizers' engagements with concepts of environmental sustainability in relation to sponsors and corporate actors that participate or contribute to the realization of these events. More broadly, the chapter asks whether we can rethink, reconfigure, or radically alter Pride Events in light of the looming climate crisis that threatens the planet, and what implications a process of radical rethinking of Pride Events would have for LGBTQIA+ persons around the world.

Pride Events often represent a beacon of hope and optimism for LGBTQIA+ persons who often experience shunning and marginalization within their own local communities. As such, they are crucial sites in which to imagine the future for LGBTQIA+ persons. Precisely because of this role of Pride Events as crucibles of different social and political challenges, as well as temporal sites of future-making, it would be impossible to contemplate the future of global and local Pride politics without acknowledging the importance of the current climate crisis and the related question of environmental sustainability.

As a concept, environmental sustainability has become almost a buzzword, used to identify anything that is positive in terms of attention to the natural environment (Morelli 2011: 2). Moreover, our growing familiarity with the very concept of sustainability can also be attributed to the adoption, in 2015, of the so-called 'Sustainable Development Goals', by the United Nations. These were 17 objectives,[1] to be achieved ideally by 2030, which were agreed upon unanimously by all member states of the United Nations, to work towards peace and prosperity for people, as well as the planet (Swain 2018; Katila et al 2019).

While there is still a very long way to go to achieve these objectives, well beyond the set horizon of 2030, the language and rhetoric of sustainability has permeated many fields of social and political discourses, often in performative (Anantharaman 2022), rather than transformative, terms. So-called practices of 'greenwashing' (Miller 2017; de Freitas Netto et al 2020), for instance, have become ubiquitous tools for corporations to undertake superficial initiatives to make them appear environmentally friendly, while pursuing industrial practices that are steeped in the exploitation and degradation of the natural environment, as well as creating health hazards for individuals, communities, and entire regions, in some cases. Fossil fuel companies, such as Shell or British Petroleum (BP), for instance, have jumped on the 'greenwashing' bandwagon by emphasizing their growing use of sustainable technologies, such as wind or solar panels, while continuing to undertake polluting practices around the world and jeopardizing, in the process, human, animal, and environmental safety and security (Gelmini 2021; Speare-Cole 2023; Yılmaz and Baybars 2022).

This chapter is structured around four sections. The first section situates the discourse on environmental sustainability in the context of the global growth of Pride Events, focusing on the intersections between LGBTQIA+ activism, environmental activism, and the rise of so-called 'Queer Ecology' (Gaard 1997; Mortimer-Sandilands and Erickson 2010). The second section addresses the challenges and opportunities encountered by some of the participants to this research in trying to make their own Pride Events 'sustainable'. While the number of participants engaging with this concept in the context of this research is very low, the significance of these challenges requires an analysis that can combine the factual with the speculative, thus offering potential future avenues for further investigation. Third, the chapter adopts the framework of 'Queer Eco-Criticism'[2] to consider the problems that arise with practices of 'pinkwashing' by some sponsors and corporations supporting Pride Events, with clear opposition emerging from some LGBTQIA+ activists in relation to the inclusion of these actors. Last, the discussion moves to a speculation on the future of Pride Events from an environmental sustainability perspective, arguing that this will increasingly become an inescapable issue for Pride organizers, particularly those that create mega-events attended by hundreds of thousands of people in big urban centres, especially in the Global North.

Think green? Why environmental sustainability is a Pride issue

Although the concept of 'intersectionality' is often reduced to a trite performative articulation of the intersections between different social justice movements (Carastathis 2014, 2016; Grzanka 2020), it is crucial to emphasize the intersectional importance of Pride Events as physical and symbolic sites where different interests and experiences can converge, to imagine a more just world. Urgently, the question we may ask in this regard is whether LGBTQIA+ liberation and rights do even make sense in the context of a dying planet, and what can be done about this. Despite the paucity of research on this topic, as observed by Whitworth (2019: 487), it is useful to reflect on the existing connections and intersections between LGBTQIA+ activism and environmental activism, as they arose at roughly the same time (specifically in the Global North), during the late 1960s and early 1970s[3] (Whitworth 2019: 487). Both movements are traditionally considered to be examples of 'New Social Movements' (Melucci 1980; Touraine 1985; Offe and Offe 2019), focusing on non-materialistic and intangible values, such as equality, anti-discrimination, or preserving and saving the natural environment.

Despite this overarching commonality of interest, namely the idea of fostering values that improve the quality of life (although still firmly within an anthropocentric perspective[4]), historically there has not often been an overlap of intents between these two movements. Foster and Kerr (2024: 2), for instance, have argued that environmental activism has traditionally been unwelcoming (and sometimes outright exclusionary) of LGBTQIA+ persons and communities. These forms of exclusion are puzzling, especially considering that throughout the 1970s, some LGBTQIA+ heterogeneous groups of people, such as lesbian separatists,[5] so-called 'Radical faeries',[6] as well as ecofeminists, took part in various 'back-to-land' projects (specifically across the US), which strongly intersected with the philosophical premises of the then-nascent environmental movement (Whitworth 2019: 489).

At the same time, these experiences, as well as further theoretical elaborations, particularly in the Global North,[7] have given the impetus to the emergence of the concept of 'Queer Ecology', to describe a specific type of ecological sensibility that intersects with queer theory (Mortimer Sandilands 2005), while also building on Ecofeminism[8] (Gaard 1997; Meadows 2023: 169). While queer scholars have traditionally maintained a form of scepticism towards essentializing discourses grounded in biology because of the way in which arguments of homosexuality being 'against nature' have traditionally be deployed (Gaard 1997; Whitworth 2019), increasingly we see a proliferation of contributions that seek to articulate a queer perspective on ecology and environmental questions. Queer Ecology, together with other forms of exploration of the relationship between nature and sexuality (Mortimer-Sandilands and Erickson 2010), engages with discourses around the 'naturalization' of heterosexuality, as well as the heterosexualization of nature. One way in which these issues are raised, for instance, is through the questioning of the assumption that queer life is inherently urban, as opposed to a heterosexual (untouched/unpolluted) rurality (Mortimer-Sandilands and Erickson 2010: 21; Whitworth 2019: 488). Hence, the process of 'queering' ecology, in its most political version, raises questions on the connections between heterosexuality and environmental degradation, along the lines suggested by Mortimer-Sandilands and Erickson (2010: 30): ' "[Q]ueering ecology" involves the opening up of environmental understanding to explicitly non-heterosexual forms of relationship, experience, and imagination as a way of transforming entrenched sexual and natural practices toward simultaneously queer and environmental ends.'

Queer Ecology, as a theoretical approach to the study of the intersections between nature and sexuality, pushes us to question the hetero-anthropocentric focus on life and existence that articulates the construction of naturalness/unnaturalness, including understandings of (homo)sexuality and gender variability and diversity. By 'queering' our understanding of what is 'natural', as well as calling into question our use of the natural environment to pursue (human) domination (Gaard 1997), 'Queer Ecology' makes the question of 'the sexual' broader than the expression of fleshly desire and connects it more broadly to nature as being sentient and political.

Given these theoretical engagements with the concept of 'Queer Ecology', it might be difficult to see the connection of this type of argument with Pride Events. However, queer ecological thinking creates a form of relationality between humans and the natural environment that emphasizes what is non-linear, or 'twisted', as the Colombian ecologist Brigitte Baptiste explained in an interview (Gallón Salazar 2023):

> Ecology is a relational science and proposes that the relationship of the world is achieved through the complexity of those relationships

that are ephemeral, unstable. ... It is a boiling pot that makes people who work in ecology understand that the world is continually changing, on different scales of time and space, which is always active. ... That's where queer theory is deeply ecological, because it talks about how everything goes wrong. In such a world, full of possible paths, everything ends up being twisted. Queer theory is a theory of the deviant that, with humor and irony, suggests that identity is a fiction full of anomalies and that everything and everyone is crooked [*todos estamos chuecos*]. [Freely translated from Spanish[i]]

The relational character of Queer Ecology shows how environmental activism and LGBTQIA+ activism may be aligned: in the recognition of the 'twistedness' of human and natural existence, commonalities can be found against the hetero-anthropocentric models of culture, development, and prosperity that often converge and manifest themselves through homo/transphobic and environmental violence. One example of the significance of these connections between LGBTQIA+ and environmental activism is represented, for instance, by the ongoing fights by environmental activists, particularly in the Global South, who are at constant risk of their lives. The case of the political killing of Honduran and Lenca environmental activist Berta Cáceres on 2 March 2016, for instance, shows the intersectional value and alignment between LGBTQIA+ issues and environmental fights. In a speech (Korol 2018: 93), Cáceres highlights the importance of these intersectional alliances:

We relearn things, we learn new things too. For example, respect and teaching in the streets. That the LGBT community came out, marching from all its diverse identities alongside union or left-wing leaders, or the leaders of those political parties that are within the Resistance, that they walked and marched together, we had never seen that before. Through struggle and popular education, we learn to recognize each other. That the prostitutes came out into the streets, and [we] all together learnt that they are not a waste of humanity, that

---

[i] See original quote in Spanish: '*La ecología es una ciencia relacional y plantea que el relacionamiento del mundo se logra a través de la complejidad de esas relaciones que son efímeras, inestables. ... Es una olla en ebullición que hace que las personas que trabajamos en ecología entendamos que el mundo está continuamente cambiando, en distintas escalas de tiempo y espacio, que siempre está activo. [...] Ahí es donde la teoría queer es profundamente ecológica, porque habla de que todo se tuerce. En un mundo así, lleno de caminos posibles, todo acaba por torcerse. La teoría de lo queer es una teoría de lo desviado que, con humor y con ironía, plantea que la identidad es una ficción llena de anomalías y que todo y todos estamos chuecos.*'

they are sisters who are also committed on the refoundation [of the country], for us it is a great lesson. [Freely translated from Spanish[ii]]

Berta Cáceres' words clearly articulate the interconnectedness between different social justice issues and the commonality of intents that activists can have in 'taking the streets', as well as learning from each other. When we put into perspective the knowledge that paradigms of 'animality' or 'natural inferiority', or 'unnaturalness' have been abundantly mobilized, and have been used to oppress different groups of individuals because of their sex, sexuality, gender, gender identity, race, religion, disability, and indigenous identity (Gaard 1997; Jackson et al 2005; Rembis 2018), it appears obvious how these oppressed groups of individuals can find commonality of intent in articulating a political response to these forms of 'naturalized' oppressions. Since Pride Events, even in their most party-like articulations (which may be far from the more 'engaged' or 'politicized' editions of these events), challenge questions of 'what is normal/natural', they represent the perfect sites where these interlocking systems of oppression can be challenged, for the benefit of a wide variety of actors who have multiple investments in different social justice movements.

Cleaning up Pride: challenges and opportunities in creating sustainable Pride Events

As has already been discussed, 'Queer Ecology' engages in various ways with questions connecting sexuality to nature. One of these forms of engagements is represented by the articulation of an environmentally sustainable future that is also queer-friendly. Environmental sustainability, therefore, becomes the cipher to suggest solutions that would create a more equitable, and environmentally conscious society, one in which the impact of climate change and global warming can be slowed down or mitigated, if not halted altogether (Ekins and Zenghelis 2021). In its most pragmatic version, this form of sustainability addresses the adoption of practical measures that can bring about some form of sustainable change for communities around the world. Pride Events, particularly the longer established ones such as those

---

[ii] See original quote in Spanish: '*Reaprendemos cosas, aprendemos nuevas cosas también. Por ejemplo, el respeto y la enseñanza en la calle. Que saliera la comunidad LGTTB, marchando desde todas sus identidades diversas junto a los dirigentes gremiales o de izquierda, o a los dirigentes de esos partidos políticos que están adentro de la Resistencia, que caminaran marchando juntos, nunca lo habíamos visto antes. Desde la lucha y la educación popular, aprendemos a reconocernos. Que las prostitutas salieran a las calles, y todos juntos y juntas aprendiendo que no es un desecho de la humanidad, que son hermanas que también le apuestan a la refundación, para nosotras es una gran lección.*'

taking place in metropoles such as New York, London, São Paulo, and Sydney, attract from hundreds of thousands to millions of participants. As such, they are inevitably accompanied by an environmental impact, as well as a 'carbon footprint', that pertains to the mobility of participants, the use of resources, such as water, the decoration of the sites and venues, as well as the management of waste, both biological and non-biological. A Queer Ecological perspective invites us to centre environmentally sustainable practices in the analysis of Pride organizers' decisions regarding their events.

Despite the timeliness and relevance of this issue, specific research on the environmental impact of Pride Events is practically non-existent to date, with one notable exception in this regard – Dodds and Graci (2012). This contrasts with an extensive existing literature on the environmental impact of large-scale or mass events (Caratti and Ferraguto 2012; Case 2013; Holmes and Mair 2020), as well as tourism (Wong 2004; Holden 2016; Briassoulis 2000). As Pride Events are often both mass events and attract LGBTQIA+ tourism, these contributions in the literature are certainly useful in understanding how Pride Events can be made sustainable, although specific discussions should be had that consider the specificities of Pride Events in their multiple configurations.

At the same time, the lack of academic interest and/or attention to this specific phenomenon (as was the case for the experiences of disabled and neurodivergent LGBTQIA+ persons at Pride Events described in Chapter 7) does not mean that these conversations are not entertained elsewhere, but that academia (as often happens) needs to catch up with its social surroundings. Several Pride Events around the world currently publish their own policies on how they pledge to make their event environmentally sustainable (see for instance Pride in London,[9] or New York Pride).[10] Furthermore, this topic is increasingly discussed in both environmental and LGBTQIA+ circles (Earth Day 2022; Brown 2024; Cuellár 2024), showing its salience for a large cross-sectional public. One example of these conversations is represented, for instance, by the interview with Aurélien Guilabert (Cuellár 2024) a Mexican environmental and LGBTQIA+ activist, who explains the interconnectedness of LGBTQIA+ and environmental issues at Pride Events:

> There is a problem with the Mexico City government, which has refused to ban vehicles [used as floats] in Pride marches, and this seems to me to justify an underlying issue. What drives [the use of] vehicles is money, because there are people who charge you to bring a vehicle and the place they give you in the march depends on that. In Paris, for example, there are no longer vehicles in the marches, and in many other large cities, too. We are positioning ourselves to return to the essence of the march on foot and prevent it from being monopolized by motorists, who represent a patriarchal model and the model of

fossil fuel. After all, the fight for both sexual and gender diversity and environmental justice is against the essence of patriarchy. [Freely translated from Spanish[iii]]

For this research, considerations on environmental sustainability at Pride Events have received marginal attention from interviewees. Those who have addressed this topic have done so without being directly prompted on it, but in the broader context of their efforts of reimagining Pride Events in the aftermath of COVID-19, particularly in relation to the use of public space. In this regard, the contributions by the few activists who have engaged with themes relating to environmental policies and strategies, are largely anecdotal, and mostly pertain to decisions regarding the measures to implement.

Similar to the concerns raised by Aurélien Guilabert in the previously quoted interview (Cuellár 2024), Pride organizers participating in this research highlight the mobility element relating to the organization of Pride Events as one of their priorities, and discuss specifically the presence or absence of vans, buses, and trucks. Connor, who organizes a Pride Event in Ireland, discusses, for instance, the decisions already implemented by his organization:

> So, our overall theme this year that we want to come back better and going sustainable. The fuel floats are gone, and there are only electric vehicles and push and pull floats; and there'll be a carbon offset charge to the corporates [sponsors]; and we will also help by planting plants like forests, so very nice.

On a similar note, Günther from Germany also addresses the question of the use of trucks at Pride Events across the country, particularly in the aftermath of COVID-19:

> [During the COVID-19 pandemic] there were other Pride organizations who talked about not allowing any trucks anymore. [Now] they [have] changed it back to [allowing] trucks again. I think

---

[iii] See original quote in Spanish: 'Hay un problema con el gobierno de la Ciudad de México que se ha negado a prohibir los automotores [utilizados como carrozas] en las marchas del orgullo y esto me parece que viene a justificar un tema que está detrás. Lo que mueve a los automotores es el dinero, porque hay gente que cobra para que tú metas un automotor y de eso depende el lugar que te dan en la marcha. En París, por ejemplo, ya no hay automotores en las marchas y en muchas otras grandes ciudades tampoco. Nos estamos posicionando para volver a la esencia de la marcha a pie y evitar que sea acaparada por los automovilistas, que representan un modelo patriarcal y el modelo de los combustibles fósiles. Al fin y al cabo, la lucha tanto de la diversidad sexual y de género como de la justicia ambiental es contra la esencia del patriarcado.'

it's not modern to use a diesel truck anymore to go in on a float. … Our registration fee for an electric car is reduced almost half price than if you take a diesel car. So, we look at our responsibility for this. This is definitely a big change.

The small number of Pride organizers who have addressed the question of mobility and sustainability at Pride Events have also discussed how the COVID-19 pandemic, despite its terrible physical and psychological toll on individuals, has been an important opportunity, to some extent, because during the pandemic some small-scale events were allowed to take place without the use of vehicles and with social distancing measures. This has meant, for some, the possibility of experimenting with the inclusion of vehicles during Pride Parades, as discussed by Felipe, from Spain:

> Because we were looking for a more activist [*reivindicativo*] model, then COVID allowed us to test what would happen if there were no trucks. But if there had been no COVID, the proposal would surely have been made not to have trucks. Perhaps in ten years, the issue of vehicles may change a little due to the issue of pollution, also depending on the possibilities that electric vehicles allow and the awareness that exists. [Freely translated from Spanish[iv]]

Günther, from Germany, also discusses the changed perception about the presence of vehicles at Pride Events, but thinks that floats remain necessary in order to attract public and media attention on what is happening in the streets:

> During COVID [some organizations] did [Pride Events] a couple of times with just bikes, and they realized it's nice as well. But again, the media coverage is not as big. I don't want to say you need a big truck to, to have visibility. It's just you need some features, you know, like loud music as a feature, which raises the visibility. So, if a colourful drag queen is playing super loud music on vehicle, people are looking out of their windows and saying 'Oh there is a movement, there is a march'. If you're sitting on a bike – we have thousands of people every

---

[iv] See the original quote in Spanish: '*Porque estábamos buscando un modelo más reivindicativo, entonces el Covid nos permitió hacer la prueba de qué pasaría si no hay camiones. Pero si no hubiera habido Covid, seguramente también se hubiera hecho la propuesta de que no hubiesen camiones. Quizás de aquí a diez años, el tema de los vehículos a lo mejor sí que puede cambiar un poco por el tema de la contaminación, dependiendo también de las posibilidades que permitan las vehiculos eléctricos y la conciencia que haya.*'

day sitting on a bike in Berlin for demonstrating and it's great, I love it – the visibility is almost zero.

Günther's comments shed light on the negotiations and considerations that Pride Events organizers have to think about when deciding on their priorities. In the case of Felipe, from Spain, beyond environmental reasons to allow the participation of fossil fuel trucks during the event, another concern is, for instance, the issue of democratizing participation of groups that could not afford to rent a truck to use as a float for the event. For Günther, instead, the priority seems to be ensuring that Pride Events are as visibly impactful as possible. Against this backdrop, discussions on the growth of Pride Events and the alleged push to become 'bigger and better' (Joseph 2010: 2) seem particularly important, as they clash with efforts to rethink Pride Events to be more mindful of challenges created by attempts to make them more environmentally sustainable.

On a similar note, the commodification of Pride Events discussed in Chapter 6 is connected with questions of environmental sustainability, particularly in relation to the distribution of leaflets, plastic merchandise, and other types of gadgets. Anyone who attends a highly commodified Pride Event (see for instance, Pride in London), can witness the practice of handing out gadgets[11] and leaflets during the main parade. While there is nothing inherently malignant about wanting to give people gadgets, stickers, or leaflets, the production of litter resulting from these goods is quite considerable once the event has finished. Similarly, the use of single-use plastic cups by bars and drink vendors, creates an equally significant amount of waste that needs to be collected and recycled. The question of making Pride Events sustainable, therefore, exceeds the issue of mobility, and invests many various ambits relating to the logistics and organization of these events. In this regard, Cédric, a Pride organizer from France, gives a useful overview of the various challenges encountered:

In Arras, we have been working on increasingly eco-responsible marches for years. For example, in the associations' village, we have never used plastic cups, we have always used reusable cups. There have always been recycling bins so that people can recycle. We also have ashtrays so that people do not throw their cigarette butts in the countryside. The decoration of the floats and of the village are biodegradable. So yes, it is more expensive, but it is biodegradable. … . Also, [we] limit the number of floats and the equipment is also checked; … [we] have generators that pollute less, trucks that are a little more eco-responsible, that limit the carbon footprint. In a world today where the climate is very important, it is a subject that is transversal, no matter what you are campaigning for, what association you are in.

I think it's a priority today and that our Pride marches must also adapt to the world of tomorrow, which I think must be more eco-responsible. [Freely translated from French[v]]

While anecdotal in nature, however, these contributions show the potential to bring to the forefront, both in academic and activist circles, the question of Queer Ecology and environmental sustainability in relation to Pride Events.

At the same time, building as well on the previous discussion of the challenges experienced by disabled and neurodivergent LGBTQIA+ persons, there needs to be awareness of the pitfalls that environmental sustainability policies may have on already disadvantaged or marginalized communities. One such issue is expressed, for instance, through the concept of 'Eco-ableism' (Pledl 2021; Cram et al 2022; King and Gregg 2022) as a form of ableism that ignores the implications and impact of environmentally sustainable or friendly practices and policies on the lives of disabled and neurodivergent people: '*Eco-ableism* [original emphasis] may be defined as the marginalization of disabled people through environmental design; the exclusion of disabled people in environmental decision-making; and the discrimination against disabled people through environmental discourses, beliefs, and attitudes' (Cram et al 2022: 852).

A classic case in point, would be the ban of single-use plastic straws considered to contribute to the pollution of the land and the sea. While massive numbers of single-use plastic are certainly detrimental for the environment, disabled activists have denounced how banning them is an eco-ableist measure that affects disabled persons (Pledl 2021; Cram et al 2022; Hemsley et al 2023), since other types of straw (such as glass or metal straws) are not entirely adaptable to the needs of some disabled persons.

In the context of Pride Events, Eco-ableism can manifest itself in the adoption of environmentally sustainable practices (such as banning trucks, banning single-use plastic cups or straws, changing the route of parades or marches) that can negatively impact disabled and neurodivergent persons. For this reason, conversations about the adoption of environmentally

---

[v] See the original quote in French: '*Nous, on travaille dessus depuis des années, à Arras des marches de plus en plus écoresponsables. C'est à dire, par exemple, sur le village associatif, on n'a jamais utilisé des gobelets en plastique, on a toujours utilisé des cups. Il y a toujours eu des poubelles recyclables pour que les gens trient. On a quand même des cendriers également pour pas que les gens jettent en pleine nature leurs mégots. La décoration des chars et du village est biodégradable. Alors c'est plus cher, mais c'est biodégradable. (…). Limiter aussi le nombre de chars et le matériel aussi vérifié; (…) avoir des groupes électrogènes qui polluent moins, des camions qui sont un peu plus écoresponsables, qui limitent en l'empreinte carbone. Dans un monde aujourd'hui où le climat est très important, c'est un sujet qui est transversal, peu importe sur quoi on milite, dans quelle association on est. Je pense que c'est une priorité aujourd'hui et qu'il faut que nos marches des fiertés s'adaptent aussi dans le monde d'après, que je pense pour moi doit être plus écoresponsable.*'

sustainable practices and policies at Pride Events, and more broadly in big public gatherings and events, should include a balancing exercise to make sure that the wellbeing and welfare of disabled persons are not compromised while helping to 'save' the planet. Addressing the topic of Eco-ableism at Pride Events does not imply that Pride organizers are explicitly trying to adopt or create environmental policies for their events that disproportionately target disabled individuals and groups. However, given the ableist default character of much environmental thought (Cram et al 2022), accessibility and sustainability policies should be developed in parallel, to ensure that measures are adopted that strike a balance between being environmentally conscious and inclusive of disabled and neurodivergent persons. This intersectional approach to questions of environmental sustainability is ever-more important if we consider that environmental destruction is simultaneously a cause of disablement (Jaffee and John 2018; Erevelles and Morrow 2023), as well as disproportionately impacting disabled and neurodivergent persons, compared to able-bodied persons and communities (Hoffman 2008; Sargeant 2014; Vig and Dwivedi 2024).

Fuelling the climate crisis: Queer Eco-Criticism and greenwashing at Pride Parades

On 1 July 2023, seven peaceful protesters interrupted London Pride by spraying the tarmac, chanting slogans, and sitting in front of a truck that was being used as a float by Coca-Cola. The seven activists, who were later arrested for 'causing a public nuisance' (*The Guardian* 2023), were members of the British environmentalist group 'Just Stop Oil', famous for its direct-action initiatives aimed at raising awareness of the effects of ongoing pollution caused by fossil fuels. This had not been the first time LGBTQIA+ organizations in the UK had been targeted in connection to their relations with corporate sponsors alleged to invest and profit from fossil fuels. Just a few days earlier, on 22 June 2023, two other British organizations, 'Tipping Point UK' and 'Fossil Free Pride', had called for nominees and judges of the 2023 'British LGBT Awards' to drop out of the ceremony, over ties with companies such as BP and Shell (Gayle 2023b), whose practices of 'greenwashing' (Speare-Cole 2023), and downplaying of pollution and climate change threats (Lawson 2022) made them unsuitable, in the eyes of the protesters, to sponsor such an event. Although the event went ahead, several nominees, as well as judges, ended up withdrawing.

These two examples, although obviously limited to the context of the UK, nonetheless show the growing relevance of debates on climate change across the LGBTQIA+ and environmental activist camps, and how accountability on either side can be mobilized to achieve cross-movement justice. Beyond the issue of working towards making Pride Events environmentally (more) sustainable explored in the previous section of this chapter, the other pressing issue that is increasingly becoming the focus of LGBTQIA+ environmental groups relates to the existence of patterns of 'pinkwashing' by corporations that sponsor Pride Events while being directly or indirectly involved in polluting industrial practices, investing in polluting technologies or companies, and/or being responsible for environmental degradation and global warming.

While the term 'pinkwashing' has predominantly been used in the literature to signal practices by Israel to portray itself as 'progressive' in relation to LGBTQIA+ rights, while obscuring the human rights violations perpetrated against Palestinians (Shafie 2015: 83), the concept has also increasingly been adopted to describe the actions of corporations who use rainbow iconography, as well as sponsoring LGBTQIA+ events, such as conferences, awards, Pride Events, concerts, and other gatherings, to build a progressive reputation that effectively diverts attention from problematic corporate practices (Puar 2011; Dhoot 2015; Holmes 2022). In this regard, corporations whose activities are detrimental to the environment and contribute to fuelling climate change, may simultaneously engage in both 'greenwashing' and 'pinkwashing', by offering a glossy superficial corporate image of sustainability, while also allegedly building a 'queer-friendly' reputation.

As Pride Events are increasingly under pressure to enhance their funding to create and sustain themselves over time, as discussed in Chapters 4, 5, and 6, the temptation to accept donations or sponsorship offers from corporations is more enticing than ever. This often means that Pride organizers accept sponsorships or donations from multinational corporations whose industrial practices or investments are contributing to foster climate change, either directly or indirectly. Coming back to the previous example of 'Just Stop Oil' activists sitting in front of a Coca-Cola truck at 2023 Pride in London, for instance, it would be appropriate to ask how ubiquitous the company's participation in Pride Events around the world is (very), as well as highlighting the fact that the Coca-Cola Company has been documented as fostering water shortages in different countries, such as India (Gül Holzendorff 2013; Agha 2017), or South Africa (Marcoux 2022).

In a capitalist world where every aspect of human existence is increasingly commodified, including social movements, protests, and demonstrations, it can be difficult to try to reject the pressures of corporations trying to 'colonize' portions of public and private life. Given the meagre funds dedicated to LGBTQIA+ groups and initiatives, the existence of hostility from many sectors of society towards LGBTQIA+ causes, as well as criminalization of LGBTQIA+ identities and experiences in many parts of the world, it can definitely be tempting to accept support from corporations who can, effectively, make a difference between having enough money to create the event, and having to shelve plans. At the same time, as the climate crisis inevitably looms over us, and as individuals in marginalized communities, such as women, disabled persons, working-class persons, racialized persons, as well as LGBTQIA+ persons are more likely to feel the impact of climate change, the issue of corporations' 'pinkwashing' strategies becomes part of a broader quest towards social justice; one that requires urgent scrutiny.

One initiative that has sought to address the relationship between corporate sponsors, particularly those who invest or work in the field of the production of fossil fuel, has been the British-based initiative by the group 'Fossil Free Pride'. Since 2021, this group has sought to pressure Pride Events organizers in the UK to drop sponsorships with corporations that produce and/or invest in fossil fuels. Pride Events that can prove that they have dropped ties with such organizations officially join the list of 'fossil free' Pride Events.[12] As of 2024, in the UK, 33 Pride Events have officially joined the list of 'Fossil Free Pride' for which the minimum requirement is the refusal of sponsorship deals with Fossil Fuel Corporations, as well as further actions that can be enacted, such as not allowing these organizations to register/march in these events (with a contingent or float, for instance). Members of this network of 'Fossil Free Pride' so far count many Trans, rural, or peripheral Pride Events, while events organized in big cities still lag behind in engaging in this conversation about corporate environmental 'pinkwashing', despite representing the biggest sounding board within the LGBTQIA+ community in terms of mobilizing big crowds.

Initiatives such as this one, although they may not resolve the contradiction between raising funds for the LGBTQIA+ community and balancing environmental concerns held by activists, play the crucial role of showing how LGBTQIA+ persons can be protagonists in the fight against climate change, by demanding that organizations that create events for their own communities pay more attention to the environmental cost of corporate partnerships. While 'pinkwashing' by polluting corporations at Pride Events remains a widespread practice, and one that is not consistently challenged, pressure campaigns such as that organized by 'Fossil Free Pride' show that there is growing momentum in relation not only to the creation of 'sustainable' Pride Events, but also Pride Events that are not supported by actors who are responsible for the environmental devastation and suffering of both human and non-human beings alike.

Ecology and environmental sustainability on the Pride agenda: from margin to centre?

As the climate crisis deepens at the global level, individuals around the world are increasingly realizing the interconnectedness of the fight against climate change with other social justice issues, such as poverty, racism, ableism, sexism, and homo/transphobia. One illustration of such interconnectedness is represented by the fact that LGBTQIA+ activists participating in Pride Events or other protest events often chant or write on placards the slogan 'No Pride On a Dead Planet' (Gorecho 2022; Conlon 2023; Gayle 2023a). This slogan perfectly encapsulates what is at stake when discussing why climate change is a Pride issue. What is the future of LGBTQIA+ persons, particularly those more marginalized, going to be in the context of a climate catastrophe? Far from being just a question to be projected in a (not so) distant future, the effects of climate change are already felt by many communities around the world, including LGBTQIA+ persons, and require urgent mobilization.

Increasingly, environmental LGBTQIA+ groups are articulating their vision of a 'Queer Ecology' that addresses the specific challenges experienced intersectionally by different communities who are disproportionately affected by the climate crisis (Foster and Kerr 2024). Climate change, for instance, is more likely to impact countries that are poor or 'less' developed (Fankhauser and McDermott 2014; Nawrotzki et al 2015). In this regard, LGBTQIA+ persons living in some of the poorest countries of the world may be disproportionately impacted by the direct or indirect effects of climate change (ReportOut 2023). Homelessness also represents one of the biggest issues in relation to the safety of individuals in the context of the current climate (Bezgrebelna et al 2021; Kidd et al 2021), as people who experience homelessness are more vulnerable to the consequences of natural disasters, calamities, and extreme weather. Within this context, LGBTQIA+ persons, and particularly young people, are disproportionately affected by homelessness (Romero et al 2020; McCarthy and Parr 2022). Therefore, homeless LGBTQIA+ persons will be disproportionately impacted by the effects of climate change, particularly when unable to access safe shelter.

Furthermore, the ecological question that is presented in front of many LGBTQIA+ communities around the world today also pertains to the preservation of rural LGBTQIA+ life, which is often considered to be sub-optimal compared to urban LGBTQIA+ life, following metronormative discourses, as highlighted by Halberstam (2005). Traditionally, an urban/rural divide has led to the construction of urban spaces as sites where LGBTQIA+ persons, particularly gay men, would converge, as opposed to rural spaces which were constructed as being true spaces of rugged 'masculinity' and preservation of heteronormative principles (Mortimer-Sandilands and Erickson 2010: 19; Whitworth 2019: 488). As urban centres become more and more densely populated (Seto et al 2013), and rural and peripheral areas are increasingly 'left behind', together with LGBTQIA+ persons inhabiting these areas, it becomes imperative to connect the preservation of the natural environment to social issues of marginalization and discrimination. Sometimes, the organization of Pride Events in rural and/or peripheral locations speaks to this simultaneous desire of both addressing the situation of LGBTQIA+ persons in the specific area, as well as weaving forms of 'Eco-critique' towards the urban-centred character of contemporary LGBTQIA+ politics. Events such as the 'Festival Agrocuir de Ulloa'[13] (see also Chapter 3), a Pride festival organized in Spain, in the Galician countryside, for instance, highlight the importance of this interconnected approach between Queer Ecology and Pride politics, as it seeks to reconnect the LGBTQIA+ community to the territory, as well as raising urgent questions about sustainable ways of 'being together' as LGBTQIA+ (Barreto 2020).

As amply discussed in this book, Pride Events are multiplying and growing around the world. This global growth of Pride Events shows both the salience and the potential of these gatherings to galvanize big numbers of individuals. On the one hand, this growth and multiplication of Pride Events can be read within the context of so-called 'Kaleidoscope Modernities' discussed in Chapter 2, whereby LGBTQIA+ groups around the world engage with the idea of organizing Pride Events to embark on a journey of 'modernization' in relation to sexuality and gender. On the other hand, while in several locations small Pride Events are grassroots-based and require relatively limited material resources for their organization (as the example of the 'Festival Agrocuir de Ulloa' shows), in other contexts these gatherings have become mega-events with a huge environmental footprint, as well as problematic ties with sponsoring corporations that are responsible for pollution and environmental degradation around the world, as has been discussed in this chapter. For these reasons, Pride Events represent a nodal point where some key questions around queer ecological politics can be developed.

Recently, criticism has been levelled against the polluting impact of mega-events such as the US-based music festival 'Burning Man', traditionally held in the Black Rock Desert (Nevada), which is estimated to produce around 100,000 tons of carbon dioxide (CO_2) every year (Wayne 2023); or the spectacular concerts held by pop singer Taylor Swift, particularly because of her massive use of private jets (Mendez 2024). The reality of the impact of big events is upon us: these gatherings are often producing tons of CO_2, while offsetting practices are most times just forms of 'greenwashing'. Mega Pride Events, such as those held in big metropoles, are not very dissimilar from polluting mega-events, given their massive use of vehicles, the impact of travel for participants, the production of waste, and the creation and distribution of non-recyclable gadgets and items, as well as the 'pinkwashing' by polluting corporate sponsors. Far from suggesting that big Pride Events should not take place, the issue becomes one of rethinking what is the role of Pride Events in contemporary society, particularly in contexts, predominantly in the Global North, where these festivals have reached the size of a true behemoth. Organizers, in this regard, should not consider sustainability and practices of 'pinkwashing' as additional issues that need to be tackled in the context of organizing their events. Rather, the urgency of climate change, requires a radical rethinking of the organizational and logistical priorities for Pride Events, in order to make their environmental impact, both direct and indirect, minimal or non-existent.

In considering the economic and financial challenges faced by Pride organizers, Chapter 6 contained a discussion on whether it would be feasible or desirable to 'de-grow' Pride Events, to recuperate the grassroots element of these events, and take away power from corporations who entice activists to accept their money because of the growing organizational costs. While it is undeniable that activists are faced with tough financial decisions when organizing events for which they often have to pay for services such as police presence or cleaning services, and will therefore need some forms of sponsorship, the exponential growth of Pride Events as bigger and bigger year on year may not necessarily be in the best interest of the organizers or the LGBTQIA+ participants. This does not mean that people should not be welcome to participate, or that Pride Events should stop their natural process of evolution. However, big productions with flashy polluting floats, costly celebrity entertainment, the massive presence of a contingent of corporate sponsors, might be questionable choices when trying to rethink the purpose of Pride Events, as well as consider their financial and environmental impact.

Ultimately, a queer ecological/ecocritical approach to Pride Events requires an exercise of reimagination of what Pride Events are for. While most of us find it impossible to escape the dictates of capitalism and the effects of climate change in our personal lives, in our collective choices we may have more power than we suspect. Pride organizers have power in considering how they want to make sure that their events do not replicate the harmful effects of mega-events such as 'Burning Man', for the sake of entertainment. While managing big crowds, such as at Pride Events in big urban centres such as São Paulo, London, New York, Sydney, and Mexico City, undeniably requires huge resources, and inevitably carries with it an environmental footprint, Pride oorganizers can be at the forefront of alerting their own communities to the pitfalls of pollution and interrupt forms of complicity with polluting corporations, while engaging in rethinking how the fight for LGBTQIA+ rights can be, simultaneously, also a fight for the preservation of the natural world both within and beyond the anthropocentric horizon.

Notes

[1] For a full list of the 17 Sustainability Development Goals, please see: https://sdgs.un.org/goals.
[2] For a thorough appraisal of theories of 'Eco-Criticism', please see Mortimer-Sandilands (2010), Mortimer-Sandilands and Erickson (2010), Azzarello (2016), Seymour (2020), Rendón (2022), and Gallón Salazar (2023), among others.
[3] Whitworth (2019: 487) mentions the fact that the first Earth Day was celebrated on 22 April 1970, less than one year from the 1969 Stonewall Riots in New York City.

4   To explore non-anthropocentric perspectives on environmentalism, please see Steverson (1996), Gansmo Jakobsen (2017), and Di Paola (2024), among others.
5   In the US, Lesbian Separatism during the 1970s often took form in the creation of rural communes, where lesbian women could create their own alternative 'lesbian nation(s)'. These communes and projects often shared values proper of environmentalism, such as in the case of the Oregon Women's Land Trust (OWL Farm) (Whitworth 2019: 488–489).
6   'Radical Faeries' was the name of a movement, mostly of male-identified persons, who centred their spiritual practices around the worship of nature and nature-based rituals. Its establishment has been traditionally attributed to gay activist Harry Hay. For more on this topic, see Gaard (2021).
7   For a discussion on the Western-centric focus of Queer Ecological Theories, as well as exceptions, please see Seymour (2020: 112).
8   For a discussion on Ecofeminism, please see Shiva and Mies (2014), Madhavi and Rao (2023), and Warren (2000), among others. To explore further 'Queer Ecofeminism', please see Gaard (1997).
9   Pride in London's Sustainability Pledge, available at: https://prideinlondon.org/sustainability/, last accessed 30 August 2024.
10 New York Pride's Sustainability manifesto, available at: https://go.nycpride.org/sustainability, last accessed 30 August 2024.
11 See also the Social Media hashtag #WhoMadeMyPrideMerch, created by fashion blogger Izzy McLeod to campaign for better conditions for those who make garments for the LGBTQIA+ community, as well as more attention to sustainability in the (fast) fashion industry (Shadijanova 2022).
12 For more information on the pledge to make Pride Events 'fossil free', please see the website for 'Fossil Free Pride', available at: www.fossilfreepride.co.uk/fossil-free-pride-pledge, last accessed 2 September 2024.
13 For more information on the Festival Agrocuir de Ulloa see website: https://festivalagrocuir.wordpress.com/, last accessed 4 September 2024.

Conclusion: Pride Events between the Past and the Future: Challenges and Opportunities

Beyond party and protest: Pride Events at a global crossroads

In a world in which transphobia and homophobia are unfortunately still a reality for many LGBTQIA+ (lesbian, gay, bisexual, transgender, queer, intersex, asexual, plus) persons, across latitudes and geographical contexts, in both the Global North and the Global South, the existence of Pride Events is undeniably political, often representing an act of defiance of the cisheteronormative system. The reality of Pride Events as political 'happenings' transcends the existing diatribes between different groups or individuals on whether these events should be a 'party' or a 'protest'. Taking to the streets, sometimes in joyous and frivolous ways, other times fuelled by rage and disappointment, are both forms of sexual and gender politics that we desperately need in a world in which the possibility for LGBTQIA+ persons to be themselves without fear for their security is still a privilege and a luxury for many, and in which so-called *anti-gender politics* has become a multi-million pound organized and fully institutionalized global enterprise, eroding and jeopardizing current and future social, legal, and political protections for LGBTQIA+ persons, with the support of political, religious, and corporate actors.

This book celebrates the inherent plurality of voices, experiences, challenges, and opportunities that characterize the contemporary politics of Pride Events across their local and global configurations, to invite us to challenge received notions about what Pride Events are, who should participate, and what objectives their organization should pursue. Pride Events are the ideal sites where a truly emancipatory sexual and gender politics can be articulated, but this objective needs to be nurtured through alliances, centring social justice, and resisting corporate and institutional co-optation. The book takes stock of the enormous global success of Pride

Events, from small sites to big global cities, across both the Global North and the Global South. It does so by analysing in a nuanced and critical way the pressures faced by activists in making their events 'bigger and better' and by considering what kinds of ethical and practical dilemmas this pressure exerts on organizers, particularly in relation to the increased reliance on both corporate sponsors and/or forms of institutional support. Simultaneously, the book problematizes the role of Pride Events as a sign of entrance into the realm of liberal 'modernity', one that uses LGBTQIA+ rights as a civilizational yardstick. These two contributions are key in the book: they speak directly to our ability to imagine the future of the politics of Pride Events and invite us to think outside the box, rather than accepting trite narratives on how these events have originated, how they should take place, and how they should be seamlessly replicated around the world.

Building on the firm belief in the importance of a grassroots-based intersectional politics of Pride Events, this book claims that Pride Events should never become the preserve of a privileged group of LGBTQIA+ persons who can afford to be visible, empowered, and free to celebrate and/or protest, but should represent an opportunity for every LGBTQIA+ person to participate, if they wish to be visible. For many, Pride Events represent the most tangible demonstration of the very existence of an LGBTQIA+ community to which they can belong and feel represented and empowered. For others, Pride Events often represent sites of alienation, as the promise of inclusion that these events offer may sometimes be more performative than substantial, leaving the most marginalized segments of the community at the periphery of the celebrations. The experiences of trans persons, disabled, neurodivergent persons, racialized persons, as well as working-class persons at Pride Events are often stressful and exclusionary. This reality should persuade us to scrutinize not only how inclusive these events truly are, but also what kind of politics foregrounds their organization, and what kind of intersectional alliances are crucial to achieve LGBTQIA+ liberation.

Another window into the richness of Pride Events as a social phenomenon is represented by their multiplication in both rural and peripheral locales. This exponential multiplication offers a haven for otherwise isolated individuals and communities and calls for growing opportunities for richer and more nuanced analysis of these phenomena across different scales. In places where they have been established for a long time, such as cities and metropoles around the world, these events are growing in magnitude in an exponential manner, attracting hundreds of thousands, and sometimes millions, of participants. While this success of Pride Events represents an exciting phenomenon that allows an ever-growing number of LGBTQIA+ persons to find their own voice and community, we should adopt a more critical outlook on the ways in which these events are conceptualized, created, promoted, and managed. Pride Events, in fact, do not just merely reflect the social realities of LGBTQIA+ persons around the world, but they actively produce ideas about community, solidarity, inclusion, leisure, as well as social and political participation. The process of 'mythologization' of the 1969 Stonewall Riots by activists, academics, and the media, for instance, has led to the emergence of a single narrative about the origins of the contemporary global LGBTQIA+ movement, one that is rooted in an Anglo-American model of LGBTQIA+ activism, and subordinates the emergence of any other LGBTQIA+ liberation movement, particularly those located in the Global South, to this particular foundational moment. Bringing to the surface alternative histories of LGBTQIA+ movements around the world beyond the mould of 'the Stonewall Riots' is essential not just to pluralize the epistemologies of LGBTQIA+ politics and social movements, but also to prevent the elevation of a Western narrative on LGBTQIA+ protest above others across geographical contexts.

Simultaneously, the exponential success of Pride Events around the world, and their growing interpretation as illustrations of the progress made in the field of LGBTQIA+ rights (Ammaturo 2016b; Slootmaeckers 2017), has also meant that Pride Events are increasingly seen, by a variety of actors, as a vehicle and catalyst for sexual and gender 'modernization'. Pride organizers, NGOs, international organizations, as well as some national governments, may perceive the organization of Pride Events as an illustration of the good (or encouraging) 'track record' on LGBTQIA+ rights of a specific country or region. While it is undeniable that the organization of Pride Events brings positive developments for LGBTQIA+ communities, this development is potentially worrisome, as it can represent a very effective tool in the creation and promotion of homonationalist narratives (Puar 2007; Ammaturo 2016b; Woori 2018) that articulate the role of Western democracies as needing to 'civilize' not-so-queer-friendly countries.

With this book I want to equally reinstate the importance of Pride Events as key moments of joy, rage, empowerment, and action for LGBTQIA+ persons around the world without unnecessarily romanticizing them as these 'mythical' or 'mythologizable' phenomena. This represents an invitation for Pride organizers, activists, institutional and non-institutional actors, as well as LGBTQIA+ persons and communities more generally, to avoid taking the history, meanings, and role of Pride Events for granted, but to continuously interrogate why these events are needed, how they can best serve the communities in which they take place, and how we can prevent them from being cannibalized by capitalistic and neoliberal forces that seek to transform them into marketable products. Furthermore, this analysis also aims to address and discuss the shortcomings and the challenges that are ubiquitous in the organization of Pride Events around the world today, in order to offer food for thought to all those who are invested in the success of Pride Events and recognize the importance of these gatherings for the creation of meaningful intersectional and cross-movements alliances, particularly in light of the rise of trans/homophobic right-wing and populist politics around the world.

At no point does this analysis seek to single out the choices of activists around the world who overcome several obstacles in creating events for their communities. We should, instead, situate these individual choices, and their consequences, in the broader landscape of capitalist, neoliberal, and institutional constraints that often place Pride organizers in impossible positions in relation to the acquisition of financial, organizational, and logistical resources to carry out their activities and activism. Pride organizers operate in difficult, often stigmatizing and criminalizing environments. They are also increasingly pushed to act or organize in the guise of 'events management' companies, with the obvious repercussions that these models bring with them.

Rethinking the futures of Pride Events beyond growth and modernity

Pride organizers face serious challenges around the world in relation to their activism, although the relevance and urgency of these challenges may significantly vary depending on the local context. The existence of these challenges is directly connected with the pressures for these events to become 'bigger and better' and directly interrogate what I have called the 'Kaleidoscope Modernities' of Pride Events. Pride Events are not just polysemic (Joseph 2010: 303), holding and expressing various meanings and significance for both organizers and participants, but also crucially multidimensional, insofar as they require an engagement with social, economic, and political actors that participate to the creation, negotiation, and implementation of organizational plans, such as grassroots groups, political and institutional actors, the police and criminal justice system, corporate and economic actors, as well as oppositional forces within civil societies, such as violent or non-violent counter-protesters.

Pride organizers everywhere around the world are faced with the reality of hostile policies and discourses that seek to undermine efforts to recognize the rights of LGBTQIA+ persons, both in countries in which these legal protections have been achieved, as well as in those where this has not been the case. Many organizers interviewed for this research highlight the violence and personal dangers that they have experienced in organizing their events, including being arrested, as well as the hostility of counter-protesters that have, in some cases, openly attacked participants in these events, putting them in physical and psychological danger. As the rise of global *anti-gender politics* (Sosa 2021; Ayoub and Stoeckl 2024; O'Dwyer 2024) shows, Pride organizers often operate in environments in which anti-LGBTQIA+ hostility is well-orchestrated and well-funded and, unfortunately, often politically effective.

This means that alliances across social movements (disabled, anti-racist, feminist, environmental, and so on), as well as stronger solidarity between the different segments of the LGBTQIA+ acronym, are more important than ever to resist these transphobic and homophobic attacks, including forms of transphobia still rooted within the LGBTQIA+ community itself, such as the presence of so-called 'TERFs' (Trans-Exclusionary Radical Feminists) (Pearce et al 2020). Despite the possibility of their co-optation for homonationalist purposes (Ammaturo 2016b), human rights represent one of the main drivers and 'discursive frames' (Bennett 2017: 349) that motivate Pride organizers to create their events, and they function as a catalyst for Pride organizers to create safe and empowering spaces for participants. The worrying trend spreading across the globe that highlights the expendability of LGBTQIA+ rights in favour of nationalist, populist, and right-wing narratives, shows that Pride Events need to centre human rights ever more crucially if they want to succeed to effect that social change that they seek to obtain across different latitudes.

Centring human rights, however, should not be understood as a request to fulfil a sort of 'tick box' exercise of legislative measures to be adopted in a specific country. Countless times, these provisions have been approved and never fully implemented. The type of human rights advocacy needed at Pride Events, is one that builds solidarity not just across the different letters of the LGBTQIA+ acronym, but also – crucially! – across movements and other sectors of civil society. It is a cultural discourse of human rights, rather than just a legal one, that needs to be mobilized through and across Pride Events.

In times of so-called 'culture wars' it would be tempting to suppress internal conflicts and confrontations within the LGBTQIA+ movement, to minimize the vulnerabilities that can be exploited by those who seek to undermine the rights of these communities. For their own nature, however, Pride Events are inherently conflictual in nature (Ghaziani 2008). This fact partly clashes with the rosy and mythologized narrative of the Stonewall Riots and can often makes us uncomfortable. As the marginalization of key figures of the US LGBTQIA+ movement such as Marsha P. Johnson or Sylvia Rivera from the historiography of the Stonewall Riots, or the current attempts to erase the lives and experiences of trans people from the LGBTQIA+ history show, the genesis of the LGBTQIA+ movement, and more specifically of Pride Events, has always been characterized by divisions, forms of discrimination towards some segments of the LGBTQIA+ community (such as racialized persons, trans people, or disabled and neurodivergent persons), and overwhelming attention to the needs of cisgender gay men. These conflicts are also connected to the increasing professionalization (Butterfield 2016) of Pride organizers, that make grassroots LGBTQIA+ groups, as well as participants, feel alienated from an event that should represent them. Confronting these divisions within the movements, and in the context of the organization of and participation in Pride Events, means to confront other scourges that crisscross our communities: white supremacy, classism, ableism, misogyny, and other forms of subjugation that all too often reproduce forms of domination that should be dismantled.

The rise of alternatives to mainstream Pride Events represents a dialectical effort to confront the idiosyncrasies of LGBTQIA+ movements that very often prefer to escape or underplay the existence of conflicts, rifts, or fractures within the movement itself. The existence of trans-exclusionary discourses within LGBTQIA+ movements, and the subsequent call to 'drop' trans persons to pursue a mythical form of 'LGB' liberation, represent a worrying signal of a form of reactionary politics based on an antagonistic vision of what it means to share an identity with others and to be demarcated from others precisely because of this very identity. The rise of Alternative Pride Events, often centring a much more politically progressive platform than 'mainstream' events; the multiplication of Pride Events held in peripheral or rural locales, partly as a polemical response to the corporatization of 'mainstream' Pride Events in big cities; as well as the growing hostility towards the participation of military and/or police forces to the events in their professional capacity – particularly given the threat that these actors represent for the most marginalized segments of the LGBTQIA+ community, such as racialized persons and/or trans persons – offers a partial antidote to these reactionary temptations. Analysing and understanding the conflictual nature of Pride Events, rather than painting a rosy picture for the benefit of a heteronormative crowd, is crucial if LGBTQIA+ movements want to build lasting strategies to counter homophobia and transphobia, as well as taking seriously intersectional challenges existing in their communities in relation to issues such as racism, poverty, or ableism, to name a few.

Equally urgent for the construction of truly emancipatory LGBTQIA+ movements centred on the organization of Pride Events is the issue of the corporatization and commodification of Pride Events (Peterson et al 2018b). Across the world, we see a growing number of Pride Events being sponsored by multinational corporations, including banks, global consultancy firms, clothing brands, brands producing alcoholic and non-alcoholic beverages, weapons manufacturers, companies working in the fossil fuel sector, as well as other corporate actors with abhorrent industrial practices, such as those directly or indirectly supporting wars, conflicts, and genocide. These same corporations nonchalantly drop their sponsorships and commitment to DEI (Diversity, Equity, Inclusion) when the political climate no longer favours these types of 'performative' initiatives. In this book I address the difficult balance that Pride organizers need to strike between wanting to fund their event and provide the best experience to their communities, and protecting their ethical values, particularly when controversial sponsors are involved.

The corporatization of Pride Events represents a Gordian knot for Pride organizers as one of the most controversial issues in relation to the global and local politics of Pride Events, as discussed by many participants to this research. This sort of 'necessary evil', however, has the potential of alienating huge portions of the LGBTQIA+ community, who often see in these sponsorships a contradiction with the social justice values that they embrace. The question of whether Pride Events should endlessly grow, to persuade opponents of the validity and strength of their claims, is at the heart of the conundrum relating to the corporatization and commodification of Pride Events. A provocative call to 'de grow' Pride Events, such as the one made in this book, is effectively an invitation to meditate on what Pride Events have become and for whom, particularly through the increasing reliance on corporate funding. The question I ask is whether we can truly march behind the trucks of these sponsors at Pride Events, while they poison the environment, practise modern slavery for the creation of their goods, or finance weapons used in the commission of a genocide, such as in the case of Palestine.

Embracing the Kaleidoscope Modernities of Pride Events

As discussed across different sections and chapters of the book, issues of diversity and inclusion of different segments of the LGBTQIA+ community are still pressing, with some groups increasingly looking to organize their own events, separate from 'mainstream' Pride Events, to create a more welcoming and inclusive environment. This is the case, for instance, for Black Pride, Latino Pride, and Trans Pride, to name a few. In this context, Pride organizers face a big issue relating to the true inclusion of disabled and neurodiverse persons at Pride Events. While, increasingly, accessibility policies are created by these organizers, addressing how disabled and neurodiverse persons can access the events, inclusion is often performative, rather than substantial, leaving many disabled and neurodiverse persons still feeling excluded from the celebrations. In the book I highlight the need and urgency to bring the question of the participation of disabled and neurodivergent persons to the centre of the politics of Pride Events, in order to truly create transformative and empowering events for all members of the LGBTQIA+ community, rather than just able-bodied ones. This challenge faced by Pride organizers is one that really shows how difficult it is to truly create a Pride Event that caters for all segments of the LGBTQIA+ community and can foster an agenda based on social justice issues, rather than becoming prey to easy temptations to make events just 'bigger and better' (but for whom?). Ultimately, disability justice at Pride Events is an issue of LGBTQIA+ justice, as compulsory heterosexuality and compulsory able-bodiedness, as

McRuer (2008) discusses, mutually reinforce each other, and both create the terrain for the oppression of those who do not conform to the 'norm', be they LGBTQIA+ and/or disabled or neurodivergent persons.

Another challenge for Pride organizers that has, so far, gone largely unnoticed, is the question of environmental sustainability at Pride Events, as well as the refusal to engage with corporate sponsors that are contributing, directly or indirectly, to climate change, and seek to 'pinkwash' their reputation by giving contributions to Pride Events. Climate change undeniably represents the biggest challenge for humanity in the years to come, and progressive movements, such as the LGBTQIA+ movements, need to engage seriously with an ecological politics that does not just wink at sustainable practices, but seriously considers the alternatives to the devastation caused by humans. In this book I argue that keeping on dancing and singing while the *Titanic* is sinking – in this case while the world's climate is collapsing – is not a viable option anymore and that the effects of climate change, both on LGBTQIA+ persons and on the world in general, should become a key preoccupation for Pride organizers too. Crucially, as some Pride participants have been chanting, there is 'No Pride on a Dead Planet' and it is imperative that Pride organizers acknowledge and assume their role in helping their communities understand the magnitude of the challenge ahead, one that can be addressed only through concerted collective action, rather than through individualistic pursuit.

This book is unique in the way in which it adopts a broad perspective on a multidimensional phenomenon such as Pride Events at the global level, while also acknowledging and exploring local specificities. I believe that this approach, together with the wide geographical coverage chosen for the interviews, as well as the intentional methodological decision of pluralizing both my sources and my empirical material beyond the English language (focusing in particular on Spanish, French, Portuguese, and Italian), offers us an opportunity to reflect on how we construct and circulate knowledge about LGBTQIA+ movements around the world beyond the hegemonic Anglo-American canon. Of course, I am aware that Spanish, French, Portuguese, and Italian are still languages that are connected with colonial and imperial exploitation, but I believe that in the context of academia, which is dominated by the English language, bringing to the forefront knowledge produced in non-hegemonic languages in the academic field has huge epistemological potential in forcing us to get out of our comfort zone when we think about LGBTQIA+ movements and Pride Events. I hope that this book encourages others to produce and circulate knowledge about Pride Events that draws from a vast array of languages, to analyse Pride Events in a truly inclusive, innovative, and comprehensive manner. Furthermore, I am convinced that more needs to be done in this regard in the context of LGBTQIA+ studies, which still suffer from this Western-centric bias, and sideline the knowledge produced by marginalized segments of the community, such as racialized persons, trans people, and disabled persons. I hope the book contributes to the conversation on how to make Pride Events more inclusive beyond tokenistic temptations and practices.

Ultimately, the main contribution of this book resides in the intention to affirm the political nature of Pride Events and the need to place these multiple, multifaceted and often conflictual and contradictory events at the heart of contemporary LGBTQIA+ politics. As the biggest public gatherings for LGBTQIA+ persons around the world, and one of the biggest manifestations of collective power, Pride Events play a crucial role in helping us to reimagine a more socially just and equitable future. This move can only happen if we disentangle Pride Events from the linear narrative of Western modernity, and we recognize that these events give rise to their multifarious, multidirectional 'Kaleidoscope Modernities' across geo-political spaces.

Furthermore, in order to centre Pride Events as key sites of progressive and transformative collective politics, both in the Global North and in the Global South, we need to critically interrogate the mythology of the founding origin of the Stonewall Riots, by adopting a truly inclusive epistemological approach to the study of Pride Events beyond the Anglo-American canon, one that contributes to the ongoing and never-ending project of decolonizing our knowledge on sexual and gender diversity around the world, including in relation to LGBTQIA+ social movements.

Furthermore, although they may be attractive, corporatization, commodification, militarization, and political co-optation of Pride Events represent real threats to the ongoing success of a social movement that requires more grassroots engagement, rather than just glitter and branded vodka-sponsored gadgets, to achieve social justice for LGBTQIA+ persons at the crossroads of different personal and social positionings. While the local and global challenges faced by Pride organizers around the world are varied, and they also often reflect the political legacies of colonial, genocidal, and capitalistic violence and exploitation, the very fact of taking the streets as visibly LGBTQIA+ represents an act of political courage and defiance that should never be taken for granted, together with the possible risks and threats that it may pose to the most vulnerable within the community. For this reason, I hope that this books encourages everyone to imagine and pursue a politics of Pride Events that is fuelled by joyful rage, one that manages to be playful and celebratory, but at the same time is ignited by the awareness of the historical injustices endured by many, both within and outside the LGBTQIA+ community, and refuses to become hostage of oppressing corporate and institutional forces that seek to domesticate an urgent request and need for dignity, respect, and a truly equitable future for everyone.

References

Agha, Z. (2017). Always Coca-Cola: Why environmental exploitation should be included in the legal construction of international crimes. *Amsterdam Law Forum*, *9*: 104–114.

Altay, T. (2022). The pink line across digital publics: political homophobia and the queer strategies of everyday life during COVID-19 in Turkey. *European Journal of Women's Studies*, *29*(1_suppl): 60S–74S.

Altman, D. (1982). *The Homosexualization of America: The Americanization of the Homosexual*. St Martin's Press.

Altman, D. (1996). Rupture or continuity? The internationalization of gay identities. *Social Text*, (48): 77–94.

Altman, D. (1997). Global gaze/global gays. *GLQ: A Journal of Lesbian and Gay Studies*, *3*(4): 417–436.

Ammaturo, F.R. (2015). The 'pink agenda': questioning and challenging European homonationalist sexual citizenship. *Sociology*, *49*(6): 1151–1166.

Ammaturo, F.R. (2016a). Spaces of pride: a visual ethnography of gay pride parades in Italy and the United Kingdom. *Social Movement Studies*, *15*(1): 19–40.

Ammaturo, F.R. (2016b). *European Sexual Citizenship: Human Rights, Bodies and Identities*. Springer.

Ammaturo, F.R. (2019). 'The more South you go, the more frankly you can speak': metronormativity, critical regionality and the LGBT movement in Salento, South-Eastern Italy. *Current Sociology*, *67*(1): 79–99.

Ammaturo, F.R. (2023). Pride Events in the periphery between hyper-localisation and hyper-contextualisation: a comparison between Italy and the UK. *Journal of Policy Research in Tourism, Leisure and Events*, *15*(2): 224–239.

Ammaturo, F.R. and Burchiellaro, O. (2021). The Queer House Party: Solidarity and LGBTQI+ Community-making in Pandemic Times. In Hughes, T., Adams, L., Obijiaku, C. and Smith, G. (eds) *Democracy in a Pandemic: Participation in Response to Crisis*. University of Westminster Press, pp 83–89.

Ammaturo, F.R. and Slootmaeckers, K. (2024). The unexpected politics of ILGA-Europe's rainbow maps: (de)constructing queer utopias/dystopias. *European Journal of Politics and Gender*, *1*(aop): 1–23.

Amnesty International Press Release (2021). Georgia: the authorities' failure to protect Tblisi Pride once again encourages violence. Amnesty International, 5 July 2021. Available at: www.amnesty.org/en/latest/press-release/2021/07/georgia-the-authorities-failure-to-protect-tbilisi-pride-once-again-encourages-violence/, last accessed 18 July 2024.

Anantharaman, M. (2022). Is it sustainable consumption or performative environmentalism? *Consumption and Society*, *1*(1): 120–143.

Andrews, J., Fay, R. and White, R. (2018). From linguistic preparation to developing a translingual mindset: Possible implications of plurilingualism for researcher education. In *Plurilingualism in Teaching and Learning* Routledge, pp 220–237.

Andrews, E.E., Ayers, K.B., Brown, K.S., Dunn, D.S. and Pilarski, C.R. (2021). No body is expendable: medical rationing and disability justice during the COVID-19 pandemic. *American Psychologist*, *76*(3): 1–11.

Araque Barboza, F.Y., Méndez Jiménez, A.G., Silvera Mishell, C. and Cabana Diazgranados, C. (2023). Comunidad LGBTIQ+ en un contexto Rural y la Felicidad en tiempos de Pandemia. *Anduli: Revista andaluza de ciencias sociales*, 23: 1–18.

Armitage, L. (2020). Explaining backlash to trans and non-binary genders in the context of UK Gender Recognition Act reform. *INSEP–Journal of the International Network for Sexual Ethics and Politics*, *8*(SI): 5–6.

Armstrong, E.A. (2002). *Forging Gay Identities: Organizing Sexuality in San Francisco, 1950–1994*. University of Chicago Press.

Armstrong, E.A. and Crage, S.M. (2006). Movements and memory: the making of the Stonewall myth. *American Sociological Review*, *71*(5): 724–751.

Arondekar, A. (2020). The sex of history, or object/matters. *History Workshop Journal*, *89*: 207–213.

Ayoub, P.M. (2013). Cooperative transnationalism in contemporary Europe: Europeanization and political opportunities for LGBT mobilization in the European Union. *European Political Science Review*, *5*(2): 279–310.

Ayoub, P.M. and Stoeckl, K. (2024). *The Global Fight Against LGBTI Rights: How Transnational Conservative Networks Target Sexual and Gender Minorities*. New York University Press.

Ayoub, P.M., Page, D. and Whitt, S. (2021). Pride amid prejudice: the influence of LGBT+ rights activism in a socially conservative society. *American Political Science Review*, *115*(2): 467–485.

Azzarello, R. (2016). *Queer Environmentality: Ecology, Evolution, and Sexuality in American Literature*. Routledge.

Babu, D. (2022). Perceptions of LGBTQ elders of color on the Black Lives Matter (BLM) movement and policing. *Journal of Black Sexuality and Relationships*, *8*(3): 69–91.

Bacchetta, P. (2002). Rescaling transnational 'queerdom': lesbian and 'lesbian' identitary-positionalities in Delhi in the 1980s. *Antipode*, *34*(5): 947–973.

Baez, R. (2019). Why we need 'Reclaim Pride'. *The Gay & Lesbian Review Worldwide*, 26(3): 22–26.

Banet-Weiser, S. and Glatt, Z. (2023). 'Stop treating BLM like Coachella': The Branding of Intersectionality. In Nash, J.C. and Pinto, S. (eds) *The Routledge Companion to Intersectionalities*. Routledge, pp 499–511.

Barnartt, S.N. (2008). Social movement diffusion? The case of disability protests in the US and Canada. *Disability Studies Quarterly*, 28(1).

Barnartt, S.N. and Scotch, R.K. (2001). *Disability Protests: Contentious Politics 1970–1999*. Gallaudet University Press.

Barnes, C. and Oliver, M. (1993). *Disability: A Sociological Phenomenon Ignored by Sociologists*. University of Leeds.

Barreto, D.M. (2020). Arde Galicia: o 'agrocuir' en contra da metronormatividade do 'queer'. *Madrygal: Revista de Estudios Gallegos*, 23: 15–26.

Barthes, R. (2009). *Mythologies*. Vintage.

Baxi, U. (2007). *The Future of Human Rights*. Oxford University Press.

BBC News (2021). India's top court puts controversial farm laws on hold. *BBC News*, 12 January. Available at: www.bbc.co.uk/news/world-asia-india-55615482, last accessed 18 July 2024.

Beckh, P. and Limmer, A. (2022). The Fridays for Future Phenomenon. In Wilderer, P.A., Grambow, M., Molls, M. and Oexle, K. (eds) *Strategies for Sustainability of the Earth System*. Springer, pp 427–432.

Beemyn, B. (2013). *Creating a Place for Ourselves: Lesbian, Gay, and Bisexual Community Histories*. Routledge.

Bell, D. and Binnie, J. (2004). Authenticating queer space: citizenship, urbanism and governance. *Urban Studies*, 41(9): 1807–1820.

Bell, D. and Valentine, G. (1995). Queer country: rural lesbian and gay lives. *Journal of Rural Studies*, 11(2): 113–122.

Belmont, F. and Ferreira, A.Á. (2020). Global South perspectives on Stonewall after 50 years, Part II—Brazilian Stonewalls: radical politics and lesbian activism. *Contexto Internacional*, 42: 685–703.

Benford, R.D. and Snow, D.A. (2000). Framing processes and social movements: an overview and assessment. *Annual Review of Sociology*, 26(1): 611–639.

Bengry, J. (2020). Who is the Queer Consumer? Historical Perspectives on Capitalism and Homosexuality. In Crowley, M., Dawson, S. and Rappaport, E. (eds) *Consuming Behaviours: Identity, Politics and Pleasure in Twentieth-Century Britain*. Routledge, pp 21–36.

Bennett, S. (2017). Whose line is it anyway? The diffusion of discursive frames in Pride movements of the South. *Journal of Language and Politics*, 16(3): 345–366.

Bennett, S.L. (2024). The commodification of feminism: a critical analysis of neoliberal feminist discourse. *Studies in Social Science & Humanities*, 3(5): 47–57.

Berg, E. (2024). From silence to Pride? A feminist visual narrative analysis of the Swedish Armed Forces' Pride campaigns. *Media, War & Conflict*, 1–19 (aop).

Bernieri Ponce, E. and Larreche, J.I. (2021). Descentrar para (re) mediar: las Marchas del Orgullo en las no metrópolis argentinas. *QUID 16. Revista del Área de Estudios Urbanos*, (15): 158–178.

Bernstein, M. (1997). Celebration and suppression: the strategic uses of identity by the lesbian and gay movement. *American Journal of Sociology*, *103*(3): 531–565.

Bethke, F.S. and Wolff, J. (2020). COVID-19 and shrinking civic spaces: patterns and consequences. *Zeitschrift für Friedens-und Konfliktforschung*, *9*(2): 363–374.

Bezgrebelna, M., McKenzie, K., Wells, S., Ravindran, A., Kral, M., Christensen, J., et al (2021). Climate change, weather, housing precarity, and homelessness: a systematic review of reviews. *International Journal of Environmental Research and Public Health*, *18*(11), 5812.

Bhambra, G.K. (2007). *Multiple Modernities or Global Interconnections: Understanding the Global Post the Colonial*. In Karagiannis, N. and Wagner, P. (eds) *Varieties of World-making: Beyond Globalization* (Vol. 14). Liverpool University Press, pp 59–73.

Bhambra, G.K. (2023). *Rethinking Modernity: Postcolonialism and the Sociological Imagination*. Springer Nature.

Bilić, B. (2016). Europe ♥ Gays? Europeanisation and Pride Parades in Serbia. In Bilić, B. (ed) *LGBT Activism and Europeanisation in the Post-Yugoslav Space: On the Rainbow Way to Europe*. Palgrave, pp 117–153.

Binnie, J. (2016). Critical queer regionality and LGBTQ politics in Europe. *Gender, Place & Culture*, *23*(11): 1631–1642.

Bitman, N. (2023). 'Which part of my group do I represent?': disability activism and social media users with concealable communicative disabilities. *Information, Communication & Society*, *26*(3): 619–636.

Bliszczyk, A. (2024). 'Police simply don't belong at Pride': cops filmed punching, dragging Midsumma protestors. *Vice*, 7 February 2024. Available at: www.vice.com/en/article/bvjap4/midsumma-pride-march-police-violence-queer, last accessed 18 July 2024.

Bloom, P. and Rhodes, C. (2018). *CEO Society: The Corporate Takeover of Everyday Life*. Bloomsbury Publishing.

Blum, R. (2019). Stonewall at 50: whose movement is it anyway? *New Labor Forum*, *28*(3): 28–32.

Boellstorff, T. (2016). Some Notes on New Frontiers of Sexuality and Globalisation. In Aggleton, P., Boyce, P., Moore, H.L.L. and Parker, R. (eds) *Understanding Global Sexualities*. Routledge, pp 171–185.

Bosworth, M.L., Ayoubkhani, D., Nafilyan, V., Foubert, J., Glickman, M., Davey, C. and Kuper, H. (2021). Deaths involving COVID-19 by self-reported disability status during the first two waves of the COVID-19 pandemic in England: a retrospective, population-based cohort study. *The Lancet Public Health*, *6*(11): 817–825.

REFERENCES

Bowen, F. (2014). *After Greenwashing: Symbolic Corporate Environmentalism and Society.* Cambridge University Press.

Bowling, B. and Westenra, S. (2020). 'A really hostile environment': adiaphorization, global policing and the crimmigration control system. *Theoretical Criminology*, 24(2): 163–183.

Boyce, P. and Dasgupta, R.K. (2017). Utopia or Elsewhere: Queer Modernities in Small Town West Bengal. In Kuldova, T. and Varghese, M.A. (eds) *Urban Utopias: Excess and Expulsion in Neoliberal South Asia.* Springer, pp 209–225.

Boyd, N.A. (2003). *Wide-open Town: A History of Queer San Francisco to 1965.* University of California Press.

Bracke, S. (2012). From 'saving women' to 'saving gays': rescue narratives and their dis/continuities. *European Journal of Women's Studies*, 19(2): 237–252.

Braun, V. and Clarke, V. (2012). *Thematic Analysis.* American Psychological Association.

Bravmann, S. (1995). Queer historical subjects. *Radical Society*, 25(1): 47–68.

Bregain, G. (2013). An Entangled Perspective on Disability History: The Disability Protests in Argentina, Brazil and Spain, 1968–1982. In Barsch, S., Klein, A. and Verstraeten, P. (eds) *The Imperfect Historian: Disability Histories in Europe.* Peter Lang, np.

Briassoulis, H. (2000). Environmental Impacts of Tourism: A Framework for Analysis and Evaluation. In Briassoulis, H. and Van der Straaten, J. (eds) *Tourism and the Environment: Regional, Economic, Cultural and Policy Issues.* Springer Netherlands, pp 21–37.

Britt, L. and Heise, D. (2000). From shame to pride in identity politics. *Self, Identity, and Social Movements*, 5: 252–68.

Broad, K.L. (2017). Social movement intersectionality and re-centering intersectional activism. *Atlantis: Critical Studies in Gender, Culture & Social Justice/Études Critiques sur le Genre, la Culture, et la Justice*, 38(1).

Brown, S. (2024). Sustainable Pride. *The Inclusion Post*, 1 June. Available at: https://theinclusionpost.com/sustainable-pride/, last accessed 30 August 2024.

Browne, K. (2007). A party with politics? (Re) making LGBTQ Pride spaces in Dublin and Brighton. *Social & Cultural Geography*, 8(1): 63–87.

Browne, K. and Nash, C.J. (2014). Resisting LGBT rights where 'we have won': Canada and Great Britain. *Journal of Human Rights*, 13(3): 322–336.

Brownworth, V.A. (2019). LGBTQ disability and Pride: the case for inclusion. *Philadelphia Gay News*, 3 July 2019. Available at: https://epgn.com/2019/07/03/lgbtq-disability-and-pride-the-case-forinclusion/, last accessed 23 August 2024.

Brucker, D.L. (2020). Variations in poverty by family characteristics among working-age adults with disabilities. *Family Relations*, 69(4): 792–802.

Burchiellaro, O. (2023). *The Gentrification of Queer Activism: Diversity Politics and the Promise of Inclusion in London.* Policy Press.

Burchiellaro, O. (2024). A (queer) CEO society? Lesbians who tech and the politics of extra-ordinary homonormativity. *Sexualities, 27*(4): 998–1015.

Butterfield, N. (2016). *Discontents of Professionalisation: Sexual Politics and Activism in Croatia in the Context of EU Accession*. In Bilić, B. (ed) *LGBT Activism and Europeanisation in the Post-Yugoslav Space: On the Rainbow Way to Europe*. Palgrave Macmillan, pp 23–58.

Buyantueva, R. (2022). *The Emergence and Development of LGBT Protest Activity in Russia*. Springer.

Buyantueva, R. (2023). Russia's Authoritarian Conservatism and LGBT+ Rights. *Russian Analytical Digest, 300*: 2–5.

Camargos, M.D. (2018). O surgimento das Paradas LGBT no Brasil. In Green, J.N., Quinalha, R., Caetano, M. and Fernandes, M. (eds) *História do Movimento LGBT no Brasil*. Alameda, pp 421–434.

Cannamela, D., Mauriello, M. and Summer M. (eds) (2023). *Italian Trans Geographies*. State University of New York Press.

Capasso, V. (2019). Negra, favelada, lesbiana y feminista: activismo artístico y recursos estéticos en el espacio público: El caso de Marielle Franco. *Estudos em comunicação*, (29): 227–239.

Carastathis, A. (2014). The concept of intersectionality in feminist theory. *Philosophy Compass, 9*(5): 304–314.

Carastathis, A. (2016). *Intersectionality: Origins, Contestations, Horizons*. University of Nebraska Press.

Caratti, P. and Ferraguto, L. (2012). The Role of Environmental Issues in Mega-events Planning and Management Processes: Which Factors Count? In Hayes, G. and Karamichas, J. (eds) *Olympic Games, Mega-events and Civil Societies: Globalization, Environment, Resistance*. Palgrave Macmillan, pp 109–125.

Caro Romero, F.C.C. (2020). 'Ni Enfermos, ni Criminales, Simplemente Homosexuales': Las Primeras Conmemoraciones de los Disturbios de Stonewall en Colombia, 1978–1982. *Anuario Colombiano de Historia Social y de la Cultura, 47*(1): 201–229.

Caro Romero, F.C.C. (2023). Coming out collectively: the emotions of Latin-American homosexual liberation movements. *New Global Studies, 17*(2): 135–151.

Carolin, A. and Frenkel, R. (2019). Transnational imaginaries and the negotiation of sexual rights during the South African transition. *African Studies, 78*(4): 510–526.

Carter, D. (2004). *Stonewall: The Riots that Sparked the Gay Revolution*. Macmillan.

Carter, D. (2019). Exploding the myths of Stonewall. *Gay City News*, 27 June. Available at: https://gaycitynews.com/exploding-the-myths-of-stonewall/, last accessed 22 November 2023.

Case, R. (2013). *Events and the Environment*. Routledge.

Cavalcanti, C., Barbosa, R.B. and Bicalho, P.P.G. (2018). Os tentáculos da tarântula: Abjeção e necropolítica em operações policiais a travestis no Brasil pós-redemocratização. *Psicologia: Ciência e Profissão, 38*: 175–191.

Chakrabarty, D. (2011). The muddle of modernity. *The American Historical Review, 116*(3): 663–675.

Chang, S. (2014). The postcolonial problem for global gay rights. *Boston University International Law Journal, 32*(2): 309–354.

Chasin, A. (2000). *Selling Out: The Gay and Lesbian Movement Goes to Market*. Routledge.

Chauncey, G. (2008). *Gay New York: Gender, Urban Culture, and the Making of the Gay Male World, 1890–1940*. Hachette.

Cheded, M. and Skandalis, A. (2021). Touch and contact during COVID-19: insights from queer digital spaces. *Gender, Work & Organization, 28*: 340–347.

Chiang, H. and Wong, A.K. (2016). Queering the transnational turn: regionalism and queer Asias. *Gender, Place & Culture, 23*(11): 1643–1656.

Chisholm, K. (dir) (2016). *Pride Denied: Homonationalism and the Future of Queer Politics*. Media Education Foundation.

Cho, M. and Kim, K.M. (2022). Effect of digital divide on people with disabilities during the COVID-19 pandemic. *Disability and Health Journal, 15*(1): 101214.

Civicus Monitor. On the watchlist: LGBTQI+ EuroPride goes ahead at the last minute as journalists and LGBTQI+ activists attacked. Civicus Monitor, 22 September. Available at: https://monitor.civicus.org/explore/watchlist-lgbtqi-europride-goes-ahead-last-minute-journalists-and-lgbtqi-activists-attacked/, last accessed 16 May 2025.

Clare, E. (2015). *Exile and Pride: Disability, Queerness, and Liberation*. Duke University Press.

Cleminson, R. (2020). Stonewall and its legacy in Iberia. *History Workshop Journal, 89*: 214–219.

Coi, G. and Hernández-Morales, H. (2022). Disability rights activists fight for access to cities' Pride events. *POLITICO*, 16 June 2022. Available at: www.politico.eu/article/disability-rights-activist-lgbtq-pride-paradeevents-accessibility-cities-epoa/, last accessed 23 August 2024.

Collier, R.B. and Collier, D. (1991). *Shaping the Political Arena: Critical Junctures, the Labor Movement and Regime Dynamics in Latin America*. Princeton University Press.

Conlon, P. (2023). 'No Pride on a Dead Planet' protest takes place at Citi HQ in Dublin today. *Dublin People*, 20 June 2023. Available at: https://dublinpeople.com/news/environment/articles/2023/06/20/58597/, last accessed 2 September 2024.

Conner, C.T. and Okamura, D. (2022). Queer expectations: an empirical critique of rural LGBT+ narratives. *Sexualities, 25*(8): 1040–1057.

Conway, D. (2022). Whose lifestyle matters at Johannesburg Pride? The lifestylisation of LGBTQ+ identities and the gentrification of activism. *Sociology*, *56*(1): 148–165.

Conway, D. (2023). The politics of truth at LGBTQ+ Pride: contesting corporate Pride and revealing marginalized lives at Hong Kong Migrants Pride. *International Feminist Journal of Politics*, *25*(4): 734–756.

Conway, D. (2024). Conceptualising queer activist critiques of Pride in the Two-Thirds World: Queer activism and alternative Pride organising in South Africa, Mumbai, Hong Kong and Shanghai. *Sexualities*, (aop).

Conway, J.M. (2016). Modernity and the Study of Social Movements: Do We Need a Paradigm Shift? In Smith, J., Goodhart, M.E. and Manning, P. (eds) *Social Movements and World-system Transformation*. Routledge, pp 17–34.

Cram, E., Law, M.P. and Pezzullo, P.C. (2022). Cripping environmental communication: a review of eco-ableism, eco-normativity, and climate justice futurities. *Environmental Communication*, *16*(7): 851–863.

Crawford, P. (2015). *The Mafia and the Gays*. CreateSpace Independent Publishing Platform.

Croft, S. and Fraser, S. (2022). A scoping review of barriers and facilitators affecting the lives of people with disabilities during COVID-19. *Frontiers in Rehabilitation Sciences*, 2.

Cromwell, L.D. (2015). Vendor's Privilege: Adheret Visceribus Rei. *Louisiana Law Review*, *75*(4): 1165–1250.

Croucher, S. (2002). South Africa's democratisation and the politics of gay liberation. *Journal of Southern African Studies*, *28*(2): 315–330.

Cruz-Malavé, A. (2007). *Queer Latino Testimonio, Keith Haring, and Juanito Xtravaganza: Hard Tails*. Palgrave.

Cuellár, A. (2024). Entrevista: Aurélien Guilabert y la Lucha por la Justicia Ambiental y LGBTQ+. *Dialogue Earth*, 27 June 2024. Available at: https://dialogue.earth/es/justicia/justicia-ambiental-lgbtq-aurelien-guilabert/, last accessed 30 August 2024.

Currans, E. (2012). Claiming deviance and honoring community: creating resistant spaces in US dyke marches. *Feminist Formations*, *24*(1): 73–101.

D'Emilio, J. (1983). *Sexual Politics, Sexual Communities: The Making of a Homosexual Minority in the United States, 1940–1970*. Chicago University Press.

D'Emilio, J. (1992). *Making Trouble: Essays on Gay History, Politics, and the University*. Routledge.

D'Emilio, J. (2007). Capitalism and Gay Identity. In Parker, R. and Aggleton, P. (eds) *Culture, Society and Sexuality*. Routledge, pp 266–274.

da Costa Junior, J.V.L. (2022). Leitura de Pedro Lemebel sobre Stonewall (Ou algumas notas sobre homossexualidade, capitalismo e latinidade). *Caderno de Letras*, *42*: 165–177.

Damshenas, S. (2020). Nearly 100 Pride events have been cancelled due to coronavirus pandemic. *Gay Times*, 20 March. Available at: www.gaytimes.co.uk/life/nearly-100-pride-events-have-been-cancelled-due-to-coronavirus-pandemic/, last accessed 26 March 2024.

Davis, J.L. (2019). Refusing (mis) recognition: navigating multiple marginalization in the US two spirit movement. *Review of International American Studies*, *12*(1): 65–86.

Day, C.R. (2022). The rainbow connection: disrupting background affect, overcoming barriers and emergent emotional collectives at 'Pride in London'. *The British Journal of Sociology*, *73*(5): 1006–1024.

de Fatima Tranquilin-Silva, J. (2020). Corpos e belezas trans invadem a cidade: brechas desejantes de corpografias. *Revista de Antropologia da UFSCar*, *12*(2): 214–232.

de Freitas Netto, S.V., Sobral, M.F.F., Ribeiro, A.R.B. and Soares, G.R.D.L. (2020). Concepts and forms of greenwashing: a systematic review. *Environmental Sciences Europe*, *32*: 1–12.

de Jong, A. (2017). Unpacking Pride's commodification through the encounter. *Annals of Tourism Research*, *63*: 128–139.

DeGagne, A. (2020). Pinkwashing Pride Parades: The Politics of Police in LGBTQ2S spaces in Canada. In MacDonald, F. and Dobrowolsky, A. (eds) *Turbulent Times, Transformational Possibilities*. Toronto University Press, pp 258–281.

Delanty, G. (2016). Multiple Europes, multiple modernities: conceptualising the plurality of Europe. *Comparative European Politics*, *14*: 398–416.

Delatolla, A. (2020). Sexuality as a standard of civilization: historicizing (homo) colonial intersections of race, gender, and class. *International Studies Quarterly*, *64*(1): 148–158.

Della Porta, D. (2020). Protests as critical junctures: some reflections towards a momentous approach to social movements. *Social Movement Studies*, *19*(5–6): 556–575.

den Houting, J. (2020). Stepping out of isolation: autistic people and COVID-19. *Autism in Adulthood*, *2*(2): 103–105.

Depelteau, J. and Giroux, D. (2015). LGBTQ Issues as Indigenous Politics: Two-Spirit Mobilization in Canada. In Tremblay, M. (ed) *Queer Mobilizations: Social Movement Activism and Canadian Public Policy*. University of British Columbia Press, pp 64–81.

Dhoot, S. (2015). Pink Games on Stolen Land: Pride House and (Un)Queer Reterritorializations. In Walcott, R. (ed) *Disrupting Queer Inclusion: Canadian Homonationalisms and the Politics of Belonging*. University of British Columbia Press, pp 49–65.

Di Paola, M. (2024). Virtue, environmental ethics, nonhuman values, and anthropocentrism. *Philosophies*, *9*(1): 15–19.

Dixon, L. (2024). Illusive inclusion: destination-marketing, managing Gay Pride events and the problem with cosmopolitan inclusivity. *Tourism Management Perspectives, 51* (aop).

Dodds, R. and Graci, S. (2012). Greening of the Pride Toronto festival: lessons learned. *Tourism Culture & Communication, 12*(1): 29–38.

Domínguez Ruiz, I.E. (2019). Neither resistance nor commodification: Madrid's LGBT Pride as paradoxical mobilization. *Journal of Spanish Cultural Studies, 20*(4): 519–534.

Dommu, R. (2018). Anti-trans protestors invade London Pride parade and are allowed to lead. *Out Magazine*, 7 July. Available at: www.out.com/news-opinion/2018/7/07/anti-trans-protestors-invade-london-pride-parade-are-allowed-lead, last accessed 4 July 2024.

Donà, A. (2021). Radical right populism and the backlash against gender equality: the case of the Lega (Nord). *Contemporary Italian Politics, 13*(3): 296–313.

Duarte, B.M. and da Silva, D.M. (2023). Coletivo LGBT Sem Terra: o rural e os novos projetos de famílias homoparentais em assentamentos do MST em Minas Gerais, Brasil: Collective LGBT Sem Terra: the rural and the new projects of homoparental families in MST settlements in Minas Gerais, Brazil. *Simbiótica: Revista Eletrônica, 10*(2): 77–95.

Duberman, M. (2019). *Stonewall: The Definitive Story of the LGBTQ Rights Uprising that Changed America*. Penguin.

Duberman, M. and Kopkind, A. (1993). The night they raided Stonewall. *Grand Street*, (44): 120–147.

Duckett, C.C. (2021). Downtowns and diverted dollars: how the metronormativity narrative damages rural queer political organizing. *Tulane Journal of Law and Sexuality: A Review of Sexual Orientation and Gender Identity in the Law*, 30: 1–20.

Duffy, N. (2014). South Korea: Christian protesters disrupt Seoul Pride Festival. *PinkNews*, 8 June. Available at: www.thepinknews.com/2014/06/08/south-korea-christians-protesters-disrupt-seoul-pride-festival/, last accessed 4 July 2024.

Duggan, L. (2012). *The Twilight of Equality? Neoliberalism, Cultural Politics, and the Attack on Democracy*. Beacon Press.

Dussel, E. (1993). Eurocentrism and modernity (introduction to the Frankfurt Lectures). *boundary 2, 20*(3): 65–76.

Dutch News (2020). *Pride Board Resigns to Ensure 'Inclusive Celebration'*, Dutch News, 10 March 2020. Available at: www.dutchnews.nl/2020/03/pride-board-resigns-to-ensure-inclusive-celebration/, last accessed 10 November 2023.

Dutta, A. (2018). On queerly hidden lives: precarity and (in) visibility between formal and informal economies in India. *QED: A Journal in GLBTQ Worldmaking, 5*(3): 61–75.

Earth Day (2022). How to have an eco-friendly Pride. *Earth Day*, 8 June 2022. Available at: https://theinclusionpost.com/sustainable-pride/, last accessed 30 August 2024.

Edenborg, E. (2020). Visibility in Global Queer Politics. In Bosia, M.J., McEvoy, S. and Rahman, M. (eds) *The Oxford Handbook of Global LGBT and Sexual Diversity Politics*. Oxford University Press, pp 349–364.

Egner, J.E. (2019a). 'The disability rights community was never mine': neuroqueer disidentification. *Gender & Society*, *33*(1): 123–147.

Egner, J.E. (2019b). Hegemonic or queer? A comparative analysis of five LGBTQIA/disability intersectional social movement organizations. *Humanity & Society*, *43*(2): 140–178.

Eisenstadt, S.N. (2000). Multiple Modernities. *Daedalus*, *129*(1): 1–29.

Eisenstadt, S.N. (2002). Some Observations on Multiple Modernities. In Sachsenmaier, D., Eisenstadt, S.S.N. and Riedel, J. (eds) *Reflections on Multiple Modernities: European, Chinese and Other Interpretations*. Brill, pp 27–41.

Ejdus, F. and Božović, M. (2019). Europeanisation and indirect resistance: Serbian police and Pride Parades. *The International Journal of Human Rights*, *23*(4): 493–511.

Ekins, P. and Zenghelis, D. (2021). The costs and benefits of environmental sustainability. *Sustainability Science*, *16*: 949–965.

Eliason, M.J., Martinson, M. and Carabez, R.M. (2015). Disability among sexual minority women: descriptive data from an invisible population. *LGBT Health*, *2*(2): 113–120.

Ellis, K. and Kent, M. (eds) (2016). *Disability and Social Media: Global Perspectives*. Taylor & Francis.

Ellis, N.T. (2025). What is DEI, and why is it dividing America? *CNN*, 23 January. Available at: https://edition.cnn.com/2025/01/22/us/dei-diversity-equity-inclusion-explained/index.html, last accessed 26 February 2025.

Elshobake, M.R. (2022). Human rights violations during the COVID-19 pandemic. *International Journal of Human Rights in Healthcare*, *15*(4): 324–339.

Engebretsen, E.L. (2015). *On Pride and Visibility*. In Engebretsen, E.L. and Schroeder, W.F. (eds) *Queer/Tongzhi China: New Perspectives on Research, Activism and Media Cultures*. Nias Press, pp 89–110.

Enguix, B. (2009). Identities, sexualities and commemorations: Pride parades, public space and sexual dissidence. *Anthropological Notebooks*, *15*(2).

Enguix, B. (2017). Protest, market and identity in the LGTB Pride celebrations in Spain. *Convergencia*, *24*(73): 165–186.

Erazo-Gómez, A., Martínez-Carrillo, H. and Palta-Calambas, L.A. (2023). Entre la invisibilidad y la libertad: construir paz desde organizaciones LGBT en el norte del Cauca. *Revista CS*, (41): np.

Erevelles, N. and Morrow, M. (2023). Introduction: Intersectionality. In Rioux, M.H., Buettgen, A., Zubrow, E.B.W. and Viera, J. (eds) *Handbook of Disability: Critical Thought and Social Change in a Globalizing World*. Springer Nature Singapore, pp 1–24.

Escobar, A. (2007). Worlds and knowledges otherwise: the Latin American modernity/coloniality research program. *Cultural Studies*, 21(2–3): 179–210.

Esparza, R. (2017). Queering the homeland. *Feminist Formations*, 29(2): 147–176.

Espinosa, R.V. (2020). 50 años de orgullo. Un repaso escrito y visual por la historia del movimiento LGTBIQ+ en España. *Vínculos de Historia Revista del Departamento de Historia de la Universidad de Castilla-La Mancha*, (9): 475–497.

Etikan, I., Musa, S.A. and Alkassim, R.S. (2016). Comparison of convenience sampling and purposive sampling. *American Journal of Theoretical and Applied Statistics*, 5(1): 1–4.

Evans, D. (2013). *Sexual Citizenship: The Material Construction of Sexualities*. Routledge.

Evans, T.G. (2015). 'We are here and we will not be silenced': Sylvia Rivera, STAR, and the struggle for transgender rights, 1969–1974. *The Mellon Mays Undergraduate Fellowship Journal, 2015*: 29–32.

Evens, E., Lanham, M., Santi, K., Cooke, J., Ridgeway, K., Morales, G., et al (2019). Experiences of gender-based violence among female sex workers, men who have sex with men, and transgender women in Latin America and the Caribbean: a qualitative study to inform HIV programming. *BMC International Health and Human Rights*, 19: 1–14.

Eyerman, R. (2015). Social Movements and Memory. In Tota, A.L. and Hagen, T. (eds) *Routledge International Handbook of Memory Studies*. Routledge, pp 79–83.

Fankhauser, S. and McDermott, T.K. (2014). Understanding the adaptation deficit: why are poor countries more vulnerable to climate events than rich countries? *Global Environmental Change*, 27: 9–18.

Farris, S.R. (2017). *In the Name of Women's Rights: The Rise of Femonationalism*. Duke University Press.

Feinberg, L. (1999). *Trans Liberation: Beyond the Pink and Blue*. Beacon Press.

Financial Mirror (2022). Diplomats join fight for LGBTQI+ rights. *Financial Mirror*, 12 May. Available at: www.financialmirror.com/2022/05/12/diplomats-join-fight-for-lgbtqi-rights/, last accessed 3 April 2024.

Finkelstein, V. (1980). *Attitudes and Disabled and Neurodivergent People: Issues for Discussion* (No. 5). World Rehabilitation Fund, Incorporated.

Fish, J.N., McInroy, L.B., Paceley, M.S., Williams, N.D., Henderson, S., Levine, D.S. and Edsall, R.N. (2020). 'I'm kinda stuck at home with unsupportive parents right now': LGBTQ youths' experiences with COVID-19 and the importance of online support. *Journal of Adolescent Health*, 67(3): 450–452.

Formby, E. (2023). Exploring LGBT+ people's experiences of Pride events in the UK: contrasting safeties, celebrations, and exclusions. *lambda nordica*, *28*(2–3): np.

Foroni, C., Marcellino, M. and Stevanovic, D. (2022). Forecasting the COVID-19 recession and recovery: lessons from the financial crisis. *International Journal of Forecasting*, *38*(2): 596–612.

Forstie, C. (2020). Theory making from the middle: researching LGBTQ communities in small cities. *City & Community*, *19*(1): 153–168.

Foster, E. and Kerr, P. (2024). Queer/Green collaboration as a radical response to climate crises: foregrounding the Green Stripe. *Global Political Economy*, *3*(1): 73–91.

Foucault, M. (1990). *The History of Sexuality: An Introduction, Volume I*. Translated by Robert Hurley. Vintage.

Franke, K. (2012). Dating the state: the moral hazards of winning gay rights. *Columbia Human Rights Law Review*, *44*(1): 1–46.

Fremlova, L. (2022). *Queer Roma*. Taylor & Francis.

Gaard, G. (1997). Toward a queer ecofeminism. *Hypatia*, *12*(1): 114–137.

Gaard, G. (2021). Queering the Climate. In Pulé, P.M. and Hulltman, M. (eds) *Men, Masculinities, and Earth: Contending with the (m)Anthropocene*. Springer International, pp 515–536.

Gallón Salazar, A.M. (2023). 'El Futuro es Chueco': Brigitte Baptiste y el Ecologismo 'Queer' frente al Colapso Anunciado. *El País*, 26 March. Available at: https://elpais.com/america-futura/2023-03-26/el-futuro-es-chueco-brigitte-baptiste-y-el-ecologismo-queer-frente-al-colapso-anunciado.html#, last accessed 29 August 2024.

Galvin, R. (2003). The function of language in the creation and liberation of disabled and neurodivergent identities: from Saussure to contemporary strategies of government. *Australian Journal of Communication*, *30*(3): 83–100.

Galyon, K. (2023). *Somos qhariwarmis: La intersección del género y la indigenidad En el lenguaje de hablantes bilingües de Quechua y Español*. Doctoral dissertation, University of Georgia.

Gan, J. (2007). 'Still at the back of the bus': Sylvia Rivera's struggle. *Centro Journal*, *19*(1): 124–139.

Gansmo Jakobsen, T. (2017). Environmental ethics: anthropocentrism and non-anthropocentrism revised in the light of critical realism. *Journal of Critical Realism*, *16*(2): 184–199.

Gaona, M. and Ficoseco, V.S. (2015). Otros cuerpos y espacios en disputa: Cruces entre consignas globales y demandas históricas locales en la Marcha del Orgullo en una región de frontera argentina. *Revista Nomadias*, *20*: 211–226.

Garina, K. (2023). *Speech to EuroPride Human Rights Conference*. Available at: www.epoa.eu/kristine-garinas-speech-to-europride-human-rights-conference/, last accessed 4 April 2024.

Gauci, E. (2024). We need Pride Events that are accessible for all. *Diva Magazine*, June–July 2024, Issue 325.

Gavranovič, F. (2023). Reject modernity, embrace tradition: assessing the LGBTQI+ situation in Serbia and Republika Srpska. *Peace and Security Monitor: South-East Europe & Black Sea Region*, 8: 5.

Gayle, D. (2023a). British LGBT Awards drop sponsorship deals with Shell and BP. *The Guardian*, 22 June. Available at: www.theguardian.com/environment/2023/jun/22/british-lgbt-awards-drops-sponsorship-deals-with-shell-and-bp, last accessed 2 September 2023.

Gayle, D. (2023b). Joe Lycett backs out of award ceremony over fossil fuel links. *The Guardian*, 20 June. Available at: www.theguardian.com/culture/2023/jun/20/exclusive-joe-lycett-backs-out-award-ceremony-over-fossil-fuel-links, last accessed 2 September 2023.

Gelmini, S. (2021). We're living in the golden age of greenwashing. *Greenpeace*, 29 June. Available at: www.greenpeace.org.uk/news/golden-age-of-greenwash/, last accessed 29 August 2024.

Gevisser, M. and Reid, G. (2013). Pride or protest? Drag queens, comrades, and the Lesbian and Gay Pride March. In Cameron, E. and Gevisser, M. (eds) *Defiant Desire*. Routledge, pp 278–283.

Ghaziani, A. (2008). *The Dividends of Dissent: How Conflict and Culture Work in Lesbian and Gay Marches on Washington*. University of Chicago Press.

Ghaziani, A. (2021). People, protest and place: advancing research on the emplacement of LGBTQ+ urban activisms. *Urban Studies*, 58(7): 1529–1540.

Ghaziani, A. and Baldassarri, D. (2011). Cultural anchors and the organization of differences: a multi-method analysis of LGBT marches on Washington. *American Sociological Review*, 76(2): 179–206.

Ghaziani, A. and Fine, G.A. (2008). Infighting and ideology: how conflict informs the local culture of the Chicago Dyke March. *International Journal of Politics, Culture, and Society*, 20: 51–67.

Gill, R. (2000). Discourse analysis. *Qualitative Researching with Text, Image and Sound*, 1: 172–190.

Gill, M. and Schlund-Vials, C.J. (2016). Introduction: Protesting 'The Hardest Hit': Disability Activism and the Limits of Human Rights and Humanitarianism. In Gill, M. and Schlund-Vials, C.J. (eds) *Disability, Human Rights and the Limits of Humanitarianism*. Routledge, pp 1–14.

Girardi, R. (2022). 'It's easy to mistrust police when they keep on killing us': a queer exploration of police violence and LGBTQ+ victimization. *Journal of Gender Studies*, 31(7): 852–862.

Giulianotti, R. and Robertson, R. (2006). Glocalization, globalization and migration: the case of Scottish football supporters in North America. *International Sociology*, 21(2), 171–198.

Giwa, S., Colvin, R.A., Karki, K.K., Mullings, D.V. and Bagg, L. (2021). Analysis of 'Yes' responses to uniformed police marching in pride: perspectives from LGBTQ+ communities in St John's, Newfoundland and Labrador, Canada. *SAGE Open*, *11*(2): 1–16.

Go, J. (2013). For a postcolonial sociology. *Theory and Society*, *42*: 25–55.

Gold, M. (2019). Stonewall uprising: 50 years later, a celebration blends pride and resistance. *New York Times*, 28 June. Available at: www.nytimes.com/2019/06/28/nyregion/stonewall-inn-50-anniversary.html, last accessed 10 November 2023.

Goldberg, N.G., Mallory, C., Hasenbush, A., Stemple, L. and Meyer, I.H. (2019). Police and the Criminalization of LGBT People. In *The Cambridge Handbook of Policing in the United States*. Cambridge University Press, pp 374–391.

Goldstone, J.A. (2004). More social movements or fewer? Beyond political opportunity structures to relational fields. *Theory and Society*, *33*: 333–365.

Gonzalez, K. (2019). Stonewall's parallel Queer Latinidad. *Latin American, Caribbean, and U.S. Latino Studies Honors Program*. 6. Available at: https://scholarsarchive.library.albany.edu/lacs_honors/6, last accessed 22 November 2023.

Gonzalez, K.A., Abreu, R.L., Arora, S., Lockett, G.M. and Sostre, J. (2021). 'Previous resilience has taught me that I can survive anything': LGBTQ resilience during the COVID-19 pandemic. *Psychology of Sexual Orientation and Gender Diversity*, *8*(2): 133.

Goodley, D. (2014). *Dis/ability Studies: Theorising Disablism and Ableism*. Routledge.

Goodrow, G. (2018). Bipower, disability and capitalism: neoliberal eugenics and the future of ART regulation. *Duke Journal of Gender Law and Policy*, *26*(2): 137–156.

Gordon, A. (2005). The retrospective closet: adolescence and queer prehistory. *Historical Studies*, *36*(126): 315–331.

Gorecho, D. (2022). There is no Pride on a dead planet. *Business Mirror*, 29 June. Available at: https://t.co/H0kago7MGx, last accessed 2 September 2024.

Gorman-Murray, A., Pini, B. and Bryant, L. (2013). *Sexuality, Rurality and Geography*. Lexington Books.

Gossett, C., Gossett, R. and Lewis, A.J. (2011). Reclaiming our lineage: organized queer, gender-nonconforming, and transgender resistance to police violence. *S&F Online*, *10*.

Gray, M.L. (2009). *Out in the Country: Youth, Media, and Queer Visibility in Rural America* (Vol. 2). New York University Press.

Gray, M.L., Johnson, C.R. and Gilley, B.J. (eds) (2016). *Queering the Countryside: New Frontiers in Rural Queer Studies* (Vol. 11). New York University Press.

Greenberg, A. (2023). *Superfreaks: Kink, Pleasure, and the Pursuit of Happiness*. Beacon Press.

Greensmith, C. and Giwa, S. (2013). Challenging settler colonialism in contemporary queer politics: settler homonationalism, Pride Toronto, and two-spirit subjectivities. *American Indian Culture and Research Journal*, *37*(2): 129–148.

Greer, S. (2012). Pride and Shame: Developments in the Performance of Queer Protest. In *Contemporary British Queer Performance*. Palgrave Macmillan, pp 133–164.

Grewal, I. and Kaplan, C. (2001). Global identities: theorizing transnational studies of sexuality. *GLQ: A Journal of Lesbian and Gay Studies*, 7(4): 663–679.

Griffin, C.J. and McDonagh, B. (2018). *Remembering Protest in Britain since 1500: Memory, Materiality and the Landscape*. Springer International Publishing.

Griffiths, C. (2014). Between triumph and myth: gay heroes and navigating the schwule Erfolgsgeschichte. *Helden. Heroes. Héros. E-Journal zu Kulturen des Heroischen*, 1: 55–61.

Grotz, J., Dyson, S. and Birt, L. (2020). Pandemic policy making: the health and wellbeing effects of the cessation of volunteering on older adults during the COVID-19 pandemic. *Quality in Ageing and Older Adults*, *21*(4): 261–269.

Grzanka, P.R. (2020). From buzzword to critical psychology: an invitation to take intersectionality seriously. *Women & Therapy*, *43*(3–4): 244–261.

Gu, K. (2023). 퀴어 문화 축제 방해 잔혹사. *News & Joy*, 26 June. Available at: www.newsnjoy.or.kr/news/articleView.html?idxno=305443, last accessed 4 July 2024.

Guberman, J. (2023). # ActuallyAutistic Twitter as a site for epistemic resistance and crip futurity. *ACM Transactions on Computer-Human Interaction*, *30*(3): 1–34.

Guerrero, A. (2019). Cuba y la Guerra Fría del siglo XXI. *Foro Cubano-Divulgación*, *2*(11).

Guerrero, J.H.O., Soto, N.N.C., Ninanya, W.E.M. and Gerónimo, M.S.R. (2022). El fenómeno del feminicidio: una revisión sistemática. *Revista Latinoamericana de Derechos Humanos*, *33*(2): 129–144.

Gül Holzendorff, D. (2013). Living on the Coke side of thirst: The Coca-Cola Company and responsibility for water shortage in India. *Journal of European Management & Public Affairs Studies*, *1*(1): 1–4.

Gupta, A. (2006). Section 377 and the dignity of Indian homosexuals. *Economic and Political Weekly*, *41*(46): 4815–4823.

Gurok, K. (2022). *Smooth operators? Ambassadors' engagement in Pride parades*. Master's thesis. Available at: https://gupea.ub.gu.se/handle/2077/70405, last accessed 26 March 2024.

Habermas, J. and Ben-Habib, S. (1981). Modernity versus postmodernity. *New German Critique*, (22): 3–14.

Hafford-Letchfield, T., Toze, M. and Westwood, S. (2022). Unheard voices: a qualitative study of LGBT+ older people experiences during the first wave of the COVID-19 pandemic in the UK. *Health & Social Care in the Community*, *30*(4): 1233–1243.

Hagen-Smith, L. (1997). Politics and celebration: manifesting the rainbow flag. *Ethnologies*, *19*(2): 113–121.

Hákun Leo, J. (2018). New survey: the northeast is the Faroese Bible belt while Tórshavn is the secular cradle. *Local*, 15 February. Available at: https://local.fo/divided-islands-northerners-believe-personal-god-many-torshavners-dont/, last accessed 4 July 2024.

Halberstam, J.J. (2005). *In a Queer Time and Place: Transgender Bodies, Subcultural Lives* (Vol. 3). New York University Press.

Haller, B.A. (2017). Social Media Reinvigorates Disability Rights Activism Globally. In Tumber, H. and Waisbord, S.R. (eds) *The Routledge Companion to Media and Human Rights*. Routledge, pp 300–308.

Halperin, D.M. and Traub, V. (eds) (2009). *Gay Shame*. University of Chicago Press.

Halvorsen, S. (2015). Taking space: moments of rupture and everyday life in Occupy London. *Antipode*, *47*(2): 401–417.

Han, C.W. (2022). Gay Racism: The Institutional and Interactional Patterns of Racism in Gay Communities. In Fischer, N.L., Westbrook, L. and Seidman, S. (eds) *Introducing the New Sexuality Studies*. Routledge, pp 233–243.

Han, E. and O'Mahoney, J. (2018). *British Colonialism and the Criminalization of Homosexuality: Queens, Crime and Empire*. Routledge.

Hanes, R., Brown, I. and Hansen, N.E. (eds) (2018). *The Routledge History of Disability*. Routledge.

Hatfield, J.E. (2023). Stonewall forever: queer monumentality in the age of augmented reality. *Critical Studies in Mass Communication*, *41*(1): 7–20.

Hemsley, B., Darcy, S., Given, F., Murray, B.R. and Balandin, S. (2023). Going thirsty for the turtles: plastic straw bans, people with swallowing disability, and Sustainable Development Goal 14, Life Below Water. *International Journal of Speech-Language Pathology*, *25*(1): 15–19.

Hernández Mosquera, Y.G. (2015). *Movimientos (Trans) Feministas del Ecuador: El caso de la Marcha de la putas-Quito*. Bachelor's thesis. Available at: https://dspace.ups.edu.ec/bitstream/123456789/9895/1/QT07699.pdf, last accessed 18 June 2024.

Herndon, M. (2016). *Soy Moderno y No Quiero Locas: Modernity and LGBT(Queer) Perú*. Undergraduate Humanities Forum 2015–2015, University of Pennsylvania.

Herring, S. (2010). *Another Country: Queer Anti-Urbanism*. New York University Press.

Hilderbrand, L. (2023). *The Bars Are Ours: Histories and Cultures of Gay Bars in America, 1960 and After*. Duke University Press.

Hines, S. (2019). On Trans and Feminism. *The Routledge Handbook of Contemporary Feminism*. Routledge.

Hoad, N. (2018). Arrested Development or the Queerness of Savages: Resisting Evolutionary Narratives of Difference. In Mason, C.L. (ed) *Routledge Handbook of Queer Development Studies*. Routledge, pp 73–101.

Hoffman, S. (2008). Preparing for disaster: protecting the most vulnerable in emergencies. *UC Davis Law Review*, 42: 1491.

Holden, A. (2016). *Environment and Tourism*. Routledge.

Holmes, A. (2019). Exploring activist framing in Vancouver's uniformed police debate: should police march in Pride parades? *Sojourners*, 11: 1–23.

Holmes, A. (2021). Marching with Pride? Debates on uniformed police participating in Vancouver's LGBTQ Pride parade. *Journal of Homosexuality*, 68(8): 1320–1352.

Holmes, A. (2022). Resisting Pinkwashing: Adaptive Queerness in Vancouver Pride Parades. In Rodó-Zárate, M., Pitoňák, M., Ramdas, K. and Myrdahl, T.M. (eds) *Mapping LGBTQ Spaces and Places: A Changing World*. Springer International Publishing, pp 445–463.

Holmes, K. and Mair, J. (2020). Event Impacts and Environmental Sustainability. In Page, S.J. and Connell, J. (eds) *The Routledge Handbook of Events*. Routledge, pp 457–471.

Holt, L., Bowlby, S. and Lea, J. (2019). Disability, special educational needs, class, capitals, and segregation in schools: a population geography perspective. *Population, Space and Place*, 25(4): 1–11.

Holzberg, B., Madörin, A. and Pfeifer, M. (2022). The Sexual Politics of Border Control: An Introduction. In Holzberg, B., Madörin, A. and Pfeifer, M. (eds) *The Sexual Politics of Border Control*. Routledge, pp 1–22.

Horton, C. (2022). 'Of course, I'm intimidated by them. they could take my human rights away': trans children's experiences with UK gender clinics. *Bulletin of Applied Transgender Studies*, 1(1–2): 47–70.

Hossain, A. (2017). The paradox of recognition: hijra, third gender and sexual rights in Bangladesh. *Culture, Health & Sexuality*, 19(12): 1418–1431.

Howard, J. (2001). *Men Like That: A Southern Queer History*. University of Chicago Press.

Hrynyk, N. (2021). 'No sorrow, no pity': intersections of disability, HIV/AIDS, and gay male masculinity in the 1980s. *Disability Studies Quarterly*, 41(2).

Huang, S. (2019). Fifty years since Stonewall: beyond the borders of the United States. *QED: A Journal in GLBTQ Worldmaking*, 6(2): 69–75.

Hudley, A.H.C. (2016). Language and Racialization. In García, O. (ed) *The Oxford Handbook of Language and Society*. Oxford University Press, pp 381–402.

Human Rights Campaign (2023). HRC condemns Alabama governor for signing discriminatory anti-transgender sports ban; becomes state's second ban and fourth anti-LGBTQ+ law in two years. *Human Rights Campaign*, 30 May. Available at: www.hrc.org/press-releases/hrc-condemns-alabama-governor-for-signing-discriminatory-anti-transgender-sports-ban-becomes-states-second-sports-ban-and-fourth-anti-lgbtq-law-in-two-years, last accessed 2 July 2024.

ILGA World Database (2024). *Legal Frameworks: Criminalisation of Consensual Same-sex Acts*. Available at: https://database.ilga.org/criminalisation-consensual-same-sex-sexual-acts, last accessed 26 March 2024.

IMETAC (2024). Sexualidad, Diversidad Sexual y Discapacidad: una Intersección Invisibilizada. *IMETAC*. Available at: https://imetac.mx/2024/06/sexualidad-diversidad-sexual-y-discapacidad-una-interseccion-invisibilizada/, last accessed 23 August 2024.

Ingstad, B. (1990). The disabled and neurodivergent person in the community: social and cultural aspects. *International Journal of Rehabilitation Research*, 13(3): 187.

InterPride (2017). *2016–2017 Pride Radar Report*. Available at: www.interpride.org/prideradar/, last accessed 13 June 2024.

Invalid, S. (2016). *Skin, Tooth, and Bone: The Basis of Movement Is Our People: A Disability Justice Primer*. Self-published.

Iriarte, E.G., Mcconkey, R. and Gilligan, R.H. (eds) (2016). *Disability and Human Rights: Global Perspectives*. Macmillan Education.

Irvine, J.M. and Irvine, J.A. (2017). The queer work of militarized prides. *Contexts*, 16(4): 32–37.

Irwin, R.M. (2000). The famous 41: the scandalous birth of modern Mexican homosexuality. *GLQ: A Journal of Lesbian and Gay Studies*, 6(3): 353–376.

Ishak, R. (2021). A lack of accessibility in queer spaces rushes community pride. *Hello Giggles*, 9 June. Available at: https://hellogiggles.com/disabled and neurodivergentpeople-pride-events-lgbtq/, last accessed 23 August 2024.

Isufi, A. (2021). Kosovo Pride Parade hears calls for freedom, equality. *Balkan Insight*, 1 July. Available at: https://balkaninsight.com/2021/07/01/kosovo-pride-parade-hears-calls-for-freedom-equality/, last accessed 2 July2024.

Itakura, K. (2015). Making Japan 'out-and-proud' through not-yet-consensual translation: a case study of Tokyo Rainbow Pride's website. *Queer Cats Journal of LGBTQ Studies*, 1(1).

Jackson, J.P., Weidman, N.M. and Rubin, G. (2005). The origins of scientific racism. *The Journal of Blacks in Higher Education*, 50(50): 66–79.

Jaffee, L. and John, K. (2018). Disabling bodies of/and land: reframing disability justice in conversation with indigenous theory and activism. *Disability and the Global South*, 5(2): 1407–1429.

Janoff, D.V. (2022). *Queer Diplomacy: Homophobia, International Relations and LGBT Human Rights*. Palgrave Macmillan.

Jarrett, B.A., Peitzmeier, S.M., Restar, A., Adamson, T., Howell, S., Baral, S. and Beckham, S.W. (2021). Gender-affirming care, mental health, and economic stability in the time of COVID-19: a multi-national, cross-sectional study of transgender and nonbinary people. *PloS One*, 16(7): 1–17.

Jill-Peterson, J. (2023). Trans of Color Liberation: An Unauthorized History of the Future. In Nash, J.C. and Pinto, S. (eds) *The Routledge Companion to Intersectionalities*. Routledge, pp 325–334.

Johns Hopkins Bloomberg School of Public Health (2020). Inside Taiwan's Response to COVID-19. Available at: https://publichealth.jhu.edu/events/covid-19-events-and-briefings/inside-taiwans-response-to-covid-19, last accessed 25 July 2024.

Johnson, C.W. and Samdahl, D.M. (2005). 'The night they took over': misogyny in a country-western gay bar. *Leisure Sciences*, 27(4): 331–348.

Johnston, L. (2007a). Mobilizing pride/shame: lesbians, tourism and parades. *Social & Cultural Geography*, 8(1): 29–45.

Johnston, L. (2007b). *Queering Tourism: Paradoxical Performances of Gay Pride Parades*. Routledge.

Johnston, L. and Waitt, G. (2016). The Spatial Politics of Gay Pride Parades and Festivals: Emotional Activism. In Paternotte, D. and Tremblay, M. (eds) *The Ashgate Research Companion to Lesbian and Gay Activism*. Routledge, pp 105–120.

Jones, T. (2024). United States of hate: mapping backlash Bills against LGBTIQ+ youth. *Sex Education: Sexuality, Society and Learning*, 24(6): 816–835.

Jones, Z.C. (2021). Disability activists push for more inclusive Pride celebrations. *CBS News*, 29 June. Available at: www.cbsnews.com/news/disabilityactivists-push-for-more-inclusive-pride-celebrations/, last accessed 23 August 2024.

Joseph, L. (2010). *The production of Pride: institutionalization and LGBT Pride organizations*. Doctoral dissertation, State University of New York at Stony Brook.

Jukes, J. (2024). Toward Asexual Geographies: Void-Publics and Spaces of Refusal. In Cerankowski, K.J. and Milks, M. (eds) *Asexualities: Feminist and Queer Perspectives* (revised and expanded ten-years anniversary edition). Taylor & Francis, pp 181–196.

Kalitenko, O., Anikinar, G., Spasova, E. and Shahaka, O. (2021). The restrictions of the freedom of information during the COVID-19 pandemic. *Cuestiones Políticas*, 39(70): 426–445.

Kameny, F. (1965). Does research into homosexuality matter? *The Ladder*, 9(8): 14–20.

Kates, S.M. and Belk, R.W. (2001). The meanings of lesbian and gay pride day: resistance through consumption and resistance to consumption. *Journal of Contemporary Ethnography*, *30*(4): 392–429.

Katila, P., Colfer, C.J.P., De Jong, W., Galloway, G., Pacheco, P. and Winkel, G. (eds) (2019). *Sustainable Development Goals*. Cambridge University Press.

Kazyak, E. (2011). Disrupting cultural selves: constructing gay and lesbian identities in rural locales. *Qualitative Sociology*, *34*: 561–581.

Kempapidis, T., Heinze, N., Green, A.K. and Gomes, R.S. (2023). Queer and disabled and neurodivergent: exploring the experiences of people who identify as LGBT and live with disabilities. *Disabilities*, *4*(1): 41–63.

Kendall, E., Ehrlich, C., Chapman, K., Shirota, C., Allen, G., Gall, A., et al (2020). Immediate and long-term implications of the COVID-19 pandemic for people with disabilities. *American Journal of Public Health*, *110*(12): 1774–1779.

Kennedy, E.L. (1997). Telling Tales: Oral History and the Construction of Pre-Stonewall Lesbian History. In Duberman, M. (ed) *A Queer World: The Center for Lesbian and Gay Studies Reader*. New York University Press, pp 181–198.

Kennedy, E.L. and Davis, M.D. (2014). *Boots of Leather, Slippers of Gold: The History of a Lesbian Community*. Routledge.

Kent, M. (2019). Social Media and Disability: It's Complicated. In Ellis, K., Goggin, G., Haller, B. and Curtis, R. (eds) *The Routledge Companion to Disability and Media*. Routledge, pp 264–274.

Kenttamaa Squires, K. (2019). Rethinking the homonormative? Lesbian and Hispanic Pride events and the uneven geographies of commoditized identities. *Social & Cultural Geography*, *20*(3): 367–386.

Kidd, J.D., Jackman, K.B., Barucco, R., Dworkin, J.D., Dolezal, C., Navalta, T.V., et al (2021). Understanding the impact of the COVID-19 pandemic on the mental health of transgender and gender nonbinary individuals engaged in a longitudinal cohort study. *Journal of Homosexuality*, *68*(4): 592–611.

Kidd, S.A., Hajat, S., Bezgrebelna, M. and McKenzie, K. (2021). The climate change–homelessness nexus. *The Lancet*, *397*(10286): 1693–1694.

Kilic, O. (2023). 'Every parade of ours is a pride parade': exploring LGBTI+ digital activism in Turkey. *Sexualities*, *26*(7): 731–747.

Kilic, O. (2024). Digitalizing sexual citizenship: LGBTI+ resistance at digital spaces in pandemic times. *Feminist Media Studies*, (aop): 1–19.

King, M.M. and Gregg, M.A. (2022). Disability and climate change: a critical realist model of climate justice. *Sociology Compass*, *16*(1): e12954.

Kissack, T. (1995). Freaking fag revolutionaries: New York's Gay Liberation Front, 1969–1971. *Radical History Review*, (62): 104–134.

Kitchin, R. (1998). 'Out of place', 'knowing one's place': space, power and the exclusion of disabled and neurodivergent people. *Disability & Society*, *13*(3): 343–356.

Klapeer, C.M. (2018). Dangerous Liaisons? (Homo) Developmentalism, Sexual Modernization and LGBTIQ Rights in Europe. In Mason, C.L. (ed) *Routledge Handbook of Queer Development Studies*. Routledge, pp 102–118.

Kochi, S. (2024). Fact check: The Biden Administration has flown Pride flags in Muslim-majority countries. *USA Today*, no date. Available at: https://eu.usatoday.com/story/news/factcheck/2022/06/21/fact-check-us-embassies-muslim-majority-countries-had-pride-flags/7661028001/, last accessed 5 July 2024.

Kondakov, A. (2013). Resisting the silence: the use of tolerance and equality arguments by gay and lesbian activist groups in Russia. *Canadian Journal of Law and Society/La Revue Canadienne Droit et Société*, *28*(3): 403–424.

Kondakov, A. (2020). Regulating Desire in Russia. In Ashford, C. and Maine, A. (eds) *Research Handbook on Gender, Sexuality and the Law*. Edward Elgar Publishing, pp 396–408.

Kondakov, A.S. (2022). *Violent Affections: Queer Sexuality, Techniques of Power, and Law in Russia*. UCL Press.

Kondakov, A.S. (2023). Challenging the logic of progressive timeline, queering LGBT successes and failures in Ireland and Russia. *Sexualities*, *26*(1–2): 105–124.

Konduru, D. and Hangsing, C. (2018). Socio-cultural exclusion and inclusion of transgenders in India. *International Journal of Social Sciences and Management*, *5*(1): 10–17.

Koné, M. (2016). Transnational sex worker organizing in Latin America: RedTraSex, labour and human rights. *Social & Economic Studies*, *65*(4): 87–108.

Kong, T.S. (2019). Transnational queer sociological analysis of sexual identity and civic-political activism in Hong Kong, Taiwan and mainland China. *The British Journal of Sociology*, *70*(5): 1904–1925.

Konnoth, C. (2020). Supporting LGBT Communities in the COVID-19 Pandemic. In Burris, S., De Guia, S., Gable, L., Levin, D.E., Parmet, W.E. and Terry, N.P. (eds) *Assessing Legal Responses to COVID-19*. Public Health Law Watch, University of Colorado Law Legal Studies Research Paper, No. 20-47.

Korol, C. (2018). *Las Revoluciones de Berta*. América Libre.

Kubal, T. and Becerra, R. (2014). Social movements and collective memory. *Sociology Compass*, *8*(6): 865–875.

Kuhar, R. and Švab, A. (2014). The only gay in the village? Everyday life of gays and lesbians in rural Slovenia. *Journal of Homosexuality*, *61*(8): 1091–1116.

Kulpa, R. and Mizielinska, J. (eds) (2016). *De-centring Western Sexualities: Central and Eastern European Perspectives*. Routledge.

Kunzel, R. (2018). The Rise of Gay Rights and the Disavowal of Disability in the United States. In Rembis, M., Kudlick, C.J. and Kim Nielsen, K. (eds) *The Oxford Handbook of Disability History*. Oxford University Press, pp 459–476.

Kuriakose, A. and Alex, G.J. (2018). Queering space, (trans) forming Kerala: an analysis of the cultural politics in the emergent Queer Pride Parades and allied trans-beauty pageants. *Littcrit, 44*(2): 88–96.

Kynn, J., Boyke, H. and Holloway, B.T. (2023). We'll Make Our Own Space: Making LGBTQ+ Spaces Accessible. In Kattari, S.K. (ed) *Exploring Sexuality and Disability*. Routledge, pp 299–317.

La Fountain-Stokes, L. (2021). The Life and Times of Trans Activist Sylvia Rivera. In Ramos-Zaya, A.Y. and Rúa, M.M. (eds) *Critical Dialogues in Latinx Studies: A Reader*. New York University Press, pp 241–253.

Lachance, E.L. (2021). COVID-19 and its impact on volunteering: moving towards virtual volunteering. *Leisure Sciences, 43*(1–2): 104–110.

Lalor, K. (2020). Diplomacy, Conditionality and Transnational LGBTI Rights. In Ashford, C. and Maine, A. (eds) *Research Handbook on Gender, Sexuality and the Law*. Edward Elgar Publishing, pp 32–44.

Lamond, I.R. (2018). The challenge of articulating human rights at an LGBT 'mega-event': a personal reflection on Sao Paulo Pride 2017. *Leisure Studies, 37*(1): 36–48.

Lamusse, T. (2016). Politics at pride? *New Zealand Sociology, 31*(6): 49–70.

Langlois, A.J. (2016). International relations theory and global sexuality politics. *Politics, 36*(4): 385–399.

Langlois, A.J. (2020). Making LGBT Rights into Human Rights. In Bosia, M.J., McEvoy, S. and Rahman, M. (eds) *The Oxford Handbook of Global LGBT and Sexual Diversity Politics*. Oxford University Press, pp 75–88.

Laperrière, M. and Lépinard, E. (2016). Intersectionality as a tool for social movements: strategies of inclusion and representation in the Québécois women's movement. *Politics, 36*(4): 374–382.

Lavers, M.K. (2016). Editor of Bangladesh LGBT magazine hacked to death. *Washington Blade*, 25 April. Available at: www.washingtonblade.com/2016/04/25/editor-of-bangladesh-lgbt-magazine-hacked-to-death/, last accessed 4 July 2024.

Lawrence, A. (2013). *Imperial Rule and the Politics of Nationalism: Anti-colonial Protest in the French Empire*. Cambridge University Press.

Lawson, A. (2022). Government urged to act after oil giants accused of misleading public. *The Guardian*, 16 September. Available at: www.theguardian.com/business/2022/sep/16/oil-giants-shell-bp-climate-crisis, last accessed 2 September 2024.

Leary, A. (2020). How LGBTQ+ disabled people are celebrating Virtual Pride. *Rooted in Rights*, 12 June. Available at: https://rootedinrights.org/how-lgbtq-disabled-people-are-celebrating-virtual-pride/, last accessed 27 August 2024.

Lebrasseur, A., Fortin-Bédard, N., Lettre, J., Bussières, E.L., Best, K., Boucher, N., et al (2021). Impact of COVID-19 on people with physical disabilities: a rapid review. *Disability and Health Journal*, *14*(1): 101014.

Lee, M. and Murdie, A. (2021). The global diffusion of the# MeToo movement. *Politics & Gender*, *17*(4): 827–855.

Lewis, C. and Vorobjovas-Pinta, O. (2021). Out of the Closet and into the Streets: Reflections on the Considerations in Hosting Rural Pride Events. In Vorobjovas-Pinta, O. (ed) *Gay Tourism: New Perspectives*. Channel View Publications, pp 211–223.

Liang, A. (2023). China crackdown pushes LGBT groups into the shadows. *BBC News*, 27 June. Available at: www.bbc.co.uk/news/business-65806846, last accessed 5 July 2024.

Liinason, M. and Sasunkevich, O. (2023). Tensions and ambivalences of Pride politics in uncertain times. *lambda nordica*, *28*(2–3): 7–22.

Lippert, L. (2012). Transnational Imagined Communities? Retelling the Stonewall Myth in Vienna. In Hermann, S.M., Hofmann, C.A., Kanzler, K. and Usbeck, F. (eds) *Participating Audiences, Imagined Public Spheres: The Cultural Work of Contemporary American (ized) Narratives*. Leipzig Universitätsverlag, pp 115–130.

Lockett, O. and Lewis, C. (2022). Not the only gay in the village: towards the development of a framework for the organization of LGBTQI+ pride events in rural communities. *Event Management*, *26*(3): 629–645.

López Sánchez, E. and Rodríguez Domínguez, E. (2023). Las protestas del orgullo LGBTIQ+ en escenarios locales mexicanos. *Revista Estudos Feministas*, *31*(1).

Love, H. (2009). *Feeling Backward*. Harvard University Press.

Lugones, M. (2016). The Coloniality of Gender. In De Souza Lima, L., Otero Quezada, E. and Roth, J. (eds) *Feminisms in Movement: Theories and Practices from the Americas*. Verlag, pp 35–58.

Luibhéid, E. (2023). Sexual citizenship, pride parades, and queer migrant im/mobilities. *Ethnic and Racial Studies*, *46*(9): 1877–1897.

Luksyte, A., Dunlop, P.D., Holtrop, D., Gagné, M., Kragt, D. and Farid, H.M. (2021). The challenges of volunteering during the COVID-19 pandemic. *Industrial and Organizational Psychology*, *14*(1–2): 286–289.

Mackenzie, J. (2024). LGBT troops on Ukraine's front line fight homophobia at home. *BBC News*, 25 June. Available at: www.bbc.co.uk/news/articles/cd1140yv03po, last accessed 2 July 2024.

Mad in Asia Pacific. (2021). Are Pride marches accessible for queer people with disabilities? *Mad in Asia Pacific*, 24 September. Available at: https://madinasia.org/are-pride-marches-accessible-for-queer-people-with-disabilities-mad-in-asia-pacific/, last accessed 23 August 2024.

Madhavi, B. and Nageswar Rao, D.K. (2023). Decolonizing nature: an in-depth analysis of ecofeminism. *Journal of English Language and Literature*, *10*(2): 138–144.

Maire, T. (2020). La Marcha del Orgullo en El Salvador: (re) construcción de la memoria, del mito fundador a la realidad histórica. *Controversia*, (215): 161–199.

Mambrín, A.A. (2024). Las mujeres en el espacio público urbano. *De Prácticas y Discursos: Cuadernos de Ciencias Sociales*, *13*(21): 6.

Manalansan IV, M.F. (1995). In the shadows of Stonewall: examining gay transnational politics and the diasporic dilemma. *GLQ: A Journal of Lesbian and Gay Studies*, *2*(4): 425–438.

Marche, G. (2015). Memoirs of gay militancy: a methodological challenge. *Social Movement Studies*, *14*(3): 270–290.

Marcoux, S. (2022). Coca-Cola's Cape Town crisis: examining companies' water rights obligations in a changing climate. *Business and Human Rights Journal*, *7*(2): 298–302.

Marcus, E. (2009). *Making Gay History: The Half-century Fight for Lesbian and Gay Equal Rights*. Harper Collins.

Markwell, K. and Waitt, G. (2009). Festivals, space and sexuality: gay pride in Australia. *Tourism Geographies*, *11*(2): 143–168.

Marple, L. (2005). Rural queers? The loss of the rural queer. *Canadian Woman Studies*, *24*(2): 71–74.

Martens, K. (2019). Why Accessibility Measurement Is Not Merely an Option, but an Absolute Necessity. In Silva, C., Pinto, N. and Bertollini, L. (eds) *Designing Accessibility Instruments*. Routledge, pp 37–51.

Martin, F., Jackson, P., McLelland, M. and Yue, A. (2008). *Asia PacifiQueer: Rethinking Genders and Sexualities*. University of Illinois Press.

Martino, A.S. (2020). Also Here, Also Queer: The Work of LGBT+ Disabled Activists/Scholars in 'Cripping' sexualities. In Toft, A. and Franklin, A. (eds) *Young, Disabled and LGBT+: Voices, Identities and Intersections*. Routledge, pp 13–28.

Massad, J.A. (2008). *Desiring Arabs*. University of Chicago Press.

Matebeni, Z. (ed) (2014). *Reclaiming Afrikan: Queer Perspectives on Sexual and Gender Indentities*. Modjaji Books.

Matebeni, Z. (2017). Southern perspectives on gender relations and sexualities: a queer intervention. *Revista de Antropologia*, *60*(3): 26–44.

Mattlin, B. (2022). *Disability Pride: Dispatches from a Post-Ada World*. Beacon Press.

Mbasalaki, P.K. (2022). Through a Decolonial Lens: Homonationalism in South Africa and the Cape Town Gay Pride Parade. In Sifaki, A., Quinan, C.L. and Lončarevic, K. (eds) *Homonationalism, Femonationalism and Ablenationalism: Critical Pedagogies Contextualised*. Routledge, pp 48–65.

McAdam, D. (1988). *Freedom Summer*. Oxford University Press.

McCann, E., Lee, R. and Brown, M. (2016). The experiences and support needs of people with intellectual disabilities who identify as LGBT: a review of the literature. *Research in Developmental Disabilities*, 57: 39–53.

McCartan, A. (2024). Glasgow's contested LGBT pride spaces: examining dimensions of variegated homonormativities. *Social & Cultural Geography*, 25(1): 68–86.

McCartan, A. and Nash, C.J. (2023). Creating queer safe space: relational space-making at a grassroots LGBT pride event in Scotland. *Gender, Place & Culture*, 30(6): 770–790.

McCarthy, D. (2020). Why there is still a need for Pride celebrations in Ireland? *Irish Association for Counselling and Psychotherapy*, 20(4): 11–14.

McCarthy, L. and Parr, S. (2022). Is LGBT homelessness different? Reviewing the relationship between LGBT identity and homelessness. *Housing Studies*, (aop): 1–19.

McClintock, A. (2013). *Imperial Leather: Race, Gender, and Sexuality in the Colonial Contest*. Routledge.

McFarland Bruce, K. (2016). *Pride Parades: How a Parade Changed the World*. NYU Press.

McLean, N. (2019). (Re) considering the Rainbow. *International Journal of Critical Diversity Studies*, 2(1): 24–40.

McNeill, Z. and Smith, K. (2021). Whose Pride Is This Anyway? The Quare Performance of the #Black Pride4. In Rosenberg, T., D'Urso, S. and Winget, A.R. (eds) *The Palgrave Handbook of Queer and Trans Feminisms in Contemporary Performance*. Palgrave Macmillan, pp 203–222.

McRuer, R. (2008). *Crip Theory: Cultural Signs of Queerness and Disability*. New York University Press.

McRuer, R. and Cassabaum, E. (2021). *Crip Theory*. Oxford Bibliographies. Available at: www.oxfordbibliographies.com/display/document/obo-9780190221911/obo-9780190221911-0109.xml, last accessed 22 August 2024.

Meadows, R. (2023). Queer ecologies and apocalyptic soundings: the Caribbean artivism of Rita Indiana. *Latin American Music Review*, 44(2): 167–198.

Mee-yoo, K. (2022). Embassies show solidarity at Seoul Queer Culture Festival. *The Korea Times*, 19 July. Available at: www.koreatimes.co.kr/www/nation/2024/04/113_332932.html, last accessed 3 April 2023.

Meghji, A. (2021). *Decolonizing Sociology: An Introduction*. John Wiley & Sons.

Melamed, I. (2020). El Ladrillo que Conquistó una Revolución: Stonewall y la Liberación Cuir en América Latina. *CiderX*. Available at: https://ciderxuniandes.wixsite.com/inicio/post/el-ladrillo-que-conquisto-una-revolucion-stonewall-y-la-liberacion-cuir-en-america-latina, last accessed 15 November 2023.

Melucci, A. (1980). The new social movements: a theoretical approach. *Social Science Information*, 19(2): 199–226.

Mendez, L. (2024). Taylor Swift claims she offsets her travel carbon footprint – how does that work? *BBC*, 13 February. Available at: www.bbc.com/travel/article/20240213-taylor-swift-private-jet-flight-travel-carbon-footprint, last accessed 4 September 2024.

Merton, R.K. (1972). Insiders and outsiders: A chapter in the sociology of knowledge. *American Journal of Sociology*, 78(1): 9–47.

Meyer, D.S. and Tarrow, S.G. (eds) (1998). *The Social Movement Society: Contentious Politics for a New Century*. Rowman & Littlefield.

Mignolo, W.D. (2007). Delinking: the rhetoric of modernity, the logic of coloniality and the grammar of de-coloniality. *Cultural Studies*, 21(2–3): 449–514.

Miles-Johnson, T. (2013). Confidence and trust in police: how sexual identity difference shapes perceptions of police. *Current Issues in Criminal Justice*, 25(2): 685–702.

Miller, T. (2017). *Greenwashing Culture*. Routledge.

Mkhize, G. (2015). Problematising rhetorical representations of individuals with disability: disabled or living with disability? *Agenda*, 29(2): 133–140.

Moran, D., Turner, J. and Schliehe, A.K. (2018). Conceptualizing the carceral in carceral geography. *Progress in Human Geography*, 42(5): 666–686.

Moreau, J. and Currier, A. (2018). Queer Dilemmas: LGBT Activism and International Funding. In Mason, C.L. (ed) *Routledge Handbook of Queer Development Studies*. Routledge, pp 223–238.

Morelli, J. (2011). Environmental sustainability: a definition for environmental professionals. *Journal of Environmental Sustainability*, 1(1): 1–9.

Morris, A. (2022). Alternative view of modernity: the subaltern speaks. *American Sociological Review*, 87(1): 1–16.

Mortimer-Sandilands, C. (2005). Unnatural passions? Notes toward a queer ecology. *Invisible Culture: An Electronic Journal for Visual Culture*, 9. Available at: www.invisibleculturejournal.com/pub/unnatural-passions-notes-toward-a-queer-ecology/release/1, last accessed 29 August 2024.

Mortimer-Sandilands, C. (2010). Whose there is there, there? Queer directions and ecocritical orientations. Ecozon@: European Journal of Literature, Culture and Environment, 1(1).

Mortimer-Sandilands, C. and Erickson, B. (2010). *Queer Ecologies: Sex, Nature, Politics, Desire*. Indiana University Press.

Mouzakitis, A. (2017). Modernity and the idea of progress. *Frontiers in Sociology*, 2(3): 1–11.

Muedini, F. (2018). *LGBTI Rights in Turkey: Sexuality and the State in the Middle East*. Cambridge University Press.

Munt, S.R. (2019). Gay shame in a geopolitical context. *Cultural Studies*, 33(2): 223–248.

Muparamoto, N. and Moen, K. (2022). Gay, ngochani, ordaa, gumutete and mwana waEriza: 'globalised' and 'localised' identity labels among same-sex attracted men in Harare, Zimbabwe. *Culture, Health & Sexuality*, 24(1): 48–62.

Murray, C. and Bohannon, M. (2025). State street drops corporate board diversity requirement: here are all the companies cutting DEI programmes. *Forbes*, 1 March. Available at: www.forbes.com/sites/conormurray/2025/03/01/state-street-drops-corporate-board-diversity-requirement-here-are-all-the-companies-cutting-dei-programs/, last accessed 3 March 2025.

Murji, K. and Solomos, J. (eds) (2005). *Racialization: Studies in Theory and Practice*. Oxford University Press.

Nagoshi, J.L., Hohn, K.L. and Nagoshi, C.T. (2017). Questioning the heteronormative matrix: transphobia, intersectionality, and gender outlaws within the gay and lesbian community. *Social Development Issues (Follmer Group)*, 39(3): 19–31.

Nario-Redmond, M.R., Kemerling, A.A. and Silverman, A. (2019). Hostile, benevolent, and ambivalent ableism: contemporary manifestations. *Journal of Social Issues*, 75(3): 726–756.

Navickaitė, R. (2014). Postcolonial queer critique in post-communist Europe: stuck in the Western progress narrative? *Tijdschrift Voor Genderstudies*, 17(2): 165–185.

Nawrotzki, R.J., Hunter, L.M., Runfola, D.M. and Riosmena, F. (2015). Climate change as a migration driver from rural and urban Mexico. *Environmental Research Letters*, 10(11): 114023.

Neate, R. (2017). Gays Against Guns: can the LGBTQ community curb the power of the gun lobby? *The Guardian*, 22 January. Available at: https://amp.theguardian.com/us-news/2017/jan/22/gays-against-guns-can-the-lgbt-community-curb-the-power-of-the-nra, last accessed 3 July 2024.

Nelson, J.A. (2000). The media role in building the disability community. *Journal of Mass Media Ethics*, 15(3): 180–193.

Newton, E. (2015). *Cherry Grove, Fire Island: Sixty Years in America's First Gay and Lesbian Town*. Duke University Press.

Ng, Y.S. (2017). Pride versus prudence: the precarious queer politics of Pink Dot. *Inter-Asia Cultural Studies*, 18(2): 238–250.

Nowell, C. (2025). US Park Service erases references to trans people from Stonewall Monument website. *The Guardian*, 14 February. Available at: www.theguardian.com/us-news/2025/feb/13/stonewall-website-transgender, last accessed 26 February 2025.

Nyanzi, S. (2014). Queer pride and protest: a reading of the bodies at Uganda's first gay Beach Pride. *Signs: Journal of Women in Culture and Society*, 40(1): 36–40.

O'Dowd, N. (2022). The murder that changed Ireland: the savage killing of Declan Flynn. *Irish Central*, 17 June. Available at: www.irishcentral.com/opinion/niallodowd/declan-flynn-murder-changed-ireland, last accessed 3 July 2024.

O'Dwyer, C. (2024). Backsliding versus backlash: do challenges to democracy in East Central Europe threaten LGBTQIAP empowerment? *East European Politics and Societies*, (aop).

Offe, C. and Offe, C. (2019). *New Social Movements: Challenging the Boundaries of Institutional Politics*. Springer.

Offenhartz, J. (2024). As LGBTQ+ Pride crescendo approaches, tensions over war in Gaza expose rifts. *The Independent*, 28 June. Available at: www.independent.co.uk/news/gaza-ap-new-york-new-york-city-israel-b2570402.html, last accessed 19 July 2024.

Oliver, M. (1985). The integration–segregation debate: some sociological considerations. *British Journal of Sociology of Education*, 6(1): 75–92.

Oliver, M. (1990). *The Politics of Disablement* (Critical Texts in Social Work and the Welfare State). Palgrave.

OutRight International (2023). *Beyond Rainbows and Glitter: Pride Around the World in 2023*. Available at: https://outrightinternational.org/sites/default/files/2024-09/Outright_Pride_Report_2024_v2.pdf, last accessed 13 June 2024.

Overton, L. and Hepple, J. (2022). Intersections of LGBTQ+ Social Spaces Using Gender Analysis and the Social Model. In Healy, J. and Colliver, B. (eds) *Contemporary Intersectional Criminology in the UK*. Bristol University Press, pp 204–219.

Owen, S.S., Burke, T.W., Few-Demo, A.L. and Natwick, J. (2018). Perceptions of the police by LGBT communities. *American Journal of Criminal Justice*, 43: 668–693.

Pagina 12 (2021). Documento Completo de la 30a Marcha del Orgullo. *Pagina12*, 6 November. Available at: www.pagina12.com.ar/380204-documento-completo-de-la-30-a-marcha-del-orgullo, last accessed 23 August 2024.

Parrinello, A. (2021). No country(side) for young queers: three contemporary Italian urban-rural narratives. *Whatever: A Transdisciplinary Journal of Queer Theories and Studies*, 4: 411–430.

Patchell, J. and Hayter, R. (2013). How big business can save the climate: multinational corporations can succeed where governments have failed. *Foreign Affairs*, *92*(5): 17–23.

Patel, S. (2019). 'Brown girls can't be gay': racism experienced by queer South Asian women in the Toronto LGBTQ community. *Journal of Lesbian Studies*, *23*(3): 410–423.

Paternotte, D. (2016). The NGOization of LGBT activism: ILGA-Europe and the Treaty of Amsterdam. *Social Movement Studies*, *15*(4): 388–402.

Paternotte, D. and Seckinelgin, H. (2016). 'Lesbian and gay rights are human rights': multiple globalizations and LGBTI activism. In Paternotte, D. and Tremblay, M. (eds) *The Ashgate Research Companion to Lesbian and Gay Activism*. Routledge, pp 209–224.

Patil, V. (2017). Sex, Gender and Sexuality in Colonial Modernity: Towards a Sociology of Webbed Connectivities. In Go, J. and Lawson, G. (eds) *Global Historical Sociology*. Cambridge University Press, pp 142–160.

Paul, N. (2019). Pride and Prejudice: Intersectional Perspectives on Identity Formation through Indian Pride Events. In Aneja, A. (ed) *Women's and Gender Studies in India*. Routledge India, pp 128–136.

Payne, W.J. (2021). Queer urban activism under state impunity: encountering an LGBTTTI Pride archive in Chilpancingo, Mexico. *Urban Studies*, *58*(7): 1327–1345.

Peace Pledge Union (2022). BAE Systems try to pinkwash their image by sponsoring Pride in Leeds. Peace Pledge Union, 6 August 2022. Available at: www.ppu.org.uk/news/bae-systems-try-pinkwash-their-image-sponsoring-lgbt-pride-leeds#:~:text=The%20PPU%20described%20BAE's%20sponsorship,events%20prior%20to%20the%20pandemic, last accessed 23 July 2024.

Pearce, R. (2018). *Understanding Trans Health*. Policy Press.

Pearce, R., Erikainen, S. and Vincent, B. (2020). TERF wars: an introduction. *The Sociological Review*, *68*(4): 677–698.

Pedroni, L. (2016). Selling queer rights: the commodification of queer rights activism. *Themis: Research Journal of Justice Studies and Forensic Science*, *4*(1).

Penman, M. (2017). Organizer says Pride Parade in Kiev more of a 'celebration' this year. *GBH*, 6 July. Available at: www.wgbh.org/news/2017-06-19/organizer-says-pride-parade-in-kiev-more-of-a-celebration-this-year, last accessed 3 April 2024.

Pérez, M. and Radi, B. (2020). Current challenges of North/South relations in gay-lesbian and queer studies. *Journal of Homosexuality*, *67*(7): 965–989.

Peterson, A. and Wahlström, M. (2018). Friends of Pride: Challenges, Conflicts and Dilemmas. In Peterson, A., Wahlström, M. and Wennerhag, M. (eds) *Pride Parades and LGBT Movements*. Routledge, pp 144–169.

Peterson, A., Wahlström, M. and Wennerhag, M. (2018a). 'Normalized' Pride? Pride parade participants in six European countries. *Sexualities*, *21*(7): 1146–1169.

Peterson, A., Wahlström, M. and Wennerhag, M. (2018b). *Pride Parades and LGBT Movements*. Routledge.

Petitjean, C. (2022). The French Strike Movement: Keeping Up the Struggle in Times of COVID-19. In Bringel, B. and Pleyers, G. (eds) *Social Movements and Politics During COVID-19: Crisis, Solidarity and Change in a Global Pandemic*. Bristol University Press, pp 214–222.

Picq, M.L. and Tikuna, J. (2019). Indigenous Sexualities: Resisting Conquest and Translation. In Picq, M.L. and Cottet, C. (eds) *Sexuality and Translation in World Politics*. E-International Relations Publishing, pp 57–71.

Pidd, H. (2008). Liverpool's gay community pays tribute to killed teenager. *The Guardian*, 11 August. Available at: www.theguardian.com/uk/2008/aug/11/ukcrime.gayrights, last accessed 3 July 2024.

Piepzna-Samarasinha, L.L. (2019). Disability justice/Stonewall's legacy, or: love mad trans Black women when they are alive and dead, let their revolutions teach your resistance all the time. *QED: A Journal in GLBTQ Worldmaking*, *6*(2): 54–62.

Pieri, M. (2021). Elephants in the room: chronically ill people and access to LGBTQA+ spaces. *Intersectional Perspectives: Identity, Culture, and Society*, *1*: 9–29.

Piña, D.A. (2022). White supremacy in rainbow: global pride and Black Lives Matter in the era of COVID. *New Sociology: Journal of Critical Praxis*, *3*: 1–10.

Pinckney, J. and Rivers, M. (2020). Sickness or silence: social movement adaptation to COVID-19. *Journal of International Affairs*, *73*(2): 23–42.

Piontek, T. (2006). *Queering Gay and Lesbian Studies*. University of Illinois Press.

Plakhotnik, O. (2022). On the limits of speakability: debates on homonationalism and sexual citizenship in post-Maidan Ukraine. *Feral Feminisms*, *11*: 75–92.

Plakhotnik, O. and Mayerchyk, M. (2023a). What is guarded in toilets? On transphobia, citizenship and militarisation. *Femina Politica–Zeitschrift für feministische Politikwissenschaft*, *32*(2): 96–102.

Plakhotnik, O. and Mayerchyk, M. (2023b). Pride contested. *lambda nordica*, *28*(2–30): 25–53.

Pledl, C. (2021). Eco-ableism in the environmental justice movement. *Vermont Journal of Environmental Law*, *23*(1): 1–27.

Pleyers, G. (2020). The pandemic is a battlefield: social movements in the COVID-19 lockdown. *Journal of Civil Society*, *16*(4): 295–312.

Podmore, J. (2016). Contested Dyke Rights to the City: Montreal's 2012 Dyke Marches in Time and Space. In Ferreira, E. and Browne, K. (eds) *Lesbian Geographies: Gender, Place and Power*. Routledge, pp 71–90.

Poff, M. (2022). *Negotiating 'Serbia' and 'Europe' amidst the politics of nationalism and Europeanisation: an exploration of identity contestation and utilization within the LGBT movement in Serbia*. MA dissertation, Jagellonian University in Krakow. Available at: https://dspace.ut.ee/server/api/core/bitstreams/73894bd5-efc1-442f-bf3d-b28aa6ca7e24/content, last accessed 4 July 2024.

Polsdofer, S. (2013). Pride and prejudiced: Russia's anti-gay propaganda law violates the European Convention on Human Rights. *American University International Law Review*, 29(5): 1069–1096.

Powys Maurice, E. (2021). Big brand backlash, protest and the pandemic: has the Pride 'Bubble' burst forever? *PinkNews*, 30 June. Available at: www.thepinknews.com/2021/06/30/pride-month-lgbt-future-protest/?fbclid=IwAR3oeEL7Npza_ZvyCFYjpobqvIO81ekBKo_jjog_jjpLd6ZeoVlVZOYoH18, last accessed 26 March 2024.

Pride Heroes: Celebrating Pride Month 2023. Available at: www.eeas.europa.eu/eeas/pride-heroes-celebrating-pride-month-2023_en, last accessed 3 April 2024.

Puar, J.K. (2002). Circuits of queer mobility: tourism, travel, and globalization. *GLQ: A Journal of Lesbian and Gay Studies*, 8(1–2): 101–137.

Puar, J.K. (2007). *Terrorist Assemblages: Homonationalism in Queer Times*. Duke University Press.

Puar, J.K. (2011). Citation and censorship: the politics of talking about the sexual politics of Israel. *Feminist Legal Studies*, 19(2): 133–142.

Puar, J.K. (2022). Whither Homonationalism? In Sifaki, A., Quinan, C.L. and Lončarević, K. (eds) *Homonationalism, Femonationalism and Ablenationalism: Critical Pedagogies Contextualised*. Routledge, pp 2–8.

Quéré, M. (2022). 'Lesbiennes et pédés. Ne rasons plus les murs'. Une histoire des marches homosexuelles dans la France des années 1970 et 1980. *Revue d'histoire culturelle. XVIIIe-XXIe siècles*, (4): 1–24.

Quijano, A. (1993). Modernity, identity, and utopia in Latin America. *boundary 2*, 20(3): 140–155.

Rahman, M. (2014a). Queer rights and the triangulation of Western exceptionalism. *Journal of Human Rights*, 13(3): 274–289.

Rahman, M. (2014b). *Homosexualities, Muslim Cultures and Modernity*. Palgrave Macmillan.

Rao, R. (2015a). Global homocapitalism. *Radical Philosophy*, 194: 38–49.

Rao, R. (2015b). Echoes of Imperialism in LGBT Activism. In Nicolaidis, K., Sèbe, B. and Maas, G. (eds) *Echoes of Empire: Memory, Identity and Colonial Legacies*. Bloomsbury, pp 355–372.

Rao, R. (2020). *Out of Time: The Queer Politics of Postcoloniality*. Oxford University Press.

Rembis, M. (2018). Disability and the History of Eugenics. In Remblis, M., Kidlick, C.J. and Nielsen, K. (eds) *The Oxford Handbook of Disability History*. Oxford University Press, pp 85–104.

Rendón, V.T. (2022). Repensar lo humano desde el transfeminismo antiespecista. *Analéctica*, *8*(50): 197–219.

ReportOUT (2023). A crisis of queer invisibility: climate change as a risk multiplier for LGBTQ people. *ReportOut*. Available at: www.reportout.org/green-in-the-rainbow, last accessed 4 September 2024.

Restrepo, J.C.P. (2020). Performatividad política y derechos humanos: el caso de la red comunitaria trans de Bogotá. *Ratio Juris UNAULA*, *15*(31): 669–702.

Richardson, D. (2016). Neoliberalism, Citizenship and Activism. In Paternotte, D. and Tremblay, M. (eds) *The Ashgate Research Companion to Lesbian and Gay Activism*. Routledge, pp 259–272.

Richie, J. (2010). How do you say 'come out of the closet' in Arabic? Queer activism and the politics of visibility in Israel-Palestine. *GLQ: Journal of Gay and Lesbian Studies*, *16*(4): 557–575.

Richter-Montpetit, M. and Weber, C. (2017). Queer International Relations. In *Oxford Research Encyclopedia of Politics*. Available at: https://oxfordre.com/politics/view/10.1093/acrefore/9780190228637.001.0001/acrefore-9780190228637-e-265, last accessed 16 September 2024.

Riddell, S. and Watson, N. (2014). *Disability, Culture and Identity*. Routledge.

Riedel, S. (2022). Latee Brockington, trans woman imprisoned at Rikers, sues after sexual assault. *Them*, 11 January 2022. Available at: www.them.us/story/latee-brockington-trans-woman-imprisoned-rikers-lawsuit-sexual-assault, last accessed 4 July 2024.

River, C. (2015). *The Stonewall Riots: The History and Legacy of the Protests that Helped Spark the Modern Gay Rights Movement*. CreateSpace Independent Publishing Platform.

Rivera, S. (1973). Y'all better quiet down. *Internet Archive*. Available at: https://archive.org/details/sylvia-rivera-yall-better-quiet-down-1978, last accessed 13 September 2024.

Rivers, I., Daly, J. and Stevenson, L. (2023). Homophobic and Transphobic Online Harassment: Young People in Scotland during the COVID-19 Pandemic. In Cowie, H. and Myers, C.A. (eds) *Cyberbullying and Online Harms: Preventions and Interventions from Community to Campus*. Routledge, pp 57–66.

Robinson, O.C. (2014). Sampling in interview-based qualitative research: a theoretical and practical guide. *Qualitative Research in Psychology*, *11*(1): 25–41.

Rodriguez, S.M. (2017). Homophobic nationalism: the development of sodomy legislation in Uganda. *Comparative Sociology*, *16*(3): 393–421.

Rodriguez, S.M. (2018). *The Economies of Queer Inclusion: Transnational Organizing for LGBTI Rights in Uganda*. Rowman & Littlefield.

Romero, A.P., Goldberg, S.K. and Vasquez, L.A. (2020). LGBT people and housing affordability, discrimination, and homelessness. UCLA Williams Institute. Available at: https://escholarship.org/content/qt509184bz/qt509184bz.pdf, last accessed 16 September 2024.

Roth, M. (2016). Speech of Minister of State for Europe Michael Roth at the Post-IDAHO Round Table 'Diversity and LGBTI Inclusion in the Western Balkans'. 27 June 2016. Available at: www.auswaertiges-amt.de/en/newsroom/news/160627-stm-r-postidaho/281724, last accessed 3 April 2024.

Ruez, D. (2017). 'I never felt targeted as an Asian ... until I went to a gay pub': sexual racism and the aesthetic geographies of the bad encounter. *Environment and Planning A*, 49(4): 893–910.

Rumens, N. (2017). *Queer Business: Queering Organization Sexualities*. Routledge.

Rushbrook, D. (2002). Cities, queer space, and the cosmopolitan tourist. *GLQ: A Journal of Lesbian and Gay Studies*, 8(1): 183–206.

Russell, E.K. (2018). Carceral pride: the fusion of police imagery with LGBTI rights. *Feminist Legal Studies*, 26(3): 331–350.

Russell, E.K. (2019). *Queer Histories and the Politics of Policing*. Routledge.

Russell, J. (2023). How anti-drag laws are impacting Pride celebrations across the country. *LGBTQ Nation*, 8 May. Available at: www.lgbtqnation.com/2023/05/how-anti-drag-laws-are-impacting-pride-celebrations-across-the-country/, last accessed 4 July 2024.

Sabbagh, D. (2020). BAE Systems sold £15bn worth of arms to Saudis during Yemen assault. *The Guardian*, 14 April. Available at: www.theguardian.com/business/2020/apr/14/bae-systems-sold-15bn-arms-to-saudis-during-yemen-assault, last accessed 23 July 2024.

Said, E.W. (1968). Beginnings. *Salmagundi*, 2(4) (8): 36–55.

Sajjad, T. (2022). Strategic cruelty: legitimizing violence in the European Union's border regime. *Global Studies Quarterly*, 2(2): 1–14.

Sajor, L. (2022). State Repression in the Philippines during COVID-19 and Beyond. In Bringel, B. and Pleyers, G. (eds) *Social Movements and Politics During COVID-19*. Bristol University Press, pp 52–59.

Saleh, F. (2023). Beyond queer liberalism: marginal mobilities and the future of queer politics. *Ethnic and Racial Studies*, 46(9): 1940–1946.

Sargeant, M. (2014). The vulnerable in natural, environmental and technological disasters. *JILPT Report*, 13: 63–82.

Scheffer, N. (2021). Pride de Paris: une militante trans interpellée après une altercation avec des féministes 'TERF'. *Têtu*, 28 June 2021. Available at: https://tetu.com/2021/06/28/pride-paris-2021-militante-trans-interpellee-altercation-feministes-anti-trans-terf/, last accessed 19 June 2024.

Schields, C. and Herzog, D. (eds) (2021). *The Routledge Companion to Sexuality and Colonialism*. Routledge.

Schimanski, I.D. and Treharne, G.J. (2019). 'Extra marginalisation within the community': queer individuals' perspectives on suicidality, discrimination and gay pride events. *Psychology & Sexuality, 10*(1): 31–44.

Schormans, A.F., Hutton, S., Blake, M., Earle, K. and Head, K.J. (2021). Social isolation continued: COVID-19 shines a light on what self-advocates know too well. *Qualitative Social Work, 20*(1–2): 83–89.

Schulman, S. (2013). *The Gentrification of the Mind: Witness to a Lost Imagination.* University of California.

Seed, P. (2002). Early modernity: the history of a word. *CR: The New Centennial Review, 2*(1): 1–16.

Segal, M. (2015). *And Then I Danced: Traveling the Road to LGBT Equality.* Akashic Books.

Seto, K.C., Parnell, S. and Elmqvist, T. (2013). A Global Outlook on Urbanization. In Elmqvist, T., Fragkias, M., Goodness, J., Günerap, B., Marcotullio, R.I., McDonald, Parnell, S., et al (eds) *Urbanization, Biodiversity and Ecosystem Services: Challenges and Opportunities: A Global Assessment.* Springer Nature, pp 1–12.

Seymour, N. (2020). Queer Ecologies and Queer Environmentalisms. In Somerville, S.B. (ed) *The Cambridge Companion to Queer Studies.* Cambridge University Press, pp 108–122.

Shadijanova, D. (2022). No planet, no Pride: why climate justice is LGBTQ+ justice. *Gay Times*, 21 March. Available at: www.gaytimes.com/originals/no-planet-no-pride-why-climate-justice-is-lgbtq-justice/, last accessed 3 September 2024.

Shafie, G. (2015). Pinkwashing: Israel's international strategy and internal agenda. Kohl: A Journal for Body and Gender Research, 1(1), 82–86.

Shah, S.P. (2015). Queering critiques of neoliberalism in India: urbanism and inequality in the era of transnational 'LGBTQ' rights. *Antipode, 47*(3): 635–651.

Shakespeare, T. (2017). *Disability: The Basics.* Routledge.

Shakespeare, T., Watson, N., Brunner, R., Cullingworth, J., Hameed, S., Scherer, N., et al (2022). Disabled people in Britain and the impact of the COVID-19 pandemic. *Social Policy & Administration, 56*(1): 103–117.

Shevtsova, M. (2022). Choosing to stay? Lesbian, gay, bisexual, trans and queer people and the war in Ukraine. *European Journal of Politics and Gender, 5*(3): 399–401.

Shevtsova, M. (2023). Solidarity test: challenges of forced LGBTIQ migration and activism in Central-Eastern European countries in the context of Russia's war on Ukraine. *European Societies, 26*(2): 323–345.

Shew, A. (2023). *Against Technoableism: Rethinking Who Needs Improvement.* WW Norton & Company.

Shield, A.D. (2020). The legacies of the Stonewall riots in Denmark and the Netherlands. *History Workshop Journal, 89*: 193–206.

Shiva, V. and Mies, M. (2014). *Ecofeminism*. Bloomsbury Publishing.

Shmulsky, S., Gobbo, K., Donahue, A. and Klucken, F. (2021). Do neurodivergent college students forge a disability identity? A snapshot and implications. *Journal of Postsecondary Education and Disability*, 34(1): 53–63.

Silva, M.R. and Jacobo, J. (2020). Global South perspectives on Stonewall after 50 years, Part I: South by south, trans for trans. *Contexto Internacional*, 42: 665–683.

Sipos, A. and Bagyura, M. (2024). Fighting for space within the cis- and heteronormative public sphere: an analysis of Budapest Pride. *Social Inclusion*, 12: 1–19.

Slootmaeckers, K. (2017). The litmus test of pride: analysing the emergence of the Belgrade 'ghost' pride in the context of EU accession. *East European Politics*, 33(4): 517–535.

Slootmaeckers, K. (2023). *Coming In: Sexual Politics and EU Accession in Serbia*. Manchester University Press.

Slootmaeckers, K. and Bosia, M.J. (2023). The dislocation of LGBT politics: Pride, globalization, and geo-temporality in Uganda and Serbia. *International Political Sociology*, 17(1): 1–19.

Smith, C.G. (2020). 'Where u from, who u wit?!' Black Pride Festivals as itinerant hospitality. *Journal of Canadian Studies*, 54(2–3): 395–414.

Smith, L.T. (2021). *Decolonizing Methodologies: Research and Indigenous Peoples*. Bloomsbury Publishing.

Snow, D. and Benford, R. (1999). Alternative Types of Cross-national Diffusion in the Social Movement Arena. In della Porta, D., Hanspeter Kriesim, H. and Rucht, D. (eds) *Social Movements in a Globalizing World*. Macmillan, pp 23–49.

Sopelsa, B. (2018). Following Pride events, Kenya's gay refugees fear for their lives. *NBC News*, 20 June. Available at: www.nbcnews.com/feature/nbc-out/following-pride-event-kenya-s-gay-refugees-fear-their-lives-n885136, last accessed 26 March 2024.

Sosa, L. (2021). Beyond gender equality? Anti-gender campaigns and the erosion of human rights and democracy. *Netherlands Quarterly of Human Rights*, 39(1): 3–10.

Spade, D. (2020). Solidarity not charity: mutual aid for mobilization and survival. *Social Text*, 38(1): 131–151.

Spade, D. and Belkin, A. (2021). Queer militarism?! The politics of military inclusion advocacy in authoritarian times. *GLQ: A Journal of Lesbian and Gay Studies*, 27(2): 281–307.

Spanakis, P., Peckham, E., Mathers, A., Shiers, D. and Gilbody, S. (2021). The digital divide: amplifying health inequalities for people with severe mental illness in the time of COVID-19. *The British Journal of Psychiatry*, 219(4): 529–531.

Speare-Cole, R. (2023). Shell and BP among oil firms accused of greenwashing over renewable energy. *The Independent*, 23 August. Available at: www.independent.co.uk/climate-change/news/shell-bp-oil-greenwashing-greanpeace-climate-b2397689.html, last accessed 29 August 2024.

Stallone, S. (2019). A white city turned pink: Tel Aviv as Israel's homonormative LGBTQ flagship. *Queer Studies in Media & Popular Culture*, 4(3): 257–270.

Stanley, E.A. (2021). *Atmospheres of Violence: Structuring Antagonism and the Trans/Queer Ungovernable*. Duke University Press.

Steele, L. (2024). Reparations for Segregation of Disabled and Neurodivergent People. In Hamre, B. and Villadsen, L. (eds) *Islands of Extreme Exclusion*. Brill, pp 244–264.

Stein, M. (2000). *City of Sisterly and Brotherly Loves: Lesbian and Gay Philadelphia, 1945–1972*. University of Chicago Press.

Stein, M. (2005). Theoretical politics, local communities: the making of US LGBT historiography. *GLQ: A Journal of Lesbian and Gay Studies*, 11(4): 605–625.

Stein, M. (2019). *The Stonewall Riots: A Documentary History*. New York University Press.

Stella, F. (2013). Queer space, pride, and shame in Moscow. *Slavic Review*, 72(3): 458–480.

Steverson, B.K. (1996). On the reconciliation of anthropocentric and nonanthropocentric environmental ethics. *Environmental Values*, 5(4): 349–361.

Stone, A.L. (2018). The geography of research on LGBTQ life: why sociologists should study the South, rural queers, and ordinary cities. *Sociology Compass*, 12(11).

Stonewall (2018). *LGBT in Britain – Home and Communities*. Available at: www.stonewall.org.uk/resources/lgbt-britain-home-and-communities-2018?gad_source=1&gclid=Cj0KCQjww5u2BhDeARIsALBuLnN4KXszgWO75_JLMlUB1HaE6YeCL4aAArQwhPJ4qfWXrx3BgkU7iywaAu1DEALw_wcB, last accessed 22 August 2024.

Stronach, R. (2014). Trademarking social change: an ironic commodification. *Journal of the Patent & Trademark Office Society*, 96(4): 567–599.

Sun, N., Christie, E., Cabal, L. and Amon, J.J. (2022). Human rights in pandemics: criminal and punitive approaches to COVID-19. *BMJ Global Health*, 7(2).

Svensson, J. and Strand, C. (2024). Development cooperation and the stratification of lesbian, gay, bi-and transsexual activism: international donors, elite activists and community members during Uganda Pride 2022. *European Journal of Politics and Gender*, 1(aop): 1–21.

Swain, R.B. (2018). A Critical Analysis of the Sustainable Development Goals. In Leal Filho, W. (ed) *Handbook of Sustainability Science and Research*. Springer International, pp 341–355.

Szulc, L. (2018). *Transnational Homosexuals in Communist Poland: Cross-Border Flows in Gay and Lesbian Magazines*. Routledge.

Taylor, J. (2016). Festivalizing Sexualities: Discourses of 'Pride', Counter-discourses of 'Shame'. In Woodward, I., Taylor, J. and Bennett, A. (eds). *The Festivalization of Culture*. Routledge, pp 27–48.

The Guardian (2023). Just Stop Oil protesters disrupt London Pride over 'polluting' sponsors. *The Guardian*, 1 July. Available at: www.theguardian.com/environment/2023/jul/01/just-stop-oil-protesters-disrupt-london-pride-over-polluting-sponsors, last accessed 2 September 2024.

The Indian Express (2021). Rainbow flags, balloons and placards: what Gandhinagar's first Pride parade looked like. *The Indian Express*, 10 February. Available at: https://indianexpress.com/photos/india-news/gandhinagar-pride-parade-lgbtq-members-6259061/, last accessed 18 July 2024.

Thomas, J. (2024). *A Place of Our Own: Six Spaces that Shaped Queer Women's Culture*. Virago Press.

Thomas, M. (2012). *Violence and Colonial Order: Police, Workers and Protest in the European Colonial Empires, 1918–1940*. Cambridge University Press.

Touraine, A. (1985). An introduction to the study of social movements. *Social Research*, 52(4): 749–787.

Trevisan, F. (2016). *Disability Rights Advocacy Online: Voice, Empowerment and Global Connectivity*. Routledge.

Trindade, R. (2011). O mito da multidão: uma breve história da parada gay de São Paulo. *Revista Gênero*, 11(2): 73–97.

Trindade, R. (2018). *A invenção do ativismo LGBT no Brasil: intercâmbios e ressignificações*. In J. Green, R. Quinalha, M. Caetano and M. Fernandes (eds) *História do movimento LGBT no Brasil*. Alameda, pp 227–236.

Tuo, C.E. (2015). The Italian regime of recognition of intercountry adoptions of children in light of the ECHR: what about singles? *Cuadernos Derecho Transnacional*, 7(2): 357–368.

Tzevelekos, V.P. and Dzehtsiarou, K. (2020). November. Normal as usual? Human rights in times of COVID-19. *European Convention on Human Rights Law Review*, 1(2): 141–149.

UN Convention on the Prevention and Punishment of the Crime of Genocide (1951). Available at: www.un.org/en/genocideprevention/documents/atrocity-crimes/Doc.1_Convention%20on%20the%20Prevention%20and%20Punishment%20of%20the%20Crime%20of%20Genocide.pdf, last accessed 19 July 2024.

Upadhyay, N. and Bakshi, S. (2020). Translating Queer: Reading Caste, Decolonizing Praxis. In Fernández, F. and Evans, J. (eds) *The Routledge Handbook of Translation and Politics*. Routledge, pp 336–344.

Uyan, D. (2021). Re-thinking racialization: the analytical limits of racialization. *Du Bois Review: Social Science Research on Race*, 18(1): 15–29.

Valentine, G. (2016). (Hetero) Sexing Space: Lesbian Perceptions and Experiences of Everyday Spaces. In McDowell, L. and Sharp, J. (eds) *Space, Gender, Knowledge: Feminist Readings*. London: Routledge, pp 284–299.

van Kessel, L. and van Leeuwen, F. (2019). In the end, we always have to call institutions to account: interview with Wigbertson Julian Isenia and Naomie Pieter. *Tijdschrift voor Genderstudies*, *22*(3): 285–297.

Vargas, Y. (2019). Inclusion of disabled and neurodivergent people in the LGBTQ+ community is about more than accessibility. *Rooted in Rights*, 19 July. Available at: https://rootedinrights.org/inclusion-of-disabled and neurodivergent-people-in-the-lgbtqcommunity-is-about-more-than-accessibility/, last accessed 23 August 2024.

Vasey, S. (2004). Disability Culture: The Story So Far. In Swain, J., French, S., Barnes, C. and Thomas, C. (eds) *Disabling Barriers – Enabling Environments*. Sage, pp 106–110.

Vasilev, G. (2016). LGBT recognition in EU accession states: how identification with Europe enhances the transformative power of discourse. *Review of International Studies*, *42*(4): 748–772.

Velasco, K. (2018). Human rights INGOs, LGBT INGOs, and LGBT policy diffusion, 1991–2015. *Social Forces*, *97*(1): 377–404.

Venegas Ferrin, N. (2017). 'Asi se baila en mi tierra'. Les Warmishinas dans les danses populaires andines: le cas du groupe de danse Ñuca Trans. *Horizons/Théâtre Revue d'études théâtrales*, (10–11): 78–95.

Venn, C. and Featherstone, M. (2006). Modernity. *Theory, Culture & Society*, *23*(2–3): 457–465.

Vig, S. and Dwivedi, S. (2024). Climate change and mental health: impact on people with disabilities. *Mental Health and Social Inclusion*, *28*(6): 941–949.

Von Holdt, K. (2013). The violence of order, orders of violence: between Fanon and Bourdieu. *Current Sociology*, *61*(2): 112–131.

Vorobjovas-Pinta, O. and Pearce, J. (2024). Scoping the role of LGBTQI+ festivals in regional Australia: a local community perspective. *Event Management*, *28*: 955–960.

Wagner, P. (2010). Multiple trajectories of modernity: why social theory needs historical sociology. *Thesis Eleven*, *100*(1): 53–60.

Wagner-Pacifici, R. (2017). *What Is an Event?* University of Chicago Press.

Wahab, A. (2020). Queer antiracist vigilance: pinkwatching 'queer investments' in state racist violence. *Visual Ethnography*, *9*(1).

Wahlström, M. (2018). The Meanings of Pride Parades for their Participants. In Peterson, A., Wahlström, M. and Wennerhag, M. (eds) *Pride Parades and LGBT Movements*. Taylor & Francis, pp 190–210.

Waite-Santibanez, T. (2022). *The brick*. Doctoral dissertation, Columbia University.

Waitt, G. and Gorman-Murray, A. (2008). Camp in the country: renegotiating sexuality and gender through a rural lesbian and gay festival. *Journal of Tourism and Cultural Change*, 6(3): 185–207.

Waldschmidt, A., Karačić, A., Sturm, A. and Dins, T. (2015). 'Nothing about us without us' disability rights activism in European countries: a comparative analysis. *Moving the Social*, 53: 103–138.

Waniak-Michalak, H., Leitoniene, S. and Perica, I. (2022). The NGOs and Covid 19 pandemic: a new challenge for charitable giving and NGOs' mission models. *Inžinerinė ekonomika*, 33(2): 174–187.

Ward, J. (2003). Producing 'Pride' in west Hollywood: a queer cultural capital for queers with cultural capital. *Sexualities*, 6(1): 65–94.

Wareham, J. (2020). Coronavirus could change LGBT+ Pride forever: what digital Prides teach us. *Forbes*, 22 June. Available at: www.forbes.com/sites/jamiewareham/2020/06/16/coronavirus-could-change-lgbt-pride-forever-what-can-we-learn-from-digital-prides/, last accessed 27 August 2024.

Warren, K. (2000). *Ecofeminist Philosophy: A Western Perspective on What it Is and Why it Matters*. Rowman & Littlefield.

Warren, R., Morales, J., Steinhoff, A. and Woodward, S. (2024). Speaking truth to funders: alternative accountabilities in the voluntary and community sector during the COVID-19 pandemic. *Financial Accountability & Management*, 40(4): 573–591.

Wayne, G. (2023). Burning Man needs a rebrand: instead of destroying things, help rebuild the planet. *San Francisco Chronicle*, 30 August. Available at: www.sfchronicle.com/opinion/openforum/article/burning-man-climate-change-18335011.php, last accessed 4 September 2024.

Weaver, D.A. (2024). The mortality experience of disabled persons in the United States during the COVID-19 pandemic. *Health Affairs Scholar*, 2(1): 1–9.

Webb, M. (2014). *Accessing Canal Pride: the intersection of identities for LGBT people with physical disabilities at a global event*. Undergraduate dissertation, Mount Holyhoke College. Available at: https://digitalcollections.sit.edu/isp_collection/1983/, last accessed 22 August 2024.

Weber, C. (2016). Queer intellectual curiosity as international relations method: developing queer international relations theoretical and methodological frameworks. *International Studies Quarterly*, 60(1): 1–23.

Weiss, J.T. (2012). GL vs. BT: The Archaeology of Biphobia and Transphobia within the US Gay and Lesbian Community. In Klein, F., Yescavage, K. and Alexander, J. (eds) *Bisexuality and Transgenderism*. Routledge, pp 25–55.

Weitzenfeld, A. and Joy, M. (2014). An overview of anthropocentrism, humanism, and speciesism in critical animal theory. *Counterpoints*, 448: 3–27.

White, E. (2019). *The Stonewall Reader*. Penguin.

Whitworth, L. (2019). Ecology and Environmental Issues and Activism. In Chang, H. (ed) *The Global Encyclopedia of Lesbian, Gay, Bisexual, Transgender, and Queer (LGBTQ) History*. Gale Publishing, pp 487–492.

Williams, C. (2020). The ontological woman: a history of deauthentication, dehumanization, and violence. *The Sociological Review*, 68(4): 718–734.

Wilson, N.J., Macdonald, J., Hayman, B., Bright, A.M., Frawley, P. and Gallego, G. (2018). A narrative review of the literature about people with intellectual disability who identify as lesbian, gay, bisexual, transgender, intersex or questioning. *Journal of Intellectual Disabilities*, 22(2): 171–196.

Withers, A.J. (2024). *Disability Politics and Theory*. Fernwood Publishing.

Wolowic, J.M., Heston, L.V., Saewyc, E.M., Porta, C. and Eisenberg, M.E. (2017). Chasing the rainbow: lesbian, gay, bisexual, transgender and queer youth and pride semiotics. *Culture, Health & Sexuality*, 19(5): 557–571.

Wong, P.P. (2004). Environmental Impacts of Tourism. In Lew, A.A., Hall, M. and Williams, A.M. (eds) *A Companion to Tourism*. John Wiley & Sons, pp 450–461.

Woodmass, A. (2024). Russian watchdog labels 'LGBT Public Movement' as terrorist organisation. *Jurist: Legal News and Commentary*, 24 March. Available at: www.jurist.org/news/2024/03/russia-watchdog-labels-lgbt-public-movement-as-terrorist-organization/, last accessed 26 March 2024.

Woori, H.A.N. (2018). Proud of myself as LGBTQ: The Seoul Pride Parade, homonationalism, and queer developmental citizenship. *Korea Journal*, 58(2): 27–57.

Yarborough, O.C. (2022). *Black by birth, gay by God, proud by choice: the origins and spread of DC Black Pride, 1991–2015*. Doctoral dissertation, North Carolina Central University.

Yılmaz, M.B. and Baybars, B. (2022). A Critical Perspective on Greenwashing under the Roof of Corporate Environmentalism. In Mogaji, E., Adeola, O., Adisa, I., Hinson, R.E., Mukonza, C. and Kirgiz, A.C. (eds) *Green Marketing in Emerging Economies: A Communications Perspective*. Springer International, pp 119–140.

Zajak, S. (2022). COVID-19 and the Reconfiguration of the Social Movements Landscape. In Bringel, B. and Pleyers, G. (eds) *Social Movements and Politics During COVID-19*. Bristol University Press, pp 134–140.

Zambelich, A. and Hurt, A. (2016). 3 hours in Orlando: piecing together an attack and its aftermath. *NPR*, 26 June. Available at: www.npr.org/2016/06/16/482322488/orlando-shooting-what-happened-update, last accessed 3 July 2024.

Zhou, Y.R., Sinding, C. and Goellnicht, D. (eds) (2021). *Sexualities, Transnationalism, and Globalisation: New Perspectives*. Routledge.

Żychowska-Skiba, D. (2023). Person-first language or identity-first language in relation to people with disabilities in public discourse. *Polityka Społeczna*, 587(2): 28–34.

Index

A

ableism *see* disability and accessibility
accessibility *see* disability and accessibility
accommodation (as a frame) 69
adaptation (as a frame) 69
agency 45, 47, 70
Albanians 122
Alternative Inclusive Pride Network 76
Alternative Pride Events
   corporatization and
     commodification 133, 135
   and human rights issues 86–87, 89, 90
   and the police 117–118
   rise of 7, 10–11, 64, 104, 119–123, 195
   types of 64, 76–78
   see also individual Events
Altman, D. 125
ambassadors (diplomatic) 51, 98–99, 117
American Psychiatric Association 156
Amsterdam 21, 157
anti-gender movements 74, 83, 190, 193
anti-speciesism 120
Argentina 34, 72, 78
armed forces, participation of 76–77, 100–101, 114–119
Armstrong, E.A. 7–8, 21, 29, 75
Arondekar, A. 35
assimilationist framing 75, 76
Atzmoni, Yoav 61n14
Australia 134–135

B

Bacchetta, P. 33
back-to-land projects 174
BAE Systems 130–131
Baldassarri, D. 70, 74, 128
Ball of the 41 (*El Baile de los 41*) 109
Bangladesh 78, 86, 90, 91, 99, 134, 139
banning Pride events 47, 50, 68, 99, 117
Baptiste, Brigitte 175–176
Barclays Bank 129, 132
Barreto, D.M. 73, 187
Barthes, R. 23, 30–31
Baxi, U. 33

Becerra, R. 27
Belgium 1
Belgrade 50, 68, 93
Belmont, F. 35
Ben-Habib, S. 43, 60n3
Benford, R.D. 69, 123
Bennett, S. 40, 49, 66, 67, 69–70, 85, 88, 194
Bhambra, G.K. 43, 57
Bill, Dita von 93
Black Lives Matter 77, 89, 108
Black Panthers Party 38n13
Black Pride 10, 64, 77, 119, 196
Bologna 158–159
Bosia, M.J. 66
Bosnia and Herzegovina 50
Bravmann, S. 23, 31, 33–34
Brazil 23, 34, 35, 78
Brighton 80n15, 119, 121, 133
British LGBT Awards (2023) 183
British Petroleum (BP) 173
Britt, L. 74
Browne, K. 80n15
Brussels 1
Burchiellaro, O. 129, 130
Burning Man festival 187

C

Cáceres, Berta 176–177
Canada
   Alternative Pride Events 77, 120–121
   corporatization and commodification 129, 131, 137–138
   disability and accessibility 160, 164
   local communities 108
   online Pride Events 164
   rural settings 111
   World Pride 67
cancellation of Pride Events 47, 68, 95, 99, 141, 163
Cannamela, D. 35
capitalism
   homocapitalism 54, 59, 68, 126
   see also corporatization
     and commodification
carceral pride 114, 115

INDEX

Caro Romero, F.C.C. 34
Carter, D. 26, 37n9
Causer, Michael 88
Chauncey, G. 32
Chiang, H. 46
Chile 34
Chilpancingo, Mexico 36, 72
China 33, 46, 97–98, 99, 117, 142
Chisholm, K. 67, 120–121, 129
Christianity 36, 52, 72, 93, 117
Christopher Street Day Parade, US 26
chrononormativity 45, 56, 57
Cirinnà Law 91–92
cis-washing 25–26
civilizational narratives 9, 39, 41, 45, 49, 53–54, 55–56, 66, 84
Clare, Julian 51
climate crisis *see* environmental sustainability
Coca-Cola 133, 146, 183, 184
collective memory 27
Colombia 23, 34, 35, 54, 78, 98, 132
  grassroots activism 106
  and human rights issues 85, 89
colonialism 33, 42–45, 57, 58
coming out 32, 48
  coming out scripts 70, 74, 128
commodification *see* corporatization and commodification
community-building 10, 59, 103–124
  Alternative Pride Events 119–123
  beyond the Pride Events 108–109
  and the police 114–119
  and professionalization 10, 105–110
  and Stonewall Myth 109–110
compulsory able-bodiedness 11, 153, 156, 170, 196–197
conflict
  and corporatization and commodification 129
  and issue of identity 75, 76, 77, 119–120
  sources of 64, 69–70, 74–78, 119–120, 122–123, 194–195
  and strategic framing 75–77, 119–120
  as vital part of Pride Events 62
consensus collective memory 27
Conway, D. 63, 76, 130, 136, 138
Conway, J.M. 39, 44, 48
Copenhagen/Malmö World Pride 67–68, 69
corporatization and commodification 5, 11, 76, 125–147, 195–196, 198
  and activism 130, 132–133
  and COVID-19 pandemic 140–146
  cultural change within corporations 136–137
  DEI (Diversity, Equality, and Inclusion) policies 140, 146
  environmental sustainability 188
  grants 133–134
  greenwashing 131, 173, 183–185, 187
  and modernity 54, 55, 59, 145–146
  organizers' dilemmas 135–140
  pinkwashing 2, 11, 97, 99, 128, 137–138, 174, 184–185, 187
  problematic or unethical sponsors 130–132
  processes of 127–132
  public or corporate sponsorship 132–135
  and rise of Alternative Pride Events 119–120
  size of donations 130
  terminology 128–129
counter-protesters 68, 93, 101, 102n11, 115, 116, 117, 193
COVID-19 pandemic 88, 108, 111, 112
  and disability and accessibility 161, 163–166
  and environmental sustainability 180
  and funding of Pride Events 140–146
  and human rights issues 94–96
Crage, S.M. 7–8, 21, 29
Cram, E. 182
criminalization of homosexuality 37n9, 44, 47, 91, 92, 184
Crip Theory 153
Cuéllar, A. 178–179
cultural anchors 70, 74, 128
cultural capital 55–56
culture wars 194
Currier, A. 147n7
Czechia 97–98, 107–108, 120

D

da Costa Junior, J.V.L. 34
Dalli, Helen 68
Davis, J.L. 123n2
decolonization 14, 28, 42–43, 198
de-growing Pride Events 146–147, 188, 196
DEI (Diversity, Equality, and Inclusion) policies 5, 83, 140, 146
D'Emilio, J. 8
denial of coevalness 45
Denmark 51, 67–68, 69, 91, 110–111
developmental model of homosexuality 51
diffusion of the frame of Events 66, 69–70
Digital Pride Events 163–167
diplomatic personnel 51, 98–99, 117
disability and accessibility 11, 59–60, 151–171, 191, 196–197
  contextualizing 155–157
  and COVID-19 pandemic 161, 163–166
  and disability justice 167–171
  Disability Pride 152
  Ecoableism 182–183
  homosexuality and disability 155–157
  hostility at Pride Events 167–168
  medical model of disability 153, 155
  and public spaces 153–154

social model of disability 153
Stonewall Riots 25
strategies and challenges 158–162
and technology 162–167
disability justice 167–171
Disability Pride 152
Ditsie, Beverly 80n23
Dodds, R. 178
drag queens 92, 93
Duberman, M. 25, 37n8
Dublin 88
Duggan, L. 91
Dyke Marches 64, 77–78

E

Ecoableism 182–183
ecofeminism 174, 175
Ecuador 72–73
Edenborg 13, 68–69
Eisenstadt, S.N. 41, 56–57
El Salvador 34, 35
embassies 51, 98–99, 117
emotional contagion 74
emplacement of Pride Events 71
entelechia 43–44, 56
environmental sustainability 11–12, 59–60, 172–189, 197
  challenges and opportunities 177–183
  COVID-19 pandemic 180
  Ecoableism 182–183
  environmental impact of Pride Events 178
  and future of Pride Events 185–188
  as a Pride issue 174–177
  Queer Eco-Criticism and greenwashing 183–185
  Queer Ecology 175–177, 178, 186, 187, 188
  rural and peripheral settings 73, 185, 186–187
equality normalization discourse 80n20
Erickson, B. 175
Eristavi, Maxim 52–53
Escobar, A. 42
Esparza, R. 80n25
Espinosa, R.V. 35
European Pride Organisers Association (EPOA) 52
European Union 61n9, 68, 95
Europeanization 50, 68, 72, 96
Europride 52, 67, 68, 93, 164
Evans , D. 126
exclusion 28–29, 55, 135–136
  see also Alternative Pride Events; disability and accessibility; trans people

F

far-right protesters 68, 74, 93, 95, 101, 115
Faroe Islands 110–111

Farris, S.R. 60n4
feminicidios 89
femonationalism 60n4
Ferreira, A.Á 35
Festival Agrocuir de Ulloa, Spain 73, 187
festivalization 107, 129, 170
FHAR (*Front Homosexuel d'Action*) 36–37
financial challenges *see* corporatization and commodification
Floyd, George 89, 118
Flynn, Declan 88
Formby, E. 135, 146
Fossil Free Pride 183, 185
fossil fuel companies 147n4, 173, 183, 185
Foster, E. 174
Foucault, M. 31
Fouratt, Jim 38n13
fragmentation *see* multiplication and fragmentation
frame diffusion 66, 69–70
France 36–37, 142, 144, 178, 181–182
Free-K Pride 119, 120, 133
freedom of expression and assembly 49, 56, 58, 92–96, 115
funding of Pride Events *see* corporatization and commodification

G

Gaard, G. 175
Gallón Salazar, A.M. 175–176
Gandhinagar, India 116
Garina, K. 52
Gay Activist Alliance (GAA) 26
gay bars 147n1
Gay Liberation Front (GLF) 25, 26, 27, 38n12–13
Gay Power 26, 75
Gay Pride 75
Gay Rights 75
Gay Shame 76, 120
Gays Against Guns 89
Gaza 41, 53, 120–121
generational differences 123n3
Germany 34, 50, 77, 95, 101, 122
  environmental sustainability 179–180, 180–181
Gevisser, M. 36
Ghaziani, A. 64, 70, 71, 74–75, 80n17, 103, 119, 128
ghost pride 50, 68
Giulianotti, R. 72
global homocapitalism 59, 126
global homogenization 42
Global North *see* Global South; Western-centric approach; *see individual countries*
Global Pride 79n4, 163–164
Global South
  colonialism 33, 42–45, 57, 58

corporatization and commodification 136, 138, 146, 147n7
environmental sustainability 176
and modernity 42, 44–46, 49, 54, 57, 58
opposition to mainstream events 76, 78
researching 13–14
and saviourism of Global North 98–100
and Stonewall Riots 22, 23–24, 33–37, 192
trans people 78
see also individual countries
Global Transphobia 88
global warming *see* environmental sustainability
globalization of Pride Events *see* multiplication and fragmentation
glocalization 72
GLOW (Gay and Lesbian Organization of Witwatersrand) 35–36
Gordon, A. 31–32
Graci, S. 178
grants 130, 133–134, 144
grassroots activism *see* community-building
greenwashing 131, 173, 183–185, 187
Griffiths, C. 23, 32
Gruppo Jump 158–159
Guardian, The 183
Guilabert, Aurélien 178–179
Gurok, K. 51

H

Habermas, J. 43, 60n3
Halberstam, J.J. 63, 71, 110, 186
Haller, B.A. 163
Hatfield, J.E. 24, 38n15
Heise, D. 74
Heritage of Pride March 105, 118, 119
Herndon, M. 46
Hijra Pride 78
Hilderbrand, L. 147n1
history of Pride Events *see* Stonewall Riots (1969)
HIV/AIDS 61n10, 157
Hoad, N. 39, 40, 45, 49, 51
homelessness 186
homocapitalism 54, 59, 68, 126
homocolonialism 33, 44–45
homogenization 72
homonationalist narratives 9, 49, 68, 84, 100–101, 114, 115, 192
homonormativity 91–92, 114, 115
homopatriarchy 78
homophobia 38n13, 47, 49, 78, 135, 193–194
and disability 157
and freedom of expression and assembly 88–89, 92–94, 98
Hong Kong 48, 76

horizontal hostility 74–75
hostile policies 193–194
Huang, S. 33
Huffnagel, Frits 21
human rights issues 10, 59, 83–102, 194
articulating grievances and issues 87–92
and COVID-19 pandemic 94–96
freedom of expression and assembly 92–96
and modernity 96–101
and visibility 84–87, 97
hyper-contextualization 48–49, 57, 63–64, 72, 93
hyper-localization 63–64, 72, 110

I

ILGA Europe 36, 52, 105
ILGA World 47, 52
inclusivity *see* disability and accessibility
India 44, 48, 76, 90, 116, 134
Indigenous people 12, 72–73, 108
institutionalization 54, 66, 76, 79n3, 100, 107, 120
see also community-building; corporatization and commodification; multiplication and fragmentation
International Association of Pride Organizers (InterPride) 47, 65, 66, 110, 164
intersectionality 25, 29, 191
and environmental sustainability 174–177, 183, 186
and human rights issues 89–90
and modernity 45
in rural settings 73
and visibility 68–69
see also disability and accessibility
Invalid, S. 169
Ireland 51, 88, 161, 179
Iriarte, E.G. 153, 171n3
Israel 41, 53, 120–121, 184
Italy 35, 72, 73
Alternative Pride Events 119, 120
corporatization and commodification 129, 133
disability and accessibility 158–159
human rights issues 91–92
and peripheral settings 111, 112
World Pride 129

J

Japan 36
Johannesburg 35–36, 49, 80n23
Johnson, Marsha P. 26
Johnston, L. 38n18
Joseph, L. 7, 11, 66, 69, 74, 75, 79n3, 107, 108, 112, 123, 128, 137
Just Stop Oil 147n4, 183, 184

K

Kaleidoscope Modernities 6, 8–9, 41, 56–60, 97, 123, 187, 193, 196–198
Kameny, F. 156
Kennedy, E.L. 32
Kenya 47
Kerr, P. 174
Khumbulani, South Africa 76
Kissack, T. 25, 38n13
Klapeer, C.K. 50, 61n10
Kong, T.S. 42, 46, 48
Kopkind, A. 25, 37n8
Korol, C. 176–177
Kosovo 50
  COVID-19 pandemic 143
  human rights issues 85–86, 89, 94, 98–99
  and the police 116–117
  prejudices within the community 121–122
Kubal, T. 27
Kunzel, R. 156–157
Kyiv 52–53, 101, 116

L

Ladder, The 156
Latino Pride 77, 196
Latinx *testimonios* 27
Lebanon 91, 117
lesbian separatists 174, 189n5
LGBTQIA+ terminology 12
litter 181–182
Liverpool 88
London 77, 94, 105, 129, 132, 135, 147n4, 178, 183, 184
López Sánchez, E. 79n12
Los Angeles 38n11, 80n18–19
Love, H. 49
Luibhéid, E. 140

M

mafia 24
Malta 52, 138
Manalansan IV, M.F. 33
Manchester 111
Mannan, Xhulaz 91, 139
Marche, G. 27
marginalization *see* disability and accessibility; human rights issues
marriage 51
Martin, F. 7, 42, 46, 57
Matebeni, Z. 80n23
Mattachine Society 38n11–12, 80n19
McAdam, D. 24
McFarland Bruce, K. 5, 75, 80n18, 85, 103, 135, 146
McRuer, R. 153, 155, 156, 96, 197
media 29, 47, 48, 52, 93, 99, 163, 166, 180
medical model of disability 153, 155
medical model of homosexuality 156
mega-events 170, 187
memorialization 22, 23, 24–28
mental illness 156–157
metronormativity 63, 71, 104, 110, 111, 113, 114, 186
Mexico 35
  COVID-19 pandemic 142–143
  environmental sustainability 178–179
  funding of Pride Events 131–132, 138–139
  and human rights issues 89, 90, 100
  and local history 36, 109
  rural and peripheral settings 36, 72, 113
Mexico City 109, 178–179
micro-politics 74
Mignolo, W.D. 43
migrants 52, 67–68, 118
Mijatović, Dunja 68
Milan 119
militarization of Pride Events 100–101, 114–119
modernity, and Pride Events 5–6, 8–9, 39–61, 191, 192
  canon for organization of Pride Events 58–59
  corporatization and commodification 54, 55, 59, 145–146
  and human rights issues 96–101
  Kaleidoscope Modernities 8–9, 41, 54–60, 97, 123, 187, 193, 196–198
  and organization of Pride Events 46–54
  progress and modernity conceptually 41–46
Montenegro 50
Monteroso, Spain 73
Moreau, J. 147n7
Mortimer-Sandilands, C. 175
motor vehicles at Pride Events 179–181
Mouzakitis, A. 42, 43, 44, 56
multi-issue events 75–76
Multiple Modernities 41, 56–57
multiplication and fragmentation 6–7, 62–80, 191
  conflict and differences 74–78
  contextualizing 65–70
  effects of globalization 66–67
  number of events 65
  rural and peripheral settings 70–74
Muslims 40, 41, 44–45, 53, 98–99
mutual aid 108
mythologization 23
  myth creation 30–31
  Stonewall Riots 28–32, 34–37, 109–110

N

National Park Service 25–26
Nelson, J.A. 163
neo-imperialism 44
Nestlé 146
Netherlands 21, 61n10, 157

INDEX

neurodivergent persons *see* disability and accessibility
New York City 89, 90, 117–118, 119, 178
  see also Stonewall Riots (1969)
New Zealand 112, 130
Newton, Huey 38n13
NGOization of LGBT activism 105
NGOs 52, 54, 61n10, 65, 100, 105
Nkoli, Simon Tseko 35–36
non-binary 12
Norway 160, 161
Ñuca Trans symbol, 72–73

O

older people 87, 109, 120, 161–162
Oldham, UK 111
Oliver, M. 153
online Pride Events 91, 96, 99, 141, 163–167
Oregon 95
OutRight International 39, 47, 65, 110

P

Palestine 41, 53, 120–121, 184
parenting rights 88, 91–92
Paris 36–37
Paternotte, D. 105
pathologization 153, 155, 156, 169, 171n10
Patil, V. 44
Payne, W.J. 36
perfection 43–44
peripheral settings *see* rural and peripheral settings
Peru 46
Peterson, A. 66, 70, 75–76, 80n20, 96, 129
Philippines 33, 141
Picq, M.L. 44
Piepzna-Samarasinha, L.L. 1, 168, 170
Pieri, M. 157, 158–159
Piña, D.A. 79n4
pink-testing 45
pinkwashing
  by corporations 2, 11, 97, 99, 128, 137–138, 174, 184–185, 187
  by Israel 41, 53, 120–121, 184
  by the police 115
Piontek, T. 24, 33
Podgorica 50
police
  ineffectiveness of 93–94, 115
  and modernity 100–101
  pinkwashing 115
  presence and participation 76–77, 114–119
  and riots/uprisings 29, 38n21
  role of 104
  and Stonewall Riots 24–25, 28, 30–31, 37n8
politics of essentialism 38n18

pollution *see* environmental sustainability
polysemic character of Pride Events 13, 15–16, 69–70, 170, 193
Portugal 36
postcolonialism 42–43, 44
Prague 120
Pride Denied (documentary) 67, 120–121, 129
Pride Events (overview) 190–198
  complexities of researching 12–15
  at a global crossroads 190–193
  globalization of 6–7, 39–40
  growth in magnitude 3, 5, 6–7, 11, 39
  rethinking the futures of 193–196
  tensions and conflicts 9–12
  terminology used 13
Pride Literacy 55–56, 70
Pride Parades 13
Pristina 50, 85–86
professionalization of organizers and activists 10, 54, 65–66, 97, 104, 105–110, 133, 194
Puar, J.K. 53, 84, 100, 129
public funding 132–135
Puglia 111, 112

Q

queer cultural capital 55–56
Queer Eco-Criticism 73, 183–185
Queer Ecology 175–177, 178, 186, 187, 188
queer hybridization 7, 42, 46, 48, 57
Quijano, A. 43–44

R

race
  and ableism 169
  Alternative Pride Events 10, 64, 76, 77, 119, 121, 196
  Black Lives Matter 77, 89, 108
  Black Panthers Party and GLF 38n13
  Black Pride 10, 64, 77, 119, 196
  and community-building 108
  and gay bars 147n1
  human rights issues 89
  Johannesburg Pride 35–36, 49, 80n23
  migrants 67–68, 69
  and the police 114, 117–118
  racialization 12–13
  Stonewall Riots 25, 38n15
  white supremacist framing 77, 80n23, 169
  whitewashing 25–26, 38n15
radical faeries 174, 189n6
Rahman, M. 40, 42, 44–45
Rainbow Imaginaries 67, 70
Rainbow Maps 52
rainbow symbolism 55, 67, 128
Rao, R. 40, 44, 45, 56, 126
reciprocation 69
Reclaim Pride movement 119, 122

recycling 181–182
Reid, G. 36
religious opposition 36, 52, 93, 98–99, 117
research methods of the study 14–15
Rivera, Sylvia 26, 27
Robertson, R, 72
Rodríguez Domínguez, E. 79n12
Rodwell, Craig 29
Roma community 122, 164
Rome 129
Roth, M. 50
rural and peripheral settings 10
  and community-building 104, 110–114
  critical social geography 71–73
  environmental sustainability 73, 185, 186–187
  funding of Pride Events 135
  multiplication of 63–64, 191, 195
Russell, E.K. 115
Russia 47, 52, 60n6, 92

S

safe spaces 92
Said, E. 37n5
Saleh, F. 69
Salento, Italy 73
Sarajevo 50
Saudi Arabia 98–99
saviourism of Global North 98
Schulman, S. 130
Seed, P. 43
Segal, M. 27
Seoul 51, 93, 99, 117
Serbia 36, 41, 50, 61n7, 68, 93, 95, 115
Shakespeare, T. 165–166
Shanghai 99
Shell 173
Shew, A. 165, 166
Shield, A.D. 23, 35
single-issue parades 75–76
single-use plastic 181, 182
Slootmaeckers, K. 41, 50, 66, 68
Slovakia 99–100, 159
Smith, L.T. 14, 28
Snow, D. 69, 123
social capital 74
social media 53, 96, 163, 166
social model of disability 153
social theory 42–43
South Africa 76, 80n23, 89, 90, 98
  funding of Pride Events 142
  and the police 116
  and race 35–36, 48–49
  rural settings 111
South Korea 51, 93, 94, 99, 117
Soweto 76
Spain 35, 36, 73
  corporatization and commodification 132

environmental sustainability 180, 181, 187
grassroots activism 106–107
sponsorship *see* corporatization
  and commodification
STAR (Street Transvestite Action Revolutionaries) 26
Stonewall Riots (1969) 7–8, 21–38
  decentering 32–37
  and disability 168
  effects of mythologization 31–32
  and Global South 22, 23–24, 33–37, 192
  historiography of 24–25
  and Kaleidoscope Modernities 58
  memorialization 22, 23, 24–28
  Multiple Modernities 57
  myth creation 30–31
  mythologization 23, 28–32, 34–37, 57, 58, 109–110, 192
  problematized and contextualized 21–23
  riot or uprising 27–28
  Stonewall Metaphors 23–24, 35, 37
Stronach, R. 127–128
sustainability *see* environmental sustainability
Sustainable Development Goals, United Nations 173
Sweden 67–68, 69
symbolic capital 128

T

Taiwan 46, 89–90, 134, 141
TAVIS (Toronto Anti Violence Intervention Strategy) 67
Taylor, J. 76, 107, 129
technoableism 165
technology, disability and accessibility 162–167
temporal strategies 66
Tequila Sauza 131
Thomas, J. 147n1
Tijuana 100
Tikuna, J. 44
Tipping Point UK 183
Tokyo 36
Toronto 67, 77, 120–121, 129
trademarking social change 128
Trans Exclusionary Radical Feminists (TERFS) 78, 94
trans people
  access to healthcare 90–91
  Alternative Pride Events 72–73, 77–78
  and environmental sustainability 185
  and Gay Liberation Front (GLF) 27
  human rights issues 86–91
  and the police 114
  Stonewall Riots 25–26, 27, 38n15
  trans-exclusionary discourses 195
  Trans Exclusionary Radical Feminists (TERFS) 78, 94

INDEX

Trans Marches 1, 78
Trans Pride 77, 78, 86–87, 90, 119, 121, 160
transphobia 78, 83, 88–89, 90–91, 94, 121, 194
visibility 86–87
travellers 117, 164
Trojan 129
Trump, Donald 26, 83, 99
Turin 119, 120
Turkey 92

U

Uganda 40, 45, 47, 67–68, 69, 96
Ukraine 36, 52–53, 101, 116
Union for the Physically Impaired Against Segregation (UPIAS) 153
United Arab Emirates 98–99
United Kingdom 72, 80n15
  Alternative Pride Events 122
  colonialism 44
  corporatization and commodification 129, 130–131, 132, 133, 135, 137, 143–144, 147n4
  COVID-19 pandemic 143–144
  disability and accessibility 160–161, 164
  environmental sustainability 183, 184, 185
  online Pride Events 164
  peripheral settings 111
  and the police 117
  and professionalization 106, 107
  Trans Pride 86–87, 90, 119, 121, 160
  transphobia 90, 94, 121
  violence 88
United Nations 173
United States
  Alternative Pride Events 76, 77, 119, 120, 121
  collaboration with international actors 100
  community-building 108, 109
  conflict 80n17
  corporatization and commodification 129–130, 134, 136–137, 140, 142
  COVID-19 pandemic 95
  DEI initiatives 83, 140
  disability and accessibility 159
  environmental sustainability 174

homophile politics 80n19
human rights issues 83, 98–99
and the police 117–118
and professionalization 107
transphobia 90
violence 89
see also Stonewall Riots (1969)

V

van Dalen, Frank 65
Vietnam 141
violence
  atmospheres of violence 69
  and colonialism 44, 58
  instances of 68–69, 88–90, 92, 93, 193
  and the police 24–25, 77, 92, 114–115
  visibility 13, 32, 48, 84–87, 97
  and violence and harassment 68–69
volunteers 105, 106, 133, 139, 144
Vučić, President 68

W

Wahlström, M. 101n3, 129
Waitt, G. 38n18
Waldschmidt, A. 162
Western-centric approach 7, 8, 9, 12, 23, 192
  and modernity 40, 41–46, 48, 50, 51, 54, 54–55, 56–57
  Stonewall Riots (1969) 29, 33–37
  see also multiplication and fragmentation
Whan, Del 80n18
White, E. 27
white supremacist framing 77, 80n23, 169
whitewashing 25–26, 38n15
Whitworth, L. 174
women
  Alternative Pride Events 77–78, 80n23
  feminicidios 89
  femonationalism 60n3
  and gay bars 147n1
  lesbian separatists 174, 189n5
  Stonewall Riots 25
  Trans Exclusionary Radical Feminists (TERFS) 78, 94
Wong, A.K. 46
World Pride 67–68, 121, 129